Indexicalism

# Speculative Realism

Series Editor: Graham Harman

Editorial Advisory Board
Jane Bennett, Levi Bryant, Patricia Clough, Iain Hamilton Grant, Myra Hird, Adrian Johnston, Eileen A. Joy

## Books available

*Onto-Cartography: An Ontology of Machines and Media*, Levi R. Bryant
*Form and Object: A Treatise on Things*, Tristan Garcia, translated by Mark Allan Ohm and Jon Cogburn
*Adventures in Transcendental Materialism: Dialogues with Contemporary Thinkers*, Adrian Johnston
*The End of Phenomenology: Metaphysics and the New Realism*, Tom Sparrow
*Fields of Sense: A New Realist Ontology*, Markus Gabriel
*Quentin Meillassoux: Philosophy in the Making*, Second Edition, Graham Harman
*Assemblage Theory*, Manuel DeLanda
*Romantic Realities: Speculative Realism and British Romanticism*, Evan Gottlieb
*Garcian Meditations: The Dialectics of Persistence in* Form and Object, Jon Cogburn
*Speculative Realism and Science Fiction*, Brian Willems
*Speculative Empiricism: Revisiting Whitehead*, Didier Debaise, translated by Tomas Weber
*Letting Be Volume I: The Life Intense: A Modern Obsession*, Tristan Garcia, translated by Abigail RayAlexander, Christopher RayAlexander and Jon Cogburn
*Against Continuity: Gilles Deleuze's Speculative Realism*, Arjen Kleinherenbrink
*Speculative Grammatology: Deconstruction and the New Materialism*, Deborah Goldgaber
*Letting Be Volume II: We Ourselves: The Politics of Us*, Tristan Garcia, translated by Abigail RayAlexander, Christopher RayAlexander and Jon Cogburn
*New Ecological Realisms: Post-Apocalyptic Fiction and Contemporary Theory*, Monika Kaup
*Indexicalism: Realism and the Metaphysics of Paradox*, Hilan Bensusan

## Forthcoming books

*Letting Be Volume III: Let Be and Make Powerful*, Tristan Garcia, translated by Christopher RayAlexander, Abigail RayAlexander and Jon Cogburn
*After Quietism: Analytic Philosophies of Immanence and the New Metaphysics*, Jon Cogburn
*Infrastructure*, Graham Harman
*The External World*, Maurizio Ferraris, translated by Sarah De Sanctis
*Object-Oriented Living in Artificially Intelligent Times: The Use of the Real*, Yoni Van Den Eede

Visit the Speculative Realism website at: edinburghuniversitypress.com/series-speculative-realism.html

# Indexicalism

Realism and the Metaphysics of Paradox

Hilan Bensusan

Edinburgh University Press is one of the leading university presses in
the UK. We publish academic books and journals in our selected subject
areas across the humanities and social sciences, combining cutting-edge
scholarship with high editorial and production values to produce academic
works of lasting importance. For more information visit our website:
edinburghuniversitypress.com

© Hilan Bensusan, 2021

Edinburgh University Press Ltd
The Tun – Holyrood Road
12(2f) Jackson's Entry
Edinburgh EH8 8PJ

Typeset in 11/13 Adobe Sabon by
Servis Filmsetting Ltd, Stockport, Cheshire,
and printed and bound in Great Britain.

A CIP record for this book is available from the British Library

ISBN 978 1 4744 8029 1 (hardback)
ISBN 978 1 4744 8032 1 (webready PDF)
ISBN 978 1 4744 8030 7 (paperback)
ISBN 978 1 4744 8031 4 (epub)

The right of Hilan Bensusan to be identified as the author of this work has been
asserted in accordance with the Copyright, Designs and Patents Act 1988, and
the Copyright and Related Rights Regulations 2003 (SI No. 2498).

# Contents

| | |
|---|---|
| Series Editor's Preface | viii |
| Preface | xi |
| | |
| Introduction: Reality and Speculation | 1 |
|    Speculative Realism and the Great Outdoors | 1 |
|    Totality and Speculation | 7 |
|    Other Dialogues | 10 |
|    The Paradox of Deictic Speculation | 11 |
| | |
| 1. Indexicalism: A Paradoxico-Metaphysics | 14 |
|    Indexicalism | 14 |
|    Paradoxico-Metaphysics | 18 |
|    The Routes to Indexicalism (and Paradox) | 19 |
|    Situated Metaphysics | 21 |
|    Monadologies | 23 |
|    Totality | 28 |
|    Demonstratives and Proper Names | 34 |
|    Tense Realism and Baroque Realism | 39 |
|    Horizon | 42 |
|    Measurement | 44 |
|    Exteriority and Externalism | 48 |
|    Proximity | 53 |
|    Object-oriented | 59 |
|    Tentacular Thinking | 66 |
| | |
| 2. The Metaphysics of the Others | 78 |
|    The Others | 78 |
|    The *Physis* of the Others | 81 |
|    Perspectivism | 84 |

vi    Indexicalism

> The Metaphysics of the Others in the Age of the
>     Correlate                                          89
> After Speculation                                      96
> The Priority of the Others                             99
> The Interrupted Nexus                                 103
> Process Metaphysics of the Others                     111
> Robinsonology and Transcendental Xenology             114
> From the Other to the Great Outdoors                  118
> Perception and Supplement                             126

3. The Hospitality of Perception                        134
> Doors of Perception                                   135
> Hospitality and the Given                             138
> The Complexities of Receptivity                       145
> Importance and Supplement                             150
> Perceiving is Responding                              154
> Metaphysical Empiricism                               159
> Pan-perceptualism                                     161
> Proximity, Conversation and Experience                167
> Deictic Absolutes                                     171

Coda: The Circumscription of Potosí                     184
> Epistemic Abundance                                   184
> The Potosí Principle                                  186
> *Ch'ixi*                                              191
> *Being Up for Grabs*                                  193
> Absolutely Situated                                   197

Bibliography                                            201
Index                                                   210

*La réalité est de l'autre côté du mur.*
Edmond Jabès

# Series Editor's Preface

We frequently hear calls to 'bridge the analytic–continental divide' in philosophy, usually from people who believe that they themselves embody such a bridge. The results are often disappointing: lukewarm interpretations of continental authors in terminology that happens to be socially acceptable in analytic departments. Hilan Bensusan is a different sort of animal: an author who is simply comfortable in both traditions without making much of a fuss about it.

A native of Brazil, Bensusan is currently Professor of Contemporary Philosophy at the University of Brasília, where he is followed by an unusually enthusiastic and productive group of students. In his 2016 book *Being Up for Grabs: On Speculative Anarchaeology*, Bensusan displayed his prominent interest in turning from substance to accident and from necessity to contingency.[1] Among the chief philosophical references of that book were Alfred North Whitehead, Gilbert Simondon, Saul Kripke and Quentin Meillassoux, though it concluded with a nod to Richard Rorty and Bruno Latour.[2]

The present work by Bensusan, *Indexicalism*, arguably makes an even bolder break with traditional ontologies. In the author's own fine phrase, the book now before you 'breaks with the spirit of a world of ultimate substantives presided over by an identity alien to the curvature of circumstances'.[3] Grammatically speaking, an indexical is a word whose meaning depends entirely on its context: 'you', 'me', 'here' and 'there' are classic examples,

---

[1] Hilan Bensusan, *On Being Up for Grabs: On Speculative Anarchaeology* (London: Open Humanities Press, 2016).
[2] Bensusan, *On Being Up for Grabs*, pp. 195–6.
[3] See this book, p. xi.

though Bensusan lays additional stress – for reasons that will soon become clear – on 'beyond', 'different' and 'other'. For in fact, the intellectual core of this book is Bensusan's attempt to reconcile Whitehead's process metaphysics with the theory of radical otherness found in the philosophy of Emmanuel Levinas. As discussed most famously by Jacques Derrida in 'Violence and Metaphysics', there is something paradoxical in speaking about an otherness beyond presence, since in doing so we are nonetheless obliged to make it present in language.⁴ In other words, to think something outside thought requires turning it into a thought. In continental philosophy there has been a good deal of wrangling over this point among the various camps of Speculative Realism, and on this point Bensusan is considerably closer to Meillassoux than to Object-Oriented Ontology.⁵ In an analytic context, it is Graham Priest who has pushed this paradox to the point of unapologetic 'dialetheism', or the acceptance of true contradictions, though Bensusan informs us that his book draws less from Priest than might be expected.⁶

Indeed, it is clear that Bensusan is not so much interested in paradox for its own sake as driven into paradox through his commitment to otherness in philosophy. This is due not only to his interest in Levinas; there are also Brazilian roots to this concern, with explicit reference to the work on Amerindian cosmologies by Bensusan's well-known countryman Eduardo Viveiros de Castro.⁷ The slogan Bensusan chooses for his version of this enterprise is 'the metaphysics of the others'. In somewhat Derridean fashion, Bensusan claims that any metaphysics of otherness will soon run up against the problem of metaphysics itself. There are many different forms of otherness, he tells us, ranging from Levinasian alterity to Meillassoux's 'Great Outdoors' to Heideggerian

---

⁴ Jacques Derrida, 'Violence and Metaphysics: An Essay on the Thought of Emmanuel Levinas', in *Writing and Difference*, trans. A. Bass (Chicago: University of Chicago Press, 1978), pp. 79–158.

⁵ For Meillassoux's defence of the 'correlational circle', see especially his remarks in Ray Brassier, Iain Hamilton Grant, Graham Harman and Quentin Meillassoux, 'Speculative Realism', *Collapse* III (2007), pp. 408–35. For an object-oriented rejoinder, see Graham Harman, 'The Only Exit from Modern Philosophy', *Open Philosophy* 3 (2020), pp. 132–46.

⁶ Graham Priest, *Beyond the Limits of Thought*, 2nd edn (Oxford: Clarendon Pres, 2003). A rare continental case for Priest can be found in Timothy Morton, *Realist Magic: Objects, Ontology, Causality* (Ann Arbor: Open Humanities Press, 2013).

⁷ Eduardo Viveiros de Castro, *Cannibal Metaphysics*, trans. P. Skafish (Minneapolis: Univocal, 2017).

being-towards-death to the sudden shocks of everyday life perhaps best explored in the *Grenzsituationen* of Karl Jaspers. Yet Bensusan seems most interested in the approach of Levinas's forerunner, Franz Rosenzweig, with his adamant opposition to all forms of totality. Bensusan turns all of this in a direction he likens to a 'Jewish animism'.

Bensusan's style is unique and frequently refreshing. While his argumentation is rigorous and demanding, he slices his train of thought into numerous small sections; this allows readers ample opportunity to catch their breath before scaling the next rock wall on the mountain. He frequently makes unusual formulations that stick in the mind for a long while after one is finished reading. Having had the good fortune to meet Bensusan once, in Cairo, on the very eve of the 2011 Arab Spring, I can say that he speaks in the same memorable style that one finds in his writing. Above all, I am aware of no comparable effort at a simultaneous combination of analytic philosophy, Jewish thought and recent Amerindian anthropology with the concerns of Speculative Realism. We warmly welcome this book to the series, and can promise the reader something entirely unforeseen in the previous trajectory of recent continental thought. There is a groundswell of new Speculative Realist work emerging from Brazil, and this book will likely not be the last taste of it.

Graham Harman<br>
Long Beach, California<br>
January 2021

# Preface

This is a book about the others as others. They belong, more than to any particular story, to 'the Great Outdoors' which lies at the limits of any story. These limits are often understood as the barely conceivable frontier where knowledge or thought cannot reach. The Great Outdoors does indeed set limits but it also provides shape from outside. The book endeavours to be metaphysically faithful to this exteriority instead of trying merely to accommodate it in a suitable description. The outdoors appears, then, as a landscape of others.

The indexicalist project emerges from an encounter between the philosophy of organism of Alfred Whitehead – with its attention to experience as ubiquitous and to the immanence of process – and the transcendence of the Other in the thought of Emmanuel Levinas. In a nutshell, indexicalism is the claim that absolutes are deictic – they are like such words as 'there', 'out', 'beyond', 'different'. It breaks with the spirit of a world of ultimate substantives presided over by an identity alien to the curvature of circumstances. The project's attempt to think metaphysically about the others as others proves to be a route to a paradox which is not so much the end of the road but the stone that paves it.

However, more than addressing a metaphysics of paradox for its own sake, this book is thrown into paradox indirectly through its attempt to think through exteriority.[1] Indexicalism chooses to embrace paradox to avoid substantive, totalising and non-situated alternatives that leave no room for what is other. The very idea that one should make room for what is outside is the kernel of

---

[1] Once paradox is pushed to the point of no return, Graham Priest's view that there are *dialetheias* (true contradictions) is one way forward, but by no means a compulsory one. In fact, little is said about Priest's project in what follows.

a metaphysics of paradox – and it is precisely why indexicalism cannot be less than both a metaphysics and a criticism of it. The book is therefore about the (paradoxical) limits to any metaphysical outlook that does justice to genuine exteriority.

The quest for such justice is what I call 'the metaphysics of the others'. The expression recalls a lecture I heard given by Eduardo Viveiros de Castro several years ago at a conference on the ontological turn. He thought the external world was akin to those others who are 'the ones that think us through'. In my usage, the others are those who resist the attempts to do a metaphysics (of them). The metaphysics of the others is therefore also itself a criticism of the very idea of a metaphysics. Indexicalism has therefore much in common with Amerindian perspectivism: in both cases, *deixis* resists being thought as a substantive.

A (paradoxical) metaphysics of the others is guided by an anathema: it cannot be metaphysically about the others because their exteriority is not merely a starting point. Genuine exteriority comes in many forms: the Great Outdoors, the unexpected, the absolute Other, the horizon of death. Franz Rosenzweig looked at the most intimate horizon of death to exorcise the philosophical effort to place an All above every personal reality. His revolt against the unspoken presupposition that he found in every philosophy – that there is an altar of totality on which reality is often to be sacrificed – led him to a thought of the absolute as an excluding All, oblivious to any completeness. Levinas brought this transcending absolute to the heart of philosophy – bringing a foreign, Jewish dialect to the Greek language, in the image that Jacques Derrida once offered.[2] Indexicalism is an attempt to thoroughly dismiss any overarching All by pointing towards a situated metaphysics. I like to think of it as an exercise in Jewish animism – everything is animated not by an internal agenda that could be exposed in a complete view of what exists, but rather by the impact of a transcending other. It is a form of perspectivism: whatever exists is situated.

In its effort to dismantle substantive universalities, indexicalism highlights the circumscription within which I have lived most of my life. Latin America was forged both by claims of generality coming from somewhere else and by the continuing efforts of integration. As my friend and co-author Julio Cabrera has poignantly explained, it is a continent where the universal is seen as an

[2] Derrida, 'Violence and Metaphysics', in *Writing and Difference*, pp. 79–158.

imported product. It is nevertheless a place of struggle. The struggle is not between two poles that are themselves substantive, but is itself an indexical category. There are parallels with the efforts of Ernesto Laclau and Chantal Mouffe to envisage political struggle as an ongoing condition, local and independent of pre-established goals. The situated metaphysics recommended in this book is a plea for the local – a commitment to the complexities of proximity.

\*

I am greatly indebted to two Levinasian friends: Adriana Menassé and Gabriela Lafetá. I share with them both an enthusiasm for the way Levinas thought through the contrast between totality and the infinity of the Other, and a drive to go beyond some of his predicaments. With Adriana I had a correspondence on our responsibility towards the non-human.[3] I had the honour to supervise Gabriela's PhD thesis where she examined Derrida's Levinas. We also shared the conviction that Levinas's rapport with the Other inaugurated something novel and refreshing within philosophy.

The main project of the book began to take shape in 2016 when I visited GECO, Université Libre de Bruxelles. There I started rethinking process philosophy in Levinasian terms. Our discussions of Whitehead and his convergences and departures from a Leibnizian monadological metaphysics were crucial to my elaboration of the idea that a further step in (roughly) the same direction was needed. Next came a visit to Jon Cogburn at the Louisiana State University where I became acquainted with his work on paradoxico-metaphysics and we both explored ways to shed light on some debates about perception through this notion. My two stays at the Performance Arts Forum (PAF) at St Erme gave me time to conceive the unavoidable friction between totality and perception – partly a consequence of the long-diagnosed tension between knowing and experiencing.

The structure of the argument became clear during my course on Levinas at the University of Brasilia in 2017. I began writing the final manuscript during a stay close to the Sumaq Orqo, in Potosí, early in 2018. The writing carried on throughout 2018 in Brasília and in a residence close to an exuberant jabuticaba tree (*Plinia cauliflora*) at Suyan de Mattos house at Olhos d'Água. I thank Suyan and the fruits for their generosity. My gratitude

---

[3] Menassé and Bensusan, '¿Es tiempo de abandonar el barco humano?'

goes also to my surroundings in Brasília: Devrim, my housemates, Gisel Carriconde, Hannah Prado, Judith Zuquim, Krishna Passos, Phil Jones and Raísa Curty, intimate housemate, and my familiar neighbours, Nurit Bensusan and Ariê Baylão-Bensusan. Finally, I am indebted to several people and groups with whom I discussed the ideas in the book and who provided the atmosphere that led to it. In particular, thanks to Ahanon, Alice Gabriel, André Arnaut, Barbara de Barros, Bianca de Oliveira, Damares Pinheiro, Dylan O'Brian, Eli Minor, Elzahrã Omar Osman, Fernando Silva e Silva, Fran Demétrio, Greg Carneiro, Guilherme da Silva, Jan Araújo, Janina Moninska, Jadson Alves de Freitas, J.-P. Caron, John Protevi, Juliana Fausto, Leo Cacochen, Marco Antonio Valentim, Moysés Pinto, Olga Shaumyan, Otavio Maciel, Rainri Back, Ray Cruz, Rodrigo Nunes and all those who attended my lectures and talks, to the ANARCHAI research group and to the Contemporary Ontologies work group. Damares Pinheiro also helped me with the preparation of the manuscript which was revised by Stephanie Mitchell – thanks to both.

I also acknowledge the work Graham Harman made to improve the manuscript, and Carol Macdonald, who helped me through the stages of publication. Some ideas in this book were published in two papers in 2018, and I'm greatly indebted to the reviewers and readers of these articles.[4] Conversations were crucial for this book – not only as a product of an intersection of conversations in different rhythms, at multiple speeds, in many sorts of media and in numerous tonalities, but also in the shape of unending conversations as a key feature of the metaphysics of the others that this book recommends. To be sure, conversations have no single author. But I believe they are the stuff philosophy is made of.

---

[4] Bensusan, 'Towards an Indexicalist Paradoxico-Metaphysics', and Bensusan, 'O realismo especulativo e a metafísica dos outros'.

# Introduction: Reality and Speculation

## Speculative Realism and the Great Outdoors

Speculative realism is a philosophical movement for our times. I believe it speaks to us today for at least three general and intertwined reasons. First, it endeavours with concentrated effort to step out of the closed oyster of our own cognitive and thinking practices and to break out towards the Great Outdoors. This realist drive fulfils what I take to be an obligation of philosophy today: that of being relevant to the issues that challenge our established practices with growing magnitude and intensity: issues such as the future of the planet and the rapid disappearance of numerous forms of life, as can be seen in the dwindling of both human and non-human diversity.

Second, speculative realism addresses the big picture through an appeal to speculation. However the speculative procedure is understood within various parts of the movement, Graham Harman points out in the opening pages of his general book on speculative realism that it is importantly distinct from commonsensical realism.[1] Current times arguably crave for speculation, at least as a way to strive against the narrowing of the future associated with the frustrations of common sense. Philosophy, if it looks forward, has to harbour a commitment to boldness and to intrepid thinking that the speculative realism movement has brought to the contemporary scene. The attachment to speculation creates an ethos of openness to dare the weird and to leave common presuppositions aside. This in itself brings about an atmosphere of constructive thought that encourages philosophy to engage in new beginnings. As Alfred North Whitehead often emphasised, philosophy is less about following consequences, and more about giving rise to enlightening postulates.

Finally, speculative realism was born in the plural. To be fair, it is possible to track aims and assumptions shared both by its original proponents and its latecomers, and I'll address these commonalities below. However, the movement has attracted people from different corners of thinking, and perhaps as a consequence it has quickly developed into a fruitful diaspora. More than a school of thought that carefully sows its seeds, the movement is an event that spreads through unpredictably fertile soil. This is perhaps because of the loose incisiveness of its common message – it aims at stepping into the Great Outdoors, but assumes little as to what is to be reached when one steps that far out. This book belongs to the constellation of speculative realism in the sense that it takes up its challenge, endorses its ethos, and engages with the multiple landscapes that shaped it as a movement. Indeed, the ideas in this book would have been impossible or have taken a very different form without speculative realism. They are, nevertheless, no less its offspring than a departure from it.

I think that an important tenet of the movement is that it breaks with the claim, associated with the philosophies of immanence of the late twentieth century, that reality is somehow transparent. Transparency can be illustrated by Whitehead's philosophy of organism. Actual entities are the building blocks of what exists, and are drops of experience – they are both *percipi* and *percipere* and, as a consequence, every actuality is transparent (at least) to some other. Transparency makes reality converge with the appearances displayed in experience, and is taken by Whitehead to be entailed by a rejection of the bifurcation of nature. If, he thinks, nature is not divided into what is there to be experienced and what is there to experience, everything is available to *some* experience. Accordingly, Whitehead made the notion of perceptual experience broad enough to ensure transparency, so that no actuality could go unperceived. The claim that reality is transparent is in line with the idea that experience provides a space of immanence where nothing, in principle, transcends its reach. Experience then appears as the very space where things are disputed, maintained and constituted; anything beyond experience has to be placed within the shores of experience itself – Gilles Deleuze's *transcendental empiricism* has a foothold in Whitehead's insistence that experience is all-pervasive. The guiding insight that directed Whitehead (and to some extent Deleuze) was that only by conceiving something beyond experience to ground does reality becomes indifferent to appearances.

If one assumes continuity between what is in experience and anything else that exists, there is little room for features of reality fixed once and for all – transparency seems to be an antidote to transcendence. Indeed, transparency was often coupled with the effort to exorcise transcendence and to denounce any established hierarchy as the product of a configuration of forces within a somehow flat ontology.

Speculative realists reject transparency and break with this coupling. Harman rejects transparency by taking the withdrawal of objects from direct access to be constitutive of reality. His object-oriented ontology posits a secret life for all objects by ascribing to each of them a real object that contrasts with the perceived sensual object (along with the similar pair of real and sensual qualities). Endorsing Whitehead's broad image of perceptual experience, object-oriented ontology takes the real object to be concealed from any perceptual contact – it is never exposed, and withdraws from any attempt to make it fully available. Much like Martin Heidegger's thing, which presents itself of its own accord, the real object is revealed only to some extent, and is so at its own pace. Object-oriented ontology breaks with transparency – while subscribing to a flat ontology – by postulating a reality of each object that is immune to appearances.[2] There is something inaccessible not only to human cognitive and thinking practices, but to any perceptual endeavour. While experience is pervasive, the secrecy of real objects is part of what constitutes perception – perceiving is never anything like total disclosure. Experience, like reality, is not transparent.

In a different vein, Quentin Meillassoux recommends his principle of facticity as an absolute. Everything, the principle maintains, is necessarily contingent. Facticity ensures that anything – apart from the principle of facticity itself – could necessarily be otherwise. As a consequence, things could be indefinitely different from what they appear to be. Meillassoux opposes any account of experience that makes everything transparent. For him, transparency is a way to make what Whitehead understands as experience, for example, the sole reality – and to make the correlation that excludes us from the Great Outdoors absolute. This correlation, as we will see, is what Meillassoux's speculative materialism intends to overcome – the present age is the one in which we are somehow confined to the practices through which we relate to anything else, and do not reach beyond the correlations established in these practices. Correlation is itself contingent, and this lesson is forgotten when it is assumed to be absolute – as Whitehead does when he assumes transparency. Meillassoux aims to restore a rationale behind bifurcation that is sometimes lost: that there should be something beyond appearances, beyond transparency, beyond the correlation. Facticity, for him, is what does the trick of showing that there are no appearances that cannot be deceptive. There is nothing absolute in the appearances, except that they are a result of the overall hyperchaos that makes anything possible – except a counter-example to the principle of facticity. Meillassoux argues that there is nothing necessary about the non-existence of God; this is a contingent truth and therefore not a permanent one; if God, however, comes into existence then the principle of facticity is necessarily out of his reach, and his own existence would be equally contingent. In a sense, the lack of transparency becomes, for Meillassoux, a point of departure on the road towards the absolute.

The present book is crucially embedded in the rejection of transparency. It proposes a framework for a *metaphysics of the others* that regards the Great Outdoors as thoroughly exterior – and as something other than what our cognitive and thinking practices reach, indeed as seriously opaque. This metaphysics of the others starts with the importance of the contrast between what is internal to our practices and what is exterior, what is other, what is outside. This contrast is not to be overlooked – it ensures that there is an exteriority constantly shaping what is interior. The exterior, however, is not transparent but makes a contrasting impact on what is inside, because it designs its very borders. The metaphysics of the others posits a transcending exteriority that is both inevitable for any practice and constitutive of reality. I call *indexicalism* the framework in which this metaphysics of exteriority is drawn – the claim that deixis, more than anything substantive, is basic for existence. Indexicalism claims that *outside, exterior, other* – among other deictic notions such as *there, later* or *themselves* – make up part of the ultimate reality. It makes it possible for the contrast between our cognitive and thinking practices and the Great Outdoors to be not only a heuristic distinction that is to be eventually (or ideally) abandoned, but rather the cornerstone of thinking about the world. This contrast is therefore a point of departure for the metaphysics of the others which attempts to consider the outside not as something to be included but as an interruption in the venture prompted by our practices of making things intelligible. I consider perceptual experience as the paradigmatic location of this contrast between the internal and the external. Perception is an exercise in receptivity, and hence in hospitality. To view *perception as hospitality* makes explicit that it is a process of coping with the exterior and, at the same time, makes clear that the outdoors is always in proximity. Experience is always dealing with the foreigner, the stranger – it is as such that it is a journey into peril – but it is also a central, routine, daily activity. The problem of accessing the Great Outdoors is itself not so distant from that of the blindness of sensible intuitions – the impossibility for experience to provide content directly from the outside to the interior of any understanding. The mediation required is akin to the correlation between thought and world, and needs to be thought through simultaneously with the effort to reconsider the correlation urged by speculative realism. Perception, viewed as an act of hospitality, is where mediation appears as the impact of the nearby outdoors on the reshaping of the indoors. This impact does not make the indoors irrelevant while asserting a prior exteriority.

Indexicalism, the metaphysics of the others and perception as hospitality are the main doctrines put forward in this book, and correspond to its three chapters. Perception as hospitality places perceptual experience at the centre of my metaphysical account that privileges exteriority – it is in perception that the defining contrast between any interiority and its outdoors is most evident. I take perception to be ubiquitous, and in doing so I take my position to be in line with Harman's object-oriented ontology. In fact, Whitehead's ideas are central to what I do here – if there is a transcending exteriority, it is everywhere within the reach of experience. Experience is always bordered upon and affected by what is other. The idea that the other is prior, and that thinking and cognition are hostages to something exterior around which they revolve, has been urged by Emmanuel Levinas. Levinas is a central figure in this book, as he provides the basis of the argument for the priority of the Great Outdoors. His thinking attempts to preserve exteriority carefully from the dangers of encompassing what is other in a complete view of what there is. His image of the other as incumbent upon me is also the basis for the account of experience I propose, according to which perception is not at the service of understanding in its effort to extract the intelligibility of what is experienced. Levinas, however, concentrates much of his attention on the human Other, which addresses me with words more often accompanied by a gaze. To expand his account of exteriority to the Great Outdoors more generally is a central task of this book. It is done by way of a notion of perception that makes it ubiquitous but not inclusive – exteriority is as pervasive as any contact with something different provided by experience. In this sense, the ideas of the book spring from a reading of Levinas in conjunction with Whitehead.

If the main doctrines in this book follow speculative realism in its exorcism of transparency, it departs from the movement by insisting on the importance of exteriority. In fact, Levinas understood the Other as transcendent and as forming no complete totality. To place exteriority at the centre of metaphysics is to remove totality from the scene. The metaphysics of the others, associated with indexicalism and the idea of perception as hospitality, disagrees with speculative realists about totality. Not only is our access to it limited by what is intrinsically opaque, but reality is never complete and therefore cannot do away with exterior borders. The idea of a complete or total account of things – although always tentative – flies in the face of the metaphysics of the other, for the Great Outdoors is such that it cannot be definitively tamed into an all-pervasive image. A reality with exteriority cannot harbour a general principle that would be preserved even in the supposedly extraordinary advent of God coming to existence. Likewise, exteriority is not about something veiled in a hidden place which can be located within a totality; it is the outdoors that finds no place in any image of what there is, and transcends everything. Speculative realism is certainly inclined to do justice to the Great Outdoors, but ends up including it in a totality. The metaphysics of the others is an attempt to make the Great Outdoors not only something absolute that we aim at accessing, but also a main protagonist in metaphysics.

Because the Great Outdoors itself actually becomes *the* main protagonist, the metaphysics of the others might seem less like a metaphysics than a critique of its very possibility. The Great Outdoors spells a limitation for every metaphysical effort. This limitation, however, is part of the metaphysical story that is to be told. This surely verges on paradox. It is, I argue, thoroughly paradoxical: the limits of metaphysics are part of an image of metaphysics. I defend the idea that this paradox should usher in a transformed conception of metaphysics and its limits that ensures a place for the Great Outdoors.[3] Rather than pressing us back towards totality, this paradoxical situation should make us rethink the intrinsic connections between metaphysics and its critique. Indexicalism entails both that there is no metaphysics other than a metaphysics of paradox, and that the critique of metaphysics must ultimately dwell on its paradoxical character.

The purpose of the book is therefore to put forward and recommend the paradoxical conjecture that reality upholds deictic absolutes.

## Totality and Speculation

The emphasis on exteriority, and the rejection of totality, that seems embedded in the notion of deictic absolutes appears to be especially at odds with speculation. Speculation is often understood as the tentative effort to project what is known or experienced towards what is thus far not in view. On the one hand, speculation is a method to go beyond the presumed scope of experience and knowledge in order to gain intuition about what is out of reach. It is an effort to see further, to escape from the commonsensical boundaries of what has been thought or experienced. On the other hand, in some sense speculation has something to do with transparency – it assumes that what is beyond is somehow reflected in what is already known or thought. It is connected to the reflection of mirrors that make what is still unseen transparent. As a mirror, it projects the Same on to the Other and joins them both to form a completed view that looks like a totality where nothing exterior could take place. The mirror image of what is known could complete our limited view, while at the same time obliterating the opacity of the outdoors. Specular content results from an expansion that takes what is already seen as an example. The outdoors, the other, is included within our reach as another example of something that has already been experienced. Speculation seems committed to a totality that exorcises exteriority – a totality that would be composed by the indoors and outdoors, where the deictic character of reality advocated by indexicalism would be wrong because indexicals will find their place in a totality that would no longer require metaphysics to be situated. Such a totality would exorcise the deictic addresses that are taken to be basic. Indexicalism, and its emphasis on deixis, denounces speculation as conflicting with the very contrast between internal and external that is constitutive of what is real.

By breaking with transparency, speculative realism raises the question of how the secret is reflected in the mirror. This is a question about the specular: about how what is withdrawn sees its own image reflected. The secret is located in the mirror – it becomes a spot, perhaps a blind one, that cannot be seen but has a definite place within the complete image. The specular image includes the blind spots that are the secret failures of transparency. Maybe the blind spots are like vanishing points within the image. In any case, it is as if the specular image provided a sort of cartography of the secret, a map of the borders and neighbours of what is not accessible. In contrast, the metaphysics of the others takes exteriority to be unlimited while providing the changing borders of what is indoors. Speculation seems to be at odds with exteriority – it is always closer to a totality than faithful to a recalcitrant and transcending Great Outdoors. Still, the paths opened up by speculative realism are made to address exteriority with the metaphysics of the others, even if speculation itself has to be rethought in the process.

Committed to exteriority, the metaphysics of the others understands that there is an element left out in any conception of the world. What is left out is not a vanishing point in a cartography of everything, but is rather what makes any map incomplete – and non-completable. That is, the Great Outdoors calls into question any intended full description. Its traces make metaphysics an issue of indexical addresses, a situated enterprise. Speculation is thereby called into question. It has to be limited in the sense that its task of projecting the same on to the other can be interrupted at any point by the unconditional exteriority of the other. An interrupted speculation – like a broken mirror – is one that leaves its task incomplete. Speculation has to be circumscribed by what is outdoors, what is thoroughly other. To place a mirror in a position to project something into the Great Outdoors is to betray its very nature as exterior, yet speculation can provide forays into the unknown. The metaphysics of the others is not an excuse to avoid investigation, but rather a refusal to lose sight of what lies beyond. Investigation aims not at a complete picture, but rather at an ever-supplemented and always changing landscape where exteriority is nevertheless absolute. Absolute exteriority ensures that the indoors itself is always shifting – the traces of the exterior are found not in the result speculation provides, but in the interruptions worked on the projection. The interrupted speculation leaves its marks on the investigation. Like a horizon, the Great Outdoors is never completely shown; it only sketches a contour. As a consequence, the source of realism is not speculation, but rather exteriority itself. The realism of the metaphysics of the others is not speculative, although it is enlightened by speculation. It is, rather, a realism concerning the outside.

The metaphysics of the others is also committed to the transcendence that Levinas opposed to a totality – the transcendence of the others. The attempt to avoid totality while doing justice to what is outer makes the situated metaphysics developed in this something different from a philosophy of immanence. These days, however, in order to postulate something transcendent, one has to come to terms with the numerous efforts in philosophy to dilute what transcends into a pure or overwhelming immanence. The various attempts to ensure that everything is immanent have brought about great numbers of concepts, gestures and tools that are put to use in this book. Philosophers of immanence such as Whitehead – but also Gilles Deleuze, Isabelle Stengers and Bruno Latour – aid in my account of the transcendence of the exterior. This is because what is transcendent is not a specific feature of what there is – substances, identities or other forms of stability – but rather the outer border that characterises what is real. What transcends is alterity, difference understood from a thoroughly deictic point of view. Not surprisingly, the transcendence of the exterior does not boil down to negation which promotes completeness – the result of a negation forms a totality with what is negated.[4] As Levinas points out, what is denied and what denies form a system when put together. A transcendent exterior is not a negation, but rather something other which is opaque – negating can offer a distinction with what is indoors, but what is outdoors is something else that escapes the exercise of expanding sameness and prevents a total system from being envisaged.

The situated metaphysics that follows from indexicalism associates transcendence with no substantive item of the world – what transcends has to do with deictic elements such as the outer, the other, the outside. Transcendence is relative to a position and is precisely what escapes speculation. Realism is the drive towards what is exterior, towards alterity as an ever-pressing *diaphonía* – if the metaphysics of the others is not exactly a speculative realism, it is certainly a non-commonsensical one. Reality is considered to be unavailable to a view from nowhere – there is no bifurcation between the (indexical) viewpoints from where things are seen and the place of reality outside them.

## Other Dialogues

The situated metaphysics of the others proposed in the book posits reality as intrinsically incomplete. The absence of totality can be compared with what Deleuze in his work with Félix Guattari called *n–1*, a multiplicity of conjoined elements forming no unity, and perhaps even more closely to the idea of a *pluriverse*, the coexistence of multiple worlds forming no universe.[5] The absence of a universe is central to the idea that there is no inclusion of what is exterior to the indoors, and no integration of different things into a single overarching realm. The idea of a pluriverse was put forward by the American poet Benjamin Blood – quoted by Deleuze himself in the first chapter of *Difference and Repetition*.[6] The notion has since been revived with little effect, but has nonetheless become part of the toolkit of what Boaventura Sousa Santos called *Epistemologies of the South*, especially in its attempt to make room for different territories freed from an all-encompassing global unity.[7] The paradoxical element in the idea of a pluriverse springs from its structural and infinite character – in a pluriverse, everything is a proper part. The paradox is akin to that of indexicalism: everything has something exterior to it.

Arturo Escobar engaged with the concept of the pluriverse to propose that territories are integrated networks of relations that constitute ultimate reality, as there are no *relata* prior to these networks.[8] Each network that forms a territory is hostage to the surrounding ones, yet each territory is separated from the others, and there is no possible integration that could make the territories dissolve. They could be reshaped and revamped by their neighbours, but cannot be merged into a single unified blob. Furthermore, Escobar takes a situated approach in which the pluriverse is described from the perspective of a territory in struggle – he reckons that the peripheries of the global world often look like impoverished versions of the same precisely because they are products of attempts to integrate what is ultimately other.

I intended this book to be situated in the territories of South America – a continent where colonisation and singularity seem inextricable. In the Coda, no less than in the dialogues with perspectivism and other ideas that come from the anthropology of the lower Amazon, this affiliation is made explicit. In this circumscription, the struggle for pluralism is a stance against the project of extracting the intelligibility of everything – a project that ties the origins of Western metaphysics to current artificial intelligence. If intelligibilities are themselves situated, this extraction must at least be rethought and reconsidered. The metaphysics of the others, with its commitment to the ultimate reality of the Great Outdoors, is in friction with the project of making everything ready to be artificially simulated. Since exteriority requires a position, there is no third-person perspective available from which to capture what there is with substantives that could be transported anywhere independently of their indexical grounding.

The idea of a situated metaphysics – that reality cannot be described except through some position taken on the ground – can also be understood in terms of the distinction put forward by physicist Otto Rössler between *exophysics* and *endophysics*.[9] Endophysics observes and measures the objects, properties, states and events of the world from within. It assumes the indexical vocabulary in its descriptions and in its judgements. As a situated endeavour, endophysics rejects any view from nowhere. Endophysical measurement is always done from some perspective. On the issue of measurement, considered below, situatedness attaches a circumstance to every judgement of size. As Whitehead pointed out, the idea that we can strip measurements both from the location where measuring is done and from the instruments employed is grounded on a bifurcation of nature that would require what is measured to stop short of what nature deprived of experience really is. Indeed, the issue of measurement can be an overlap between questions raised by situated epistemologies – that assume knowledge is always related to a viewpoint – and situated metaphysics such as the one rehearsed in this book. The idea of a tentacular thinking, which is arguably a development Donna Haraway pursued from her situated epistemology, is also akin to indexicalism, as I argue below. For both, reaching the world through substantive unsituated description is not conceivable. Reality, which is haunted by paradoxes, is composed of circumstances.

## The Paradox of Deictic Speculation

I close this introduction with a tentative and perhaps paradoxical remark concerning speculation and its role in indexicalism and the metaphysics of the others. Maybe speculation could take place within the very deictic framework that shapes reality – so that indexicals, but nothing substantive, could ground any speculative move. We could see indexicalism as moving speculatively within deixis.

Indeed, the paradox around indexicalism perhaps extends to speculation itself. On the one hand, indexicalism is the ground for the metaphysics of the others, posits the Great Outdoors as a component of reality, and is at odds with unchecked applications of a speculative procedure. On the other hand, indexicalism can be described as a speculative leap from the (widespread) indexical practices with which we think and talk. If reality itself is indexical, it follows that there are others (and outdoors) in it – speculation is then interrupted to make room for something fully exterior. The way towards paradox seems to be that what is exterior – which is always there perhaps as a product of a speculative move – cannot be accounted for through any speculation based on a substantive unsituated description. If there is any room for speculation, it is in thoroughly indexical terms. Maybe in deixis we can extend our view beyond what is assumed in our practices while deixis itself enables interruptions in the projection of the same on to the other. Indexicalism can be seen as engaging in an abstract (deictic) speculation which prevents other speculations. In this sense, this book claims that deixis, the very place of situatedness and to some extent relativity, is absolute.

I recently discovered the expression 'deictic absolutes' in Brian Blanchfield's book *Proxies: A Memoir in Twenty-Four Attempts*. In an essay called 'On the Near Part', Blanchfield considers conversations where deictic expressions are offered with little prospect of forthcoming clarification. This is the understanding of the notion that I employ: there is no underlying substantive reality to clarify indexicals. Deixis reaches bedrock. Even if this can be framed as a speculative conclusion, it is one that maintains that what is real always entertains the Great Outdoors in its proximity. If deixis is ultimate, proximity itself is somehow part of what there is. Deictic vocabulary could sometimes give the impression that there is something still in the air, not fully described. Indexicalism renders this incorrigible. But this should be the very allure of reality, if exteriority is irredeemably just around the corner. It is only from within that there is anything. Speculation could take us far away, but a deictic realism brings us back to where we are, facing the wall that establishes the other side.

## Notes

1. Harman, *Speculative Realism*.
2. In Chapter 1, I also consider Tristan Garcia's object-oriented ontology where there is no room for real objects. Instead, Garcia postulates two separate modes of existence for objects, a formal one where they exist in contrast with their surrounding universe and an objective one where the multiple objects access each other (Garcia, *Form and Object*). It is as if Garcia, much like Aristotle who understands the intelligible as what can be seen as such, distinguishes two modes of existence, while Harman, in a move that could be compared with Plato's, makes an extensional distinction between the real and the sensual object
3. Below, in Chapter 1, I explore Jon Cogburn's notion of a paradoxico-metaphysics in *Garcian Meditations*.
4. Benjamim Noys in *The Persistence of the Negative* argues against the late twentieth-century philosophies of immanence and diagnoses them as lacking the means to deal with negation, chiefly due to the exorcising of Hegel from the Marxist picture. Although the rejection of Hegelian ideas such as that of determinate negation made a big impact on philosophies of immanence such as those of Deleuze and Jean-François Lyotard, it is unclear that negation is the central enemy of those philosophies.
5. Deleuze and Guattari, *A Thousand Plateaus*.
6. See Blood, *Pluriverse*, and Deleuze, *Difference and Repetition*.
7. See Sousa Santos, *Epistemologies of the South*.
8. Escobar, 'Sentipensar con la Tierra'.
9. Rössler, *Endophysics*.

# Indexicalism:
# A Paradoxico-Metaphysics

*The question concerning the world is a question that addresses our proximity.*

Emmanuel Levinas[1]

## Indexicalism

*Here, there, in here, out there, this* and *that*, or maybe *this hand* and *that mountain*; resorting to pointing, I can indicate what is around me with expressions like these. I can attempt to rephrase or replace the question of why there is something rather than nothing with the question of why there is *this* rather than *that*.[2] Pointing, and using expressions that depend on some sort of pointing, deals with what is outside me in connection with what surrounds me (therefore to where I am). Because of my *standing location*, I can deal with what is external to me by pointing. If I can point at the *Great Outdoors* (or the external world, or what is outside me, or what is beyond me), it is nearby and it is around the corner, around my corner – further, it is exterior only with respect to me.

Pointing is a common practice – perhaps too common to attract much metaphysical attention. Not much has been said about the fact that reality is such that it can be pointed at. Furthermore, realism, as much as it is about going beyond one's own thinking, could be taken as a statement about pointing. Pointing can only be done from a standing location. My standing location matters because I am in the midst of things, *in media res*, to use the Latin phrase. We are in a place where we can point at the hand and at the mountain; we are among them. We can therefore think about what is around us. A distinction between kinds of belief attribution can help in understanding this dimension of being among what we are talking about – the distinction between *de re* and *de dicto* beliefs.³ Broadly speaking, we can say that *de re* thought requires a relation to what is thought. We can point at things – and think in a demonstrative, *de re* way about them – because we are in relation with them, we are not contemplating reality from nowhere. My *de re* thoughts are intelligible only from where I am.

Such thoughts are often considered to be of little importance – or of mere heuristic significance – when it comes to describing how things are out there. Expressions that perform like pointing – *this* and *that* – are perhaps sufficient to present what is around us, but are rarely more than a starting point in the business of offering an image of the furniture of the universe.⁴ An answer to that somehow grander question would involve stepping beyond my current position to reach a supposedly unbiased viewpoint. According to this line of argument, the furniture of the universe is revealed by a view from nowhere – the most impartial, the closest to how things really are and therefore the most commendable place for viewing. The line of argument follows from an account of the Great Outdoors according to which it ought to be independent from the window from which it is seen. The account is itself a corollary of the metaphysical presupposition – call it *substantivism* – according to which the world is ultimately composed of what substantives or nouns denote, such as trees, lakes, houses, artichokes, salt, lemon, wine, or matter or spirit. These substantives, which are not necessarily substances, afford purely *de dicto* thoughts. Substantivism therefore holds that talk about *this* and *that* cannot be part of a proper description of what things are. While the universe is made of whatever is denoted by 'this' and 'that', it cannot be appropriately described (or adequately accounted for) in language that assumes standing locations.

Hence, substantivism favours nouns and not demonstratives to give an account of the universe; there are hands and mountains, and as a consequence, this hand and that mountain. An account of the universe should not be given in terms of *de re* beliefs aiming at *de re* truths. The perils of positioned talk, the substantivist line continues, are manifold. One can miss the point of how things are 'out there' by confusing them with what is around – confusing the furniture of the universe with one's own surroundings, maybe one's own perceptions or perhaps one's own way of relating to what is outside. The perils go by names such as *idealism*, which is different from *subjectivism*, which are both different from *correlationism*.⁵ In order to make sure that what is out there is properly considered, the substantivist recipe is that any positioned talk must be exorcised in favour of an impersonal view from nowhere, the only way to account for how things are 'out there'.[6] To be sure, subjects, positions and points of view could be considered part of the furniture of the universe in a substantivist approach, but they would have to be treated in a *de dicto*, impersonal way in the language of substantives. One can describe subjects in terms of their capacities, or in terms of their qualities or relations, with substantives. To describe a position, a perspective or a point of view, according to substantivism, is neither to endorse it nor to accept any other.

A central contention of this book is that this, that and the other – as indexicals – belong to the ultimate furniture of the universe. (As we will see shortly, the furniture is paradoxical.) The universe is deictic or indexical, and therefore demonstratives are better equipped than substantives to deal with it, and ultimately to provide some sort of account of it. As a consequence, substantivism is rejected: although nouns can be used to provide useful accounts of a great part of what exists, they provide no more than a *façon de parler*. Substantives provide useful heuristics to disclose features of things but conceal situated presuppositions inside them – either because pointing is implicit in the use of a word or because talk of nouns conceals standing locations.

My contrasting thesis – call it *indexicalism* – is that the starting points of any metaphysical account of the universe are neither substances nor actual entities, neither objects (or subjects) nor material items, neither neutrinos nor forces, but rather this, that, in, out, same, other, here, there, horizons and other indexicals – and they are much more numerous than is often thought. There is an irreducibly deictic character in the furniture of the universe; its elements have to include something like what is around and what is away, what is internal and what is external, what is nearer and what is farther or outer, what is the same and what is different. Deictic features are therefore present everywhere. They are not a dimension of thought (or language) but a consequence of being somewhere. As a result, it is not only thought or language that can be *de re*; I am closer to claiming that *to be* is itself an indexical, or rather that to be is to be indexed. In other words, to be is to be capable of being pointed at.

Indexicalism holds that things are constituted of deictic elements. More precisely, indexicalism holds that the ultimate realities of the universe are concrete indexicals – the very structure of what is concrete is deictic. It surely can come in many flavours, as the struggle between indexicalism and substantivism can be found in several debates in the history of philosophy. In order to find it, one has to disentangle it from discussions about correlationism, subjectivism and idealism and, in general, discussions about how to access the Great Outdoors. As we will see, sometimes disentangling the issue of indexicalism from the discussions about what can be thought or known independently of who thinks or who knows is not straightforward.

One can find a possible precursor to indexicalism in Plato's Stranger in his *Sophist*, who posits five *megista gene* (greater kinds): *Same*, *Other*, *Rest*, *Movement* and *Being*. Being appears surrounded by four indexical kinds that are external to it but affect it from without. One can find here a process whereby indexicality shapes Being – whatever there is occupies a position with respect to what else exists. The Stranger promotes the parricide of Parmenides by holding that not being could be if it is simply other than being; nothingness is not itself a greater kind but a product of Other applied to Being. It is as if the Stranger comes from outside to provide Being with an address: it is only in relation to what is other than being that being is. Nothing precedes these ultimate five kinds; there is nothing substantive underneath them. They are, the five of them, equally ultimate. Moreover, at least four of the ultimate components of whatever exists are indexical – the remaining one, Being, surrounded by the other greater kinds, can hardly be considered in purely substantive terms.

In any case, indexicalism is far from a standard view in metaphysics. To spell it out and argue for it – which I will do in a more or less intertwined way – will involve a non-standard combination of input from different traditions in a composition that will bring together some central ideas from Levinas, elements of philosophical reflection on demonstratives and *de re* language, attention to perceptual experience, and insights coming from process philosophy, especially from Whitehead. In this chapter I intend to introduce the ingredients for my indexicalist mix. These ingredients themselves are enough to insinuate the finished potion, for each of them suggests that there are hidden deictic elements underneath anything substantive.

## Paradoxico-Metaphysics

Indexicalism has an air of paradox. If the furniture of the universe is deictic, both the idea of furniture – pieces that are more or less detachable – and the idea of universe – one big thing with no external borders – become weird.[7] One way to begin to come to terms with this is to take indexicalism as both a metaphysical doctrine and a way to argue that metaphysics is impossible (or ought to be severely bound). It is the latter because it attempts to show that nothing substantive can be said about what there is – at least, nothing in terms of irreducible substantives. It is only from a positioned place, and not from no place at all, that the universe can become accessible and its pieces of furniture be considered. If the metaphysical project involves giving a general account of everything at once, the project has to be abandoned or severely revised. But the project is doomed not because there are limits to our access to what there is – it is not the fault of the aspiring metaphysician. The fault is that there is no such thing as a metaphysical picture in this sense – a general account of everything at once – to be attained. This is why indexicalism is also a metaphysical doctrine: it explains why this metaphysical picture cannot be attained and therefore why the metaphysical project is impossible. It is a metaphysics that accounts for the impossibility of metaphysics. Analogously, it is a metaphysics that responds to the questions of why and how metaphysics should be overcome: there is no metaphysics of pointers unless metaphysics itself is a pointing.

Cogburn has coined the term *paradoxico-metaphysics*.[8] Such a metaphysics would establish the general features of reality that make access to the general features of reality impossible (or severely limited). He introduces the idea of a paradoxico-metaphysics as follows:

> Metaphysics aims to give a maximally general account of what reality is like such that we encounter the phenomena that we do. But what if we encounter phenomena [. . .] that seem to entail that metaphysics is impossible? Then the task of metaphysics is to give a maximally general account of what reality is like such that metaphysics is impossible.[9]

Indexicalism is such a paradoxical endeavour. To be sure, the paradoxical element can be accommodated if we consider that 'metaphysics' is being used in similar but slightly different senses.

In one sense, it is attached to an all-encompassing domain that can be absorbed in a single glance; metaphysics would entail substantivism, the thesis that substantives are the ultimate constituents of what there is. In another, it is related to what exists – in this case, a deictic furniture that makes everything positioned or situated – even if there are no ultimate substantive items. Indexicalism holds that any enclosed realm described by substantives has something beyond it – *beyond* is a constituent of reality as much as an ingredient of thought. As it is, 'metaphysics' points on one hand to an enclosed totality and on the other to its transcendence. If the furniture of the universe is indexical and involves something beyond any set of its pieces, there is no all-inclusive realm with nothing beyond it. The two senses of 'metaphysics' are entangled enough, however, to show that there is a metaphysical reason why metaphysics is impossible – a paradoxico-metaphysical reason. The reason can be spelled out in terms of a consequence of indexicalism: there is no transcendence-free totality.

### The Routes to Indexicalism (and Paradox)

Levinas is an important character in my indexicalist plot because, from his *Totality and Infinity* onwards, he focused his philosophical attention on what he understood as an irreducibly indexical element: the Other, which he treated respectfully with a capital first letter. The Other, as in Plato's *Sophist*, is external to being and, as such, provides some sort of constraint on it from without. The Other is not an operator – that would make it possible to think of myself as the Other of the Other, which would quickly lead to the view from nowhere – but a mark of exteriority.[10] Levinas has championed a struggle against postulating a transcendence-free totality that will encompass both what is within and what is without, leaving no room for anything beyond. At first glance, it seems he has an ethical problem with totality: it is unfair and violent to the Other, for it converts the Other into something substantive. In fact, his ethical project can be described as the effort to rescue the Other – an indexical in an asymmetrical relation to the Same[11] – from substantives. To describe what is other in terms of substantives is to make it less other, to bring it to a common ground in a step towards totality.

He compares the existence of the Other as such with the ontological argument: it is in the nature of the Other to exist as something exterior.[12] This is the metaphysical import of his effort: to clearly disentangle exteriority from totality. It is an error to try to achieve the exterior through a view from nowhere that sees everything while being in no place; it is a form of violence to subject the Great Outdoors to a total image that makes it less Outdoors (and maybe less Great). Interestingly, a view from nowhere is precisely what is rejected both by Parmenides in his exorcism of nothingness beyond being and by Plato's Stranger's parricide that insists that nothingness is intelligible but only as being completely other. The parricide makes room for a view from an absolute other, but not for a view from nowhere. Levinas's commitment to the Other is a commitment to exteriority that explicitly distances him from a quest for totality. In this sense, Levinas will appear in my construction of indexicalism as someone who provides a key to distinguish it from many forms of idealism, subjectivism and correlationism. To be confined in an environment of indexicals – of this and that and the like – is not to be enclosed away from anything external, precisely because the indexical environment includes the beyond, the other, the across the border. Levinas's strategy compared with the ontological argument intends to show that while those indexicals are inside an environment, their role is to point to something exterior. It is in their nature to point to something beyond. It is precisely because this element of beyond – the Other – seems not to fit in a substantive description that Levinas builds his philosophical stance on indexicals. He presents a robust contrast between the deictic character of the Other and any substantive attempt at a description.[13] This contrast is also a contrast between exteriority and totality; while the latter, at least in principle, can be captured by some sort of general description, the former requires an element beyond any description.

Drawing on the distinction between the descriptive and the demonstrative, this book will articulate and defend an image of the world according to which everything is ultimately positioned in the context of its proximity. In other words, nothing plays a role in a grand scale of things if by this grand scale we mean a transcendence-free totality. Rather, what exists is endowed with addresses and cannot be accounted for without respect to its neighbourhood. Spelling out indexicalism will require a Levinasian rejection of totality that privileges exteriority combined with a process-philosophical approach that will extend the deictic character of what exists beyond the human (and beyond living organisms). Such an approach enables attention to what is concrete instead of a focus on general principles or laws. Whitehead's term for the belief that incomplete attention to the singular circumstances of an actual existent was enough to account for what is concrete is 'the fallacy of misplaced concreteness'.[14]

The singular circumstances of an actual existent in its concreteness escape from any account of existence in general. This stance is shared by Levinas, chiefly in his *Existence and Existents*, where priority is given to the actual existent, which always shoulders the burden of existence. The concrete, anywhere, is not composed only of examples of a general description but also of all sorts of non-universal, situated environments where whatever is actual is in contact with something else that is actual alongside. In process philosophy, such a view paves the way for an understanding of humans and non-humans in similar terms. This displacement of humans from centre stage places indexicalism with contemporary metaphysical endeavours such as object-oriented philosophy and new materialism.[15]

The assembling together of process philosophy and Levinas's attention to the Other will require some care, for the former easily slips in the very direction of transcendence-free totalities that the latter intends to exorcise. Also, we will see that indexicalism has difficulties with the speculative method that informs some process philosophy – especially that of Whitehead – and some other contemporary metaphysical enterprises. With a broad brush, indexicalism has a nominalist feel to it: it attempts to exorcise universals. Also in conformity with the spirit of nominalism, the indexicalist concentration on the particularities of the concrete – together with siding with exteriority against totality – encourages experience to play a decisive role. In that sense, it departs from at least some application of the speculative method of understanding the unknown through projections from what has been experienced while welcoming attention to the concrete in experience as a place where the novel appears. Experience turns out to be more than what makes it possible to extract the meaning from what is perceived.

## Situated Metaphysics

I understand indexicalism as espousing a thoroughly situated metaphysics. This means that positions where indexicals apply are the ultimate building blocks. Indexicals, as *de re* talk, make sense only in the middle of things, from a position, from somewhere. There are indexicals only if there are positions, positions that in their turn cannot be fully described in substantives. These positions are the viewpoints where demonstratives apply: *me*, *here* and *now* point to the interior of a position, whereas *other*, *there* and *later* point outwards. They are standing locations: passing, situated and fully described through the place they are with respect to anything else. A position can be understood as composed primarily of a border that distinguishes what is inside it and what is outside. I will call these positions *interiorities* and take them to be composed by *deictic operations* that can be seen as their ultimate components.

Interiorities are not substances, nor do they in any sense tend to subsist – they are no more than standing locations. They could also be compared with bodies.[16] Each interiority is placed in an indexical environment, mapped out by deictic operations. Clearly, interiorities are not substantive realities that precede demonstrative talk; they only make sense – only have their borders drawn – through the deictic operations. As such, interiorities are units that cannot be contemplated, or considered, or counted from nowhere – they are positions mapped by demonstratives and as such they are partly determined from outside, from other positions. In an important sense, interiorities are not closed, for they are also drawn by indexicals that point outwards, not in terms of substantive descriptions of what is outside but rather in terms of demonstratives that fix positions without providing a substantive determination of what is there. Deictic operations, as we will see shortly, fix references; it is through this fixation that they establish positions (and compose interiorities). Each interiority therefore includes an exterior: each is composed of operations such as both here and away, now and later, around and elsewhere, same and other. If we see these operations as ultimately constituting particles, they draw borders that are relative to other positions; interiorities are always positions with respect to other interiorities. They have an other, an exterior, embedded in them. Exteriority is possible because there are interiorities, but these are not enclosed units; rather, they are hostages of what is exterior. These units in their turn, in line with Levinas's distinction between totality and exteriority, form no whole. Jean Wahl, reflecting on how Hegelian dialectics leads to totality, describes the process as drawing in each step on the fragmentary. In a sense, indexicalism is a way of never betraying externality by falling for the attractions of totality; each position in an indexical map has what Wahl calls 'a naked and blind contact with the Other'.[17]

Interiorities are therefore intimately marked by the exterior, but form locations that can be referred to through demonstratives. Those standing locations, according to indexicalism, are what makes predication possible. As such, they shoulder the burden of concrete existence: nothing exists without a standing location among concrete things, so every concrete existence therefore lies in an interiority. No predication can be made without a position to be predicated. It is the position, the interiority, that is predicated; in that sense, it is similar to what Aristotle in the *Organon* called a *tode ti* or an *ousia prote*.[18] Though it is what supports predication, it is not in itself any predicate (or cluster or bundle of predicates). It is a concrete position that is ultimately predicated: for example, 'being mortal' applies to an interiority that is Socrates, delimited by deictic operations. The interiorities thus delimited can also be compared with substrata, something that can make two indiscernibles – two subjects of the same predications – non-identical. If two particular entities have different substrata, they can have the same qualities and relations but still be different. We will see that the deictic operations that compose an interiority can require predicates, but once a position is fixed, it becomes somehow independent of the predicates used in its composition. The predication of something, the 'is P' of a predication, requires a subject. Levinas remarks that concrete existence is always under hypostasis – the postulation of a subject. Even 'being Spinoza's God' – the most impersonal entity he can conceive – is tied to an entity that bears the predication.[19] The subject of a predication is fixed by deictic operations; it is an interiority. According to indexicalism, *these* operations and the mapping of positions precede any predication: before any S is P, before S is anything, it is constituted as a standing location by deictic operations. Although these demonstratives are often implicit in predicates and substantives, indexicalism claims that deictic operations underlie any predication.

## Monadologies

It is instructive to compare interiorities with monads and their interaction with what different monadologies describe. This comparison will appear throughout this book, but it is time to introduce it now. I take the monadological tradition in metaphysics to have brought to the fore the importance of coexistence and the social interdependence of what exists.[20] It is a tradition championed by Leibniz, which has echoes in different accounts of coexistence and social interdependence from the twentieth century in which monads were either explicitly postulated or implicitly assumed.

As opposed to the self-grounded substances Aristotle postulated, Leibnizian monads are identical if and only if they are indiscernible. Having no substrata, they are composed of their qualities, their relations, their states and the events they participate in. Leibnizian monads depend on their relations to be what they are. They are not isolated in their predications – unlike Descartes' *res extensa*, which is independent of any thinking, and Descartes' *res cogitans*, which is indifferent to any spatial feature. Monads are interconnected units of action that together make the actual world what it is. For Leibniz, they are chosen by God with an eye to the excellence of the world that they compose. Each monad is individuated with the help of all others in a possible world – they could not subsist in a different possible world because they carry all the other world-mate monads in their interior. Monads are worldly. They are geared towards their specific society of monads.[21]

Different monadologies have discarded some of Leibniz's metaphysical assumptions – especially those having to do with the world being designed by God and therefore displaying a pre-established harmony between all events – while keeping some features specifically related to understanding the universe as made of interdependent units of action.[22] In general, however, they also tend to maintain the idea that units of action have no substrata and are defined in terms of their predicates. In principle, therefore, they could be describable in substantive terms. Indexicalism is itself not far from the idea that the universe is made of interdependent units of action. However, instead of ditching substrata to embrace predication, indexicalism does the opposite: it posits substrata as standing locations prior to any predication.

If the monadological move is to understand predication as that which connects whatever coexists, the indexicalist move is rather to find this connection in what lies underneath any predication – substrata conceived as standing locations. The idea is to engage what underlies predication, and not predication itself, to account for the connectedness of what exists. Because of the ubiquitous and irreducible deictic operations, there is no closed totality formed by the interdependence between the interiorities. The deictic relations each interiority has with the others make them part of a coexisting collection that nevertheless forms no transcendence-free totality. Interiorities do not belong to a world understood as a totality in pre-established harmony, as Leibniz's monads do. Rather, they are hostage to the exteriority that composes them, and this is what distances them from a closed totality in which predicates determine everything about each unit.

Gabriel Tarde, Alfred North Whitehead and Bruno Latour have proposed non-Leibnizian neo-monadological metaphysical systems.[23] Tarde's monadology is explicitly a sociology in which monads interact with each other through social relations; they attempt to associate in order to attain their aims. Just as in Leibniz, monads persist in time and can be defined in terms of their predicates. Among their qualities, they have aims, and as units of action they act to attain those aims. They are guided by their agendas; they can depart from pursuing them, but only when forced to by other monads with different, extrinsically distinct agendas. Something similar can be found in Whitehead. He drops the idea that units are substances, and his actual entities do not subsist in time, although they are the ultimate individuals that account for any actuality, including those of space and time. As in Leibniz, the perception of other units of action is central; actual entities are interrelated by operations of perception – each one perceives others by being affected by them from outside and not, as in Leibniz, by having them inside as a programme for action. In Whitehead, actual entities in their mutual solidarity are responsible for anything concrete through their goals, their creativity and their capacity for satisfaction.[24] As in Tarde, and by contrast with indexicalist interiorities, Whitehead's actual entities are aim-oriented, and whatever is exterior to them affects them only by affecting the aggregate course of action. Latour introduces the idea of a post-established harmony between non-substantial monads that struggle to survive in different tests of resistance. These tests are crucial, and one can only count how many units of action there are in relation to these tests of resistance.[25] He draws on Tarde to propose a monadology of social agents seeking an appropriate network that can enhance their capacity to attain their aims. In all these cases, the goal that guides the action relates to what is exterior only through a totality – a totality of a pre-selected world or of a world being composed. The exterior affects the units only to the extent that each unit depends on what is there, and therefore forms a totality encompassing each unit and its exterior.

Monadological thinking has a substantivist kernel. Each unit of action is defined by a class of predicates that includes qualities, relations, states of affairs and events, and these predicates are meaningful only by contrast with other units of action. This interconnection through predicates – through substantives – brings forth a (transcendence-free) totality. Leibniz's monads house in their interior connections to other monads, some of them clearly perceived and others only hinted at. They need no (new) information from outside, as their action is always programmed to be in harmony with the other monads in their world. In God's global choice of a world that he has chosen to be actual among infinitely many other possible worlds, each monad is selected by its predicates and characterised by them alone. It is situated among others only through the relations they have with its predicates – relations that can be described independently of any deictic operation. Leibniz's monads are endowed with a capacity to perceive their world-mate monads because their relations to all the others are inscribed within them. This provides each of them with a perspective. For example, Adam is a sinning monad, and although it is contingent since there are infinitely many possible worlds, it is determined in advance that he will find the apple and eat it.[26] The apple is unique because of its predicates, and the principle of the identity of indiscernibles. Adam knows enough of the predicates of the apple to be able to identify it – his perspective is composed of an articulation of predicates. God, in contrast, knows all the predicates of the apple and needs no pointing to fix the reference of those predicates – the apple is uniquely determined by its predicates. Furthermore, Adam himself needs no deictic operation to find the apple. The predicates he uses are made to be enough to find the apple in the right moment; this is the role of divine design. In neo-monadologies this role is dropped, but each unit still relates to the others through their predicates.

Indexicalism shares with monadologies the claim that interiorities are basic elements in the universe. Monadologies inherit from Descartes the idea that subjectivities cannot be reduced to anything that involves no interiorities, and that genuine interiorities are somehow alien to a totality formed without them.[27] Monadologies proceed to spread interiorities throughout – and through predicates make a totality of an aggregate of them.

Looking at the monadological attention to a plurality of interiorities, I'm tempted to say that the indexicalist (paradoxico-)metaphysics is a kind of non-substantivist monadology. This would do justice to the effort monadological thought makes to understand the coexistence of interiorities. But in relevant senses that will become clearer below, indexicalism contrasts with any monadology mainly because indexicalist interiorities do not have identities that can be described by a class of predicates. Rather, they are defined in terms of deictic operations; indexicalism's Cartesian heritage hinges solely on the idea that there are interiorities in the universe. Additionally, in contrast with the units of action in monadologies, these interiorities are not defined in terms of a purpose. To be clear, they can have aims, but the deictic operations that compose them precede and underlie any aim.

The friction between indexicalism and monadology is nevertheless fertile and often difficult to grasp. Whitehead, in particular, arrives at a neo-monadological way of thinking through a rejection of absolute space (and absolute time) and through an insistence on the primary character of events. He takes events and duration to constitute time systems and spatial relations. Events and relative time and space create an image of things in which they are utterly situated and relative to a deixis. Events are understood in terms of what goes on and therefore in terms of motion – and motion requires a fixed point of view. Whitehead's actual entities are themselves events capable of perceiving other events. In *The Concept of Nature*, he introduces the percipient event in terms of a *locus standi* which is 'represented in thought by the concept of "here"'.[28] The percipient event needs a duration associated with its 'here' – Whitehead calls this relation *cogredience*[29] – that can only be conceived within a time system and that is thoroughly situated. This 'here', the *locus standi* that makes possible an actual entity capable of perceiving events, is a place in the world. Nothing is more relevant to a percipient event than its location. This *locus standi* is an interiority. Whitehead's need for *loci standi* shows that interiorities are situated, as they are demarcated by deictic operations. The percipient event is what provides the foothold for any perception in the world; perception requires a point of view, a standing location. Situated interiorities, drawn by deictic operations and ascribing a position for predication, are a point of departure for indexicalism. The *locus standi* seems to be a common denominator of interiority that makes it close to a Whiteheadian neo-monadology.

This common denominator of interiorities – that they are endowed with a standing location – is, however, part of two different concoctions. Whitehead's metaphysics of events in *The Concept of Nature* is consolidated into a more general process philosophy in *Process and Reality* and other subsequent texts. The situated element associated with the primacy of events is made less intense by the stress on actual entities, their interconnectedness and their aims. They are located in a space formed by perceptions that dwell in predicates, for actual entities are oriented by their aims, pursue their satisfaction and exercise creativity. The situated dimension of standing location fades when mingled with the predicates that orient actual entities through perception – and dims when associated with an overarching goal. Indexicalism, on the other hand, emphasises the deictic operations that compose a standing location. Its central focus is the indexical environment, where there is always space for transcendence through the other, the outer, the beyond, the Great Outdoors.

## Totality

Levinas gives a central importance to (his notion of) interiority. He acknowledges that it is a Cartesian inheritance that makes him start out with interiority, while bearing in mind that exteriority and separation from what is outside are crucial to a genuine transcendence rather than a mere interdependence. He claims that separation is the very condition for me to be affected by the Other – as much as atheism is what makes religion possible, as opposed to a mere dependence on God.[30] Interdependency creates totality, while separation enables something else: the infinite exteriority of the Other. Infinity is what prevents the totalising movement – the Other cannot be encompassed by any complete account.

There are several senses of totality that emerge from this contrast with exteriority. One of them is the absence of interiority. If there is no interiority, one cannot make sense of the asymmetrical distinction between same and other, arguably of any indexical reasoning at all, and more generally of any deictic operation that cannot merely be shorthand for a relation between predicates. In any sense of interiority, there is the external element that contrasts with what is inside: the external world beyond the *res cogitans*, the other units of action in a monadology, what is beyond an ego and its intentional acts. It can be said that the indexicalist interiority is a minimum denominator that is required for an interiority to be such: the capacity to occupy a position that draws a distinction between inner and outer through deictic operations. An interiority has to have an exterior – and in that sense we can say that a totality cannot be an interiority. Leibniz's attempt to conciliate interiorities filled with predicates and the totality of a possible world assumes that worlds themselves have no interiority. (The same can be said of the totality formed by all possible worlds that Leibniz presents in the metaphor of the palace of Palas towards the end of the *Theodicy* – here, each one of the infinitely many rooms is a possible world.) Indexicalism postulates that interiorities – like exteriority – abound. There is no being that is not indexical – and if this is so, there is no such thing as a (transcendence-free) totality.

Another important sense of totality in contrast with exteriority has directly to do with asymmetry. Levinas considers that my relation with the Other cannot rest on symmetry because if it is so, then I am already seeing both myself and the Other from nowhere. I am not the Other for the Other, because it is for me that the Other is Other. This is partly shown, for Levinas, by considering how absurd and criminal it is to ask of the others what I ask of myself.[31] To respond to what is asked – and not required or commanded – is entirely my responsibility. Asking, which involves this appeal to responsibility, always comes from somewhere: there is an Other who asks me something because I can respond. The refusal of totality is the refusal to understand what is asked as coming from nowhere – this is why, in Levinas, there is no moral code that can replace the ethical stance.

In any case, asymmetry is an important feature of indexicalism, with its viewpoints and standing locations. It is not that there is the mountain-for-me, as opposed to the mountain-in-itself that could be only viewed from nowhere, and also to me-for-the-mountain; rather, there is a mountain-for-me and the other which is the mountain, seen from my point of view as external. The outer is always situated in an interiority – there is no external world independent of a viewpoint. Conflating exteriority with totality leads to the idea that realism about the external world must entail the postulation of a totality. In fact, if there is a totality there is no genuine exteriority, because there is no asymmetry between what is internal and what is external. To consider that the internal is the external for the external is to engage in something akin to what John McDowell labelled a 'sideways-on picture': a picture that would separate conceptual operations on one side from the world on the other.[32] In this case, the sideways-on picture would also produce a totality by putting the deictic operations on one side and the world on the other – or the indexicals by means of which I occupy a position and the Other are seen stereoscopically from a different (and reciprocal) set of indexicals. We can alternate between the points of view of two interiorities, but the stereoscopic view would require that we occupy both at the same time – and this is the sideways-on picture. In other words, we assume that there is a description of the external that is not phrased in terms of anyone's indexicals, just as McDowell intends to exorcise the idea that the world is alien to our conceptual operations. As a consequence of exorcising this picture, we have to be careful with third-person descriptions. If they are indexical-free, they slip into a sideways-on picture. If they are themselves made from a position, then the predicates they are using to describe the others are (implicitly) supported by the deictic operations that distinguish between the describing I and the others being described.

Totality can also spell an appeal to a common factor or a neutral predicate that would apply both to what is internal and what is external. This sense of totality is expressed by the idea that the Other is another I, an alter ego. Edmund Husserl, in the fifth of his *Cartesian Meditations*, attempts to show that the phenomenological endeavour he described in his first four meditations yields no solipsism.[33] For Husserl, thinking and acting are understood in terms of intentional acts, and there is nothing prior to or independent of them in subjectivity. A subjectivity is defined in terms of its intentional acts. The difficulty consists in the fact that the point of departure of the endeavour is the subject where intentional acts take place, and that if this is so, any other subject would also be a product of these intentional acts and therefore not an independent reality on its own. Husserl then proposes to dispel the fear of solipsism by coupling his phenomenology with a (neo-)monadology that enables him to consider the other subjects as a reflected image of 'my own' ego, source of all intentional acts; this reflected image becomes an *alter ego*. The alter ego is just like me; it is a specular image of myself and my own intentional acts. Levinas is explicit in his debt to Husserl and his phenomenological method, which allowed him to engage in a thoroughly first-person way of thinking in philosophy. Husserl is right to start out in the first person, and is also right in worrying about the danger of solipsism. However, the idea of an alter ego seems to Levinas to be the wrong path, for as he puts it, the Other as Other 'is not only an alter ego: the Other is what I myself am not'.[34] The problem with the alter ego is that it takes my deictic operations, which are implicit in my intentional acts, as predicates that can be projected on to what is exterior. As a way to avoid solipsism, the alter ego comes too late: there should be something exterior to me before any intentional act – a subjectivity is an indexical interiority before its intentional acts.

Levinas's rejection of the alter ego could seem like an extreme gesture; after all, if the external deserves respect, it is reasonable to conceive of it as an ego, as an interiority just like myself. Levinas's dissatisfaction with the idea of the Other as an alter ego arises from at least two lines of thought, both of them illustrative of an indexicalist way of thinking: first, a rejection of the totality that symmetry brings – the alter ego is a specular image of the ego that replaces exteriority with more of the same; second, a rejection of the idea that the Other stands on the same footing as me. The Other, deserving of the respect of a capital initial, is not like me, not familiar, but is precisely what is external and strange to me; this character of strangeness is brought to the fore when I acknowledge the Other as another. My intentional acts are grounded in the deictic operations that shape my interiority, and these include the distinction between same and other through which the borders of my interiority are drawn. Rather than the idea that the Other is to be seen primarily as like me – the idea of symmetry – Levinas prefers the idea that the Other is superior, asymmetrical and external to what I am. To be sure, I can take into consideration what I know about myself to understand the Other. This is not because my effort is to step into the Other's shoes, but rather because I understand the external as such only when I let the Other step into my shoes. Respect for the external is not to project me on to the Other but rather to let myself be infected by the external, by the stranger. This is what Levinas calls substitution, replacing oneself by another – acting not only towards the Other, but for the Other.[35] The possibility of substitution as a way to relate to what is external is what makes it possible for my action to depart from my agenda and my aims. In substitution, it is my course of action that is interrupted by something that transcends me; only from the point of view of totality can there be mutual transcendence.[36]

A final sense of totality to be rejected by the indexicalist is the idea that a complete description of the external world is possible. This is where indexicalism might look like a case of the impossibility of metaphysics. Here again, Levinas helps in his insistence that the Other is never fully captured by me. What is beyond is infinite. (The Great Outdoors is greater than any totality.) Every description is not only from the viewpoint of an interiority, but is also incomplete. Indexicalism holds that being is indexical, and therefore that nothing exists but as *this*, *that* or the like, from a positioned point of view.

The impossibility of a complete description – which would be like a view from nowhere – is a consequence both of the impossibility of eliminating exteriority and of existence itself being indexical. The same and the other are never only the same and the other, and no indexical will exhaust what anything is – because it can be something else when pointed at from elsewhere. But couldn't the different situated descriptions of an object – this desk-for-me and this shelter-for-the-cat – be merged together? Granted, this desk-for-me cannot be summed up in its entirety by a description oriented by my deictic operations, nor by any other situated description. But what about an aggregate of different situated descriptions? A first problem with such an aggregate totality is whether one can aggregate all the possibly infinitely many situated viewpoints to form something that could be a candidate for a complete description. Even if this aggregate is conceivable, there would be no such thing as what is described by it, since being is always indexical – a cubist view from nowhere is nonetheless still a view from nowhere. A cubist totality is still non-situated, and it provides no complete description because it extracts the deictic operations that compose being if being is indexical. From this indexicalist point of view, it cannot be a complete description, and a cubist aggregate – aside from hardly being complete – would provide no suitable (indexicalist) account.

Cogburn understands paradoxico-metaphysics as amounting to a claim that metaphysics is itself necessary and impossible. He understands that metaphysics ought somehow to tackle totalities as it addresses maximally general accounts of reality, but should also acknowledge that those totalities are often themselves paradoxical. By enclosing everything, they fail at least to enclose themselves. Cogburn understands that the only totalities that can concern metaphysics are the ones that turn out to be inconsistent. He writes:

> We cannot help but to treat the totalities of most interest to us as if they constitute the world, but in doing so we think of such totalities as both closed and transcendent, leading to contradiction. And for the paradoxico-metaphysician the world itself is the inconsistent totality that generates these contradictions when we interact with it. If our metaphysics is contradictory, that is because it accurately reflects reality.[37]

Inconsistent totalities are the staple of a paradoxico-metaphysician's diet. To envisage a maximally general account of what there is leads to paradox if something in what there is makes it impossible for a maximally general account of what there is to be given. Indexicalism holds that the outside, the outer, the beyond and the Outdoors are part of what there is, and they render impossible a maximally general account of what there is.

The limits to metaphysics provide both the shape and the content of metaphysics – it limits its reach while providing it with a crucial topic. From an indexicalist point of view, metaphysics and its critique are intertwined. In that sense, it has to deal in paradox. If there are limits to any grasp of totality, these limits are no less metaphysical than the effort to reach a totality. Paradoxico-metaphysics, viewed from the point of view of Kant's critique of traditional metaphysics, could be seen as a claim that any transcendental philosophy is inextricably committed to metaphysics. To reform metaphysics and append it with a transcendental story is therefore not enough to make it palatable, for reality itself has to be one way or another for the (appended) transcendental story to be accurate. There should be something in reality that makes it impossible for phenomena to transcend the reach of empirical judgements. Also, there should be something in reality that makes it possible to draw the limits of what is accessible – of what is knowable or thinkable. Jacques Derrida has hinted that the effort of recoiling from our empirical judgements to a transcendental sphere is only distinguishable from the attempt to go beyond our empirical judgements if we focus on the direction of the path we walk.[38] Without that, he notices, the *ultratranscendental* resembles the pre-critical. However, the importance of focusing on the direction of the path shows that any transcendental effort lapses into metaphysics if we drop a commitment to a sphere of subjectivity beyond any criticism – by positing an unquestioned presence of the (transcendental) subject. Without this commitment, the recoil

## Demonstratives and Proper Names

John Perry has advocated the idea that indexical expressions are essential, in that they cannot be fully replaced, and play a role that cannot be played without them.[39] His thesis is that beliefs and belief dynamics – and therefore elements of thought and speech – cannot be entirely understood without an appeal to indexicals. In particular, they cannot properly be accounted for in the model of propositional attitudes according to which a belief is a relation between a subject on the one hand, and a proposition that can be otherwise stated as an independent *relatum* in the relation on the other. When I come to realise that I am the one making a mess with sugar packets in the supermarket, or when I come to believe that the meeting I am scheduled to go to at noon is now, the proposition and the subject remain the same while my belief state has clearly changed. The essentiality of indexicals, for Perry, implies that beliefs are positioned and a great deal of what we think depends on *de re* content. Indexicals, he argues, challenge the very idea that there are propositions constructed in a *de dicto* manner that mediate a relation between a subject and the object of her belief. We cannot do away with the *de re* nature of belief; Perry asks the question, relevant for an argument in favour of indexicalism, of whether we can instead discard the *de dicto* element in beliefs. Doing so, he says, would imply that we 'would think of belief as a system of relations of various degrees between persons and other objects'.[40] A belief would be a relation to something that cannot be described except in the middle of things, so that there is a difference between not believing that I am making a mess while believing that someone is, and coming to believe that this someone is me – or coming to believe that noon is right now. Perry suggests that 'I stand in the relation, believing to be making a mess, to myself.'[41] Clearly, there are many ways to stand in such a relation, because there are different indexical words that would amount to the same – the relation is essentially *de re*. He then concludes that '*de dicto* belief might be seen as merely an illusion, engendered by the implicit nature of much indexicality'.[42]

The essential indexical, which Perry takes to be a problem for a model of belief involving ultimately only *de dicto* content, is also a problem for any metaphysics that assumes that its mission can be accomplished while leaving indexicals aside. The indexicalist claims that if beliefs – and thoughts and speech – are unavoidably *de re*, this is because such is the nature of reality; it cannot be understood without indexicals. Parts of the universe pointing at other parts of the universe are what give existence to both of these parts of the world. Reality is such that everything in it is in the middle of it. Not only Perry's essential indexical, but all the transformation in the philosophy of language brought about by works on direct reference by Keith Donnellan, David Kaplan, Howard Wettstein, Hilary Putnam and Saul Kripke, among others, contribute to a fleshed-out indexicalism.[43]

Wettstein summarises what he calls the revolution in the philosophy of language brought about by direct reference in a motto: *linguistic contact without cognitive contact*.[44] The idea is that one can point at something through linguistic expressions – demonstratives, proper names, natural-kind terms and even definite descriptions – without having a correct description of what is pointed at. In other words, one can appropriately refer to something without possessing a truthful description of what is referred to – or stated differently again, denoting dispenses with *de dicto* content. If this is so, then one can successfully denote $x$ without being able to position $x$ in a view from nowhere.

Kripke, embracing an analysis of names recommended by John Stuart Mill, argues that proper names are not identical to any definite description associated with them. Socrates was a philosopher in the actual world, but there should be a different possible world in which the same person was a sailor; as a consequence, one can refer to Socrates through his name without knowing anything about him, believing, for example, he was a fat miner from Potosí. Kripke's ideas on proper names followed from his work on the semantics of modal logic, in which he introduced an idea of possible worlds significantly different from Leibniz's. It is crucial for Kripke that the same Socrates could be in different possible worlds – that he has a trans-world identity, preserved in different possible worlds. The use of the name 'Socrates' in suitable circumstances refers to the individual Socrates who happens to have been a philosopher in the actual world. That individual is detached from what is true of him in the actual world, and indeed from any definite description, and in that sense individuation precedes description.

This precedence is revealing: what makes Socrates an individual is that he was first denoted by a name, 'Socrates'. It is this pointing to something through a proper name – a deictic operation – that makes Socrates an individual with a trans-world identity. This deictic operation identifies something independently of any description. Kripke understands that the phrase 'Phosphorus is the morning star' fixes the reference of the name 'Phosphorus'. This sentence, which contains explicitly indexical expressions such as 'morning', can be false as a description of what Phosphorus is – it could be discovered that a celestial body other than Venus shines first in the early morning in Earth's skies. But once the reference of 'Phosphorus' is fixed, it follows that necessarily, yet without being known *a priori*, Phosphorus is Hesperus.

Kripke uses an example from Putnam to clarify the notion of reference-fixing, which is of great importance for metaphysical indexicalism.[45] It could be discovered that cats are robots sent by extraterrestrials to spy on human domestic life. In this case, the false sentence 'cats are animals' can still fix the reference of cats. Now, if descriptions that fix reference had to be true, the consequence of the discovery would be that cats don't exist – Kripke and Putnam understand that cats are already individuated, for it is precisely because of the false sentence that the discovery that cats are robots has any content. The discovery is therefore about cats, identified by the false sentence describing them as animals. The false sentence manages to individuate something so that it fixes the reference of 'cats'. In other words, it is not the truth of a description that denotes. It is not the substantive content of a description that determines what the sentence is about; rather, it is the deictic operations carried on by the description that do the trick. The lesson for indexicalism is that reference-fixing, a linguistic deictic operation, is independent of the truth of a description – and the substantives in the description have an underlying deictic role. Indexicalism holds that being is being indexical, and that deictic operations like reference-fixing are what bring something (individuated) to existence.[46] If there is more than one reference-fixing procedure for one term, or more than one set of deictic operations for one interiority, then a convergence is discovered. To discover that Phosphorus is Hesperus, for example, is to find out something about a single position from different viewpoints. To discover such convergence is not to engage in a view from nowhere, but just to find out that one position can be viewed otherwise. I can then spot the morning star while being aware that it is also the evening star – and that I could see the same thing later in the day from another viewpoint. Sameness, or otherness and exteriority, does not imply totality.

Kripke's lesson concerning how descriptions do a reference-fixing job partly draws on earlier work by Keith Donnellan on definite descriptions having both an attributive use and a referential one.[47] In the first use, but not the second, something is attributed to what is described. In the referential use, 'the last planet in the solar system' can refer to Pluto even if it is no longer considered a true planet. The reference is already fixed, so the truth of the description becomes irrelevant, unless attributive usages are also at stake. Indexicalism, together with any approach that considers *de re* content to be primary, holds that a referential use – sometimes irrelevant – underlies any attributive use of a definite description. Attributive use of a definite description cannot be fully reduced to referential use, for a description has a truth value that determines what is satisfied by it. Still, that definite descriptions have an underlying referential usage shows that they perform deictic operations. They also point to what Perry calls 'the implicit nature of much indexicality'.[48] Expressions such as 'the last planet' and 'the solar system' are respectively an implicit demonstrative – 'last' is a position pointed to from the centre of the system – and a proper name. Terms such as *last*, *far*, *faster* and *smooth* perform implicit indexical work; they are relative to the position from which the words are uttered.

The Ancient Greek writer Sextus Empiricus compiled and organised several arguments that he understood as leading to scepticism mostly through *diaphonía* – the existence of more than one well-supported, justifiable claim about something.[49] An important part of these arguments – called 'modes' – was attributed to Aenesidemus (and a relevant condensation of his ten original modes in just five bore the name of Agrippa). The first modes of Aenesidemus show how things are far away when viewed from some perspectives but close from others, sweet to some tastes while bitter to others, small when seen from afar and bigger than the sun when seen from nearby, and so on. Many expressions seem to carry no indexical content – appearing purely substantive or *de dicto* – because of a tacit common point of view shared by many language users. So we say that the road is smooth (assuming that one will drive and not crawl on it), that the marzipan is sweet (assuming that one will not mix it with sour cream or eat it after consuming marshmallow), and that the sky is blue (assuming the ordinary daytime lighting). Several similar expressions are less than explicitly indexical because a tacit point of view in the middle of things is assumed – a point of reference or a fixed standard for measurement is implicitly established. Arguably, other deictic operations could be hidden by a shared tacit point of view. Prototypical substantives such as 'mountain', 'book', 'sky' and 'liquid' could be regarded as hardly indexical, but this is because a point of view is always tacitly assumed; a mountain can be a shelter, a book can be a source of food, the sky could include the Earth viewed from Mars, and a drop of liquid can be a solid surface for some micro-organisms. From where I utter these words, the position being assumed is taken so much for granted that alternative perspectives seem irrelevant.

Kaplan extends the Kripkean disentanglement of reference and description by further deflating the substantive character of any demonstrative expression.[50] He concocts an expression – demonstrative that, *d*that – that forces a referential use of definite descriptions. It is as if he is attempting to show how descriptions can be stripped of all attributive employment. There is, he claims, a demonstrative, indexical structure behind the interplay of descriptions. Kaplan's analysis of demonstratives has several important elements for the indexicalism I am constructing. While Kripke takes reference-fixing as something attached to a pre-existing time framework, Kaplan is more willing to free demonstratives from such a (substantive) constraint. Kripke considers that there are some essential properties of what is referred to that depend on the history of the introduction of the denoting expression. So, he says a table denoted by 'this table' cannot be the same while losing its historically defined essential properties:

> though we can imagine making a table out of another block of wood or even from ice, identical in appearance with this one, and though we could have put it in this very position in the room, it seems to me that this is not to imagine this table as made of wood or ice, but rather it is to imagine another table.[51]

This table could not be this table while being made of a different material – its material constitution is an essential property. Kaplan, by contrast, argues that demonstrative expressions such as *this table* have minimal substantive features in their content. If this table were made of ice or another block of wood, it would still be *this* table – the table denoted by the demonstrative expression. Kaplan distinguishes between the content and the character of an expression: the former is what it expresses – my name and 'me' share the same content – and the latter how it expresses it – through me saying 'I' or someone else saying my name. In indexical cases, content is just an expression's reference. If this table were made of a different material, the reference of the expression *this table* would still be the table in the position that is pointed to. Essential properties that make this table what it is – its material constitution or its origin – are substantive properties that go beyond the deictic operations that shape the border of the table denoted by the demonstrative expression. The position pointed at by the expression would be the same; the deictic operation is oblivious to any (possible) substantive essential properties of the table. The content of the indexical expression is, in any case, the table situated where it is, no matter its essential properties – *this table* points solely to a table at the pointed location.

### Tense Realism and Baroque Realism

The tension between substantives and indexicals appears also in discussions concerning the nature of time and its relation to change, prompted by John McTaggart's defence of the unreality of time.[52] McTaggart's despair concerning the reality of time stems from his conviction that a B-series of substantive, *de dicto* markers – such as twentieth century, 2018, 30th of January – is not enough to fully understand the passing of time. He deems that we also need to include an A-series of indexical markers such as *last century*, *this year* or *today*. In an A-series, we speak of past, present, future and the passing of time; it is through the A-series that we have a sense of tense. In contrast, a B-series gives us no sense of now; it provides us with a calendar viewed from nowhere, a handless clock. In order to understand change and events that take place in the passing time – they will happen, are happening and have happened – McTaggart thought we needed the indexical series. The sense of genuine change and the existence of events require a *de re* sense of time that a B-series alone cannot provide. As Whitehead stressed in his metaphysics of events, nothing can take place without a reference to a standing location.[53] It is only in reference to a position that anything takes place. McTaggart challenged the idea that a B-series is sufficient to understand time; a non-indexical, substantive series of descriptors can present myself as down the mountain in the morning, myself as up the mountain at noon and myself as back down in the evening, but it cannot make sense of the change between the states, and therefore of the event of climbing the mountain.

McTaggart, however, was no indexicalist. If an indexical A-series was needed in order for time to fully make sense, he was ready to ditch time together with change and events. His commitment to substantivism made him maintain the non-reality of time. An indexical series is incompatible with substantive reality, for it introduces positions, perspectives or incoherence. McTaggart understands reality as forming some sort of totality – neutral with respect to any point of view, absolute and not relative to a position, coherent and not having inconsistent states placed in different moments. It cannot only be real that I am on the top of the mountain; it cannot be real now that I am on the top of the mountain and real later that I am not; and it cannot be real that I am and am not on the top of the mountain. If time disturbs totality and departs from the order of substantives, it cannot be real.

Realist responses to McTaggart involved two paths: attempts to conciliate genuine change and events with the B-series – a substantivist path that agrees with McTaggart's presuppositions while trying to discard his non-realist conclusion – and indexicalist efforts to show that the A-series can be real. Kit Fine has studied the alternatives in the second path in some detail.[54] He considers how to drop each of the assumptions McTaggart makes about reality, one at a time. If we reject the view that reality is neutral, we can for example endorse presentism: only present states are real. If we reject that reality is absolute, we can endorse perspectivism: it is one way in the present and another way in the future. If we reject that it is coherent, we can say that the past and the present are somehow both real and inconsistent – which would not be enough to enable inconsistent statements in the present.[55] Fine favours the last two alternatives over the first, which gives up the idea that reality should be neutral. The problem of withdrawing the requisite of neutrality – and embracing something like presentism – is that the choice of one tense over the others is ultimately unjustified.

The third option – dropping coherence – is worked out by Fine in terms of an inconsistent totality. He posits time segments that are internally consistent – past, present and future. Reality, however, is not relative to tense, because each of these segments is a fragment of an all-encompassing totality that Fine calls *über-reality*, which he defines as being the inconsistent juxtaposition of all fragments. *Über-reality* is the inconsistent totality that aggregates all fragments, affording a cubist view of everything at a glance.[56] Fine's inconsistent totality is still ready to be viewed from nowhere. His realism endorses an indexical A-series but collapses it in an all-encompassing totality.

In contrast, an indexicalist realism would embrace the segments of tense as associated with interiorities. Tense is a deictic operation; its segments are no part of a substantive totality. Tenses can be understood only with respect to their deictic constituents such as same, exterior, different, now, earlier, sooner and later. Indexicalist realism considers the A-series a crucial element of reality, as it expresses the situated character of what exists; further, B-series expressions are themselves significant only to the extent that they conceal implicit indexicalities. So, expressions such as 'the twentieth century' make sense only with respect to deictic borders drawn in relation to a purported standing location (and with respect to a scheme of measurement, as we will see shortly). It follows that the B-series is the one that is dispensable for the understanding of time. Accordingly, reality is neither neutral – nothing can be real without deictic operations at a standing location – nor visible from nowhere. It is inconsistent only if it is seen as a substantive; reality is no more than the working of deictic operations.[57] If reality has to be taken as a substantive, it can only be the topic of a paradoxico-metaphysics.

In *The Fold*, Deleuze contrasted the *classical* taste for harmony that conceives of reality as being a consonance or even a unison – exemplified either by B-series (substantive) realism or McTaggart's (substantive) non-realism – with the *baroque* (or neo-baroque) taste for dissonance that takes reality to include multiple or even inconsistent elements.[58] Indexicalism, as much as the more substantivist versions of tense realism, is (neo-)baroque. Levinas understands the passing of time as being the very presence of the Other.[59] Time is whatever witnesses the vulnerability of the present, as something else is always to come; the present is in the future's hands, just as the Other holds an upper hand on me. Deleuze's baroque-picture reality is one in which a view from nowhere is prevented by the very nature of lighting: to make something visible is to reveal its shades, to unveil is also to conceal. A baroque realism is one in which shades alongside lighted areas compose a view that is never complete. Reality is not displayed in a landscape in which everything has its place independently of how it manages to make itself visible. The baroque prefers the movements of the shades, and therefore it rather portrays the struggle towards the salvation of a soul than the glory of redemption. The struggle is part of the reality of salvation. Analogously, deictic operations determine what is internal and what is external; they establish an outer element that is crucial for an interiority to be what it is. Baroque realism is a realism of horizons: things are placed in their coming-to-appear and in their ceasing-to-appear. If substantivism avoids dissonance by embracing the idea of a showcase totality, indexicalism conceives any view as tied to a horizon where a standing location is bordered by what transcends it.

## Horizon

The horizon accompanies a standing location in space and in time. As much as a standing location, the horizon is impermanent – it is the limit of the space given a fixed position; as I move, my horizon moves with me. There is always something beyond the horizon; it is the spatial symptom of the future. The Greeks had a geography for the borders of a position. They understood the horizon as a river, circumscribing where we are.[60] The indexical river was present whenever they were thinking about being and appearances. Martin Heidegger gives much attention to the disappearance of the horizon in the ontotheological preoccupations that departed from the focus on being that he finds among the pre-Socratic philosophers. His picture of pre-Socratic thought is one in which horizons are main characters. He claims that Anaximander's fragment speaks about what blossoms towards and what withdraws from a common space where everything is.[61] He agrees with Aristotle that Anaximander's main topic is *physis*, but he claims that his scope is not what is natural – as opposed to what is artificial in Aristotle – but rather the coming to being of everything. Anaximander was concerned with the space to which things are brought when they become and from which things vanish when they perish. What Heidegger considers the inaugural concern of Western thought involved a founding horizon, from which every existent joins everything else and departs by falling away. Heidegger therefore conceives the initial moves of Western thought as grounded in the indexical notion of horizon – whatever takes place takes place not in a showcase that can be viewed from nowhere, but rather within the horizon shared by everything else.

Only several decades after Anaximander's supposedly inaugural sentence, we find Parmenides writing his *Poem* about being and the impossibility of nothingness. Following neo-Parmenidean thinker Emanuele Severino, while one has to picture Parmenides' view of being as resolutely substantivist – everything is permanent and independent of any standing location – one cannot understand being unless one understands appearances and therefore the horizon. He holds that in Parmenides' view nothing ceases to exist, it just sets on the horizon, as the enduring sun escapes the appearances that currently present themselves to us by hiding beyond our sight.[62] Severino pictures the horizon as crucial to explaining how things appear and disappear without lapsing into nothingness. The horizon is of the order of appearances – he claims Parmenides understood the horizon structure to be associated with being so that things can either emerge or fade in a way that requires no commitment to nothingness. Nothingness was, in fact, a later addition brought about by the parricide that confined horizons to the realm of deceitful appearances. In contrast, Parmenides thought horizons were part of what being requires – as Severino interprets the last part of the *Poem* as crucial to understanding the message. The third part of the *Poem* is not about how things appear different from what they are, but rather about how their appearance and disappearance are part of the horizon of being. In this reading at least, Parmenides understood horizons – and arguably indexicals – as inextricably tied to being. The parricide, by introducing *nothingness* and therefore the quest for a view from *nowhere*, is what made substantivism possible.

Horizons are indexical environments. Heidegger ascribes to Anaximander the view that it is only because something lasts among everything else that the horizon is somehow fixed. Surely, it is only with respect to a standing location that a deictic operation such as *horizon* can work; from a fixed standing location, things appear and disappear, much like events that take place.[63] The horizon captures the happening of something from a beginning to an end – precisely what a B-series has trouble describing. It is interesting to compare horizons with maps. There are no horizons in ordinary world maps.[64] Indexicalism treats maps as convenient ways to deal with places that would produce a substantive effect because their indexicality is appropriately implicit. Furthermore, a map conceals as much as it reveals; different measurement strategies and different projections produce different maps. There is no map that can represent everything unless the map is itself what is being mapped. The indexicalist claim can be understood as follows: if things can be mapped only by things as they are in their own true scale, they cannot be mapped on to a map.

## Measurement

The problem of measurement is a way to make explicit the predicaments of a substantivist metaphysics. Karen Barad, in *Meeting the Universe Halfway*, explores the disagreements between Niels Bohr and Werner Heisenberg with respect to the principle of uncertainty. She claims that for Bohr,

> what is at issue is not that we cannot know both the position and momentum of a particle simultaneously (as Heisenberg initially argued), but rather that particles do not have determinate values of position and momentum simultaneously. [... Bohr maintains that] there is something fundamental about the nature of measurement interactions such that, given a particular measuring apparatus, certain properties become determinate, while others are specifically excluded. Which properties become determinate is not governed by the desires or will of the experimenter but rather by the specificity of the experimental apparatus.[65]

Barad endorses what she claims to be Bohr's view: that indetermination is a consequence of measurement, that there is a *diaphonía* in the measurement procedures and that this divergence cannot be dissolved by appeal to any matter of fact – or at least to any matter of fact independent of the experimental apparatus. Measurement is inextricably situated: no size, length, smoothness or speed can be measured except from a circumstance that involves both a standing location and the measuring equipment. A fragment of Heraclitus has it that 'the sun is the size of my feet', which is the result obtained using the naked eye when comparing one's feet against the sun as a measurer.[66] There is no measurement-free measure. Barad is adamant in concluding that one cannot afford not to consider the circumstance of measurement. Barad's Bohr holds that there is nothing that can be measured without the action that the experimental apparatus performs. The fact that action engages with what is being measured in a particular way cannot be ignored. Measurement appears as a deictic exercise, and furthermore, the world being measured appears as implicitly *de re*. Episodes of measurement are prototypical cases in which a standing location is *sine qua non*. The system of measurement, the equipment used and the metric geometry make sure that nothing can be measured without the contribution of the (measuring) spontaneity. A four-yard wall has four yards only if measured in yards and depending on the material used to measure – one could use a rubber ruler as easily as a metal stick. In a remark close to what guides the analysis of measurement by Whitehead (see below), Wittgenstein writes:

> How should we get into conflict with truth, if our footrules were made of very soft rubber instead of wood and steel? – 'Well, we shouldn't get to know the correct measurement of this table.' – You mean: we should not get, or could not be sure of getting, that measurement which we get with our rigid rulers. So if you had measured the table with the elastic rulers and said it measured five feet by our usual way of measuring, you would be wrong; but if you say that it measured five feet by your way of measuring, that is correct. – 'But surely that isn't measuring at all!' – It is similar to our measuring and capable, in certain circumstances, of fulfilling 'practical purposes'. (A shopkeeper might use it to treat different customers differently.)[67]

It seems as if what is taken to be appropriate measurement requires, among other things, that the material used for the purpose satisfy some conditions that have more to do with the circumstances of measurement than with the measure itself. It could appear that those circumstances of measurement carry an intolerable degree of arbitrariness: intolerable to the substantivist taste, at least.

Henri Poincaré famously held that there is nothing in nature that can help us determine the appropriate way to measure – the choice of one amid several geometries is entirely conventional. Poincaré held that measurements belong in a realm of convenience and there is no matter of fact guiding how to proceed. As merely a matter of convenience, it is taken to be distinct from the matters of fact that concern what is being measured. The conventional choice is a decision that takes place indifferent to any fact, while facts are oblivious to any convention, including those related to measurement. Whitehead discusses how Poincaré's position was ridiculed by Bertrand Russell, who insisted that there should be something in nature determining that the Earth is larger than a billiard ball.[68] Willard V. O. Quine has accommodated Russell's criticism of Poincaré by reformulating conventionalism: in his brand of the doctrine, conventionality is not confined to a specific realm and is rather spread everywhere. 'The lore of our fathers', Quine writes, 'is a fabric of sentences.' It is, he continues, 'a pale grey lore, black with fact and white with convention'.[69] He concludes that he finds no substantial reason to claim that there are entirely black or fully white threads. Matters of convention are intertwined with matters of fact such that experience can help make decisions concerning any issue and can shed light on geometrical controversies. Conventionality is not local; it is spread throughout all beliefs while leaving room for verdicts from matters of fact, which are also spread throughout. It is therefore not mere convention that decides that the billiard ball is smaller than the Earth.

Whitehead's take on the Poincaré–Russell controversy is slightly but importantly different. He claims that both positions are right. As a consequence of his rejection of the bifurcation of nature into a realm of contents for experience and a realm of experiencing, he recommends the abandonment of the distinction between natural variables and their measurements. He reckons that both Russell and Poincaré are right – there is something in nature that determines how to measure, but nothing that is alien to the act of measurement. Russell is right that there should be little controversy that the Earth is larger than the billiard ball: not because the circumstances of experience are irrelevant for measurement, but precisely because measurement is situated. To use a phrase from Wittgenstein in his *Investigations*, measurement doesn't stop anywhere short of the very facts of nature.[70] Whitehead understands these facts to be every bit as tied to the circumstances around them as their measurement; natural facts are not made of anything but what makes up experience. He argues that space and time are themselves dependent on what happens, on what takes place, instead of being prior to any event; hence there is no sense of position or duration except with respect to a class of events. It follows that measurement is an event (or a series of events) amid other events that take place only with reference to other events. Measurements of duration and position can only be done from a point of reference, from a standing location. This location being given – given the circumstances of measurement – it becomes evident how measurement ought to be done. Once there is a diversity of measurement alternatives, Whitehead recommends that we consult what indicates the peculiarities of the (situated) experience. Such indications are relative to a *locus standi*. Measurement is relative to the point from which perceptual experience takes place.

Concerning this *locus standi*, we have natural indications that are far from being conventions; they are rather exercises of a situated receptivity. These natural indications are present in experience, since nature is not alien to experience – both are composed of intertwined events. Russell is therefore right that the Earth is surely larger than the billiard ball, but it is so *for us*. Poincaré is right that there is no natural fact independent of us determining it to be so. It is not a conventional determination, but Whitehead holds that it is a situated measurement grounded in full-blown natural indicators. Since perception is not alien to nature, situated measurement has to be as much part of it as anything else. Whitehead's image of nature is not of a neutral, absolute and coherent totality but of a composition of standing locations. Locations are a crucial element of nature, and it is only from them that measurement is possible – nature is made of what perceptions of it are made of. To be sure, when we consider all the standing locations where we are concerned with human feet (or billiard balls), it is clear that the sun belongs in a much larger rank. The *diaphonía* of the different alternatives of measurement – which creates the indeterminacy that Bohr takes into account, that Poincaré somehow embraces, and that Russell is keen to refute – is noticeable only if we approach a view from nowhere. Otherwise, Barad and Whitehead would agree that a particular measuring situation makes some properties determinate while excluding some claims concerning positions and duration. Determination and exclusion are functions of the experimental situation and not of any convention. Just as with tense, issues in measurement make clear that relevant truths about what is around us cannot be formulated without an appeal to situation variables. Measurements from a standing location are part of nature, rather than being issued from any convention.

Similarly, the application of properties to instances rarely makes sense if no situational variable that enables measurement is considered: predicates such as *green, round, solid* or *is an atom* are implicit clusters of measurement procedures. What holds for measurement should therefore hold for gauging in perception that 'grass is green' or that 'the moon is round'. Again, as the first modes of Aenesidemus make clear, there is a *diaphonía* in the application of these predicates if we make no appeal to circumstances. Deprived of standing locations in perception (and the apparatus of experimentation), no application of these terms is intelligible. Whitehead considers these predicates to be 'eternal objects' independent of any event, only rendered actual when invoked in a specific claim from a situated perception – mere potentialities unless applied to specific perceptions.[71] The application of predicates in perception is an act of measurement; independent of anything that renders them actual, both *is green* and *has four yards* are on an equal footing. Perception is itself a collection of acts of measurement that can only make sense from an interiority, from a standing location. The claim that measurement and perception in general are implicitly but inextricably involved with standing locations is in line with the indexicalist aim of taking most universal thought to be best understood as tacitly *de re* and pegged to a specific situation that determines its scope. There is nothing concrete that is so universal it is not situated.

## Exteriority and Externalism

Indexicalism adopts the outcome of Levinas's ontological argument for the Other: what is exterior is, as exterior, that which draws the border of an interiority. The exterior, the outer, the Outdoors are effectively components of an interiority, which is a unit of transcendence assembled by deictic operations. Indexicalism therefore conceives thought as fully permeable to exterior elements. As a consequence of a conception of interiority as something that is not closed in itself as an independent variable, indexicalism is externalist.

Externalism about thought is a claim about the effective power something outer has on the content one thinks. Hence, elements alien to one's cognition affect thoughts. Typically, they are said to do so either by affecting the meaning of what is thought once thinking depends on public languages curated by others and not under the thinker's control, or by shaping the circumstances of the thought that are sometimes unknown to the thinker. The alien element alters the content of what is thought through impact either on the *formulation* of a thought (in public language) or on the *topic* of a thought (depending on external circumstances). The usual example of the latter is Putnam's thought experiment in which someone from Earth (where what fills rivers, lakes and oceans is H$_2$O) is secretly transported to Twin Earth (where everything looks like the same as it looks on Earth, but what fills rivers, lakes and oceans is XYZ).[72] Thoughts about water in the head of the transported earthling change from being about H$_2$O to being about XYZ without any cognitive indication. The thinker unknowingly changes topic because of the alien element present in the very constitution of one's thought. That the alien element affects the formulation of one's thought can be illustrated by several of Wittgenstein's examples in his *Investigations*.[73] This case can be made if we centre our attention on the rule-following considerations around section 185. There, the possibility of error in the pupil's understanding of the concept of 'adding 2' that is being taught is endless. One can never be sure of having learned the concept appropriately – and therefore one is always in danger of not thinking at all. Because there is no such thing as a private language that acquires meaning only through cognitive operations one does on one's own, if enough of my concepts are not properly acquired, my thought is devoid of any content. One is therefore hostage to the others who care for a public language when a thought is being formulated and, as a consequence, when a thought acquires content. Content is therefore determined externally.

Levinas's philosophy of language developed in section 1B of *Totality and Infinity* is externalist in the sense that both the topic and formulation of one's thought are vulnerable to alien elements.[74] His point of departure is that language is primarily neither a tool for representing things nor a device to cope with the world by performative acts. Rather, it is an opening to the Other. It is intrinsically geared towards the Great Outdoors because it is shaped by dialogue, by conversation, by the need to say something to someone else. It is primarily involved with *saying*, rather than with what ends up being *said*, to use the concepts he deploys later.[75] The need to say something – to respond – is the way the Other affects the workings of one's thinking. When one thinks, one is hostage to the Other that acts as our master.[76] Just as in

Wittgenstein, one is hostage to one's tutors, who provide content to one's thought – they hold the key to formulating thought, a key that can never be fully handed to any thinker because it belongs to alien elements, to the outer, to the Outdoors. My own thinking is only possible because of the lessons of the others, which render them indispensable. My spontaneity is held hostage because it can always be corrected. The transcendence that is intrinsically part of an interiority is visceral; it is a component of its inner articulations. It is only through the Other that I can formulate any thought about the Outdoors. Further, just as in Putnam, Levinas maintains that the Other as such is never fully present nor fully an object of thought – it is as if one cannot know whether the Other is Earth or rather Twin Earth. The Other – as exterior – is never exhausted by intentional acts. In any case, a thinker is always vulnerable to the infinity of the Other.

Levinas's conception of the interference of the external guides his claim that the Other's freedom (and the Other's agency) cannot depend on my own freedom and is not a product of my own sovereignty. Rather, it is an internal and constitutive limit to my spontaneity.[77] Moreover, as I am hostage to the others who have been my tutors – I can always be mistaken in following a rule I learned from others – my spontaneity is forged by my responses to them. The Other requires responses to an infinite degree – I can surrender myself to the Other up to any point. This infinite responsibility I have towards the Other extends to anything exterior that asks anything of me. This responsibility is the condition for the possibility of my freedom, which is the only way for me to be able to cope with the infinite responsibility towards what is exterior. This is an important feature of Levinas's metaphysics: what is exterior shapes my subjectivity before any intentional act. The indexicalist lesson is that interiorities are shaped from outside.

My responsibility to the Other is not a consequence of my thought but a condition of its possibility. The Other is inside an interiority, like a ground that could not have appeared due to a commitment or a decision but rather shapes every decision and commitment, either acting by means of my cognitive abilities or shaping them without being noticed. Vulnerability to the Other is not, however, sheer dependence. The Other is separate from a subjectivity and acts by asking – and the demands are themselves limitless, and therefore they can never be completely satisfied.[78] I am not obliged either to give money to a beggar or to consider anyone's argument, but a demand is placed on me that requires a response. This demand can be responded to with indifference – ignore the beggar, ignore the argument – as much as it can be responded to with complete surrender – becoming a slave of the beggar after giving her all my money, adopting the beliefs that produced the argument instead of my previous beliefs. The responsibility is infinite; the actual response is an act of my freedom. Levinas's externalism is not about being occupied by a definite Other that is present inside, but about being permanently in the hands of the traces of the Other. This is how the Other is kept exterior.

An indexicalist externalism inherits this stance towards the Outdoors. It is through what is within its external borders that an interiority can formulate and provide content to thinking. The Outdoors are kept outside. Thinking is contentful only to the extent that it is indexical. The influence of the Outdoors can also be brought to the fore by Wettstein's motto for the revolution in the philosophy of language mentioned above – which is roughly an externalist-leaning revolution. The motto holds that linguistic contact requires no cognitive contact. The contact thought establishes with its outside requires no cognitive link. Levinas describes how this tie can be structural: it is in the nature of an interiority that the exterior affects it. An interiority is open to the infinity of what is beyond it and therefore holds no identity as itself through time – it is always at the mercy of what transcends it. In that sense it is a unit of response, because its kernel is a standing location drawn by deictic operations. An interiority is not a goal-oriented unit; rather, it is as guided by what is internal as by what is external: outer and beyond are among the deictic operations that compose it as much as inner and within. Interiorities are oriented towards the Great Outdoors.

One can wonder whether by closely following Levinas's steps concerning the Other – and the ways what is exterior affects an interiority – indexicalism as I have been elaborating it loses sight of the Great Outdoors as more than a human stranger. Levinas is (sometimes) adamant in distinguishing the human and the non-human Other – he claims, for instance, that the former can contest my possession while the latter can only refuse it.[79] Independently of whether this distinction places a limit on Levinas's indexicalism – by predicating the Other – I believe indexicalism can extend the above considerations concerning the external in thought beyond

Levinas's intended scope. We will see later how the non-human Other can influence thoughts by requiring responses.[80] In any case, I claim that when I think of a tree, I am partly hostage to that tree, for it can prove my thoughts false (or even contentless). As we will see below, there is no thought of a tree that can be indifferent to the tree appearing in perception. The perceived tree is never fully present nor fully thematised. The Outdoors is accessible because it is constitutive of any interiorities, together with other deictic operations. The tree, like the human stranger, is beyond my borders, transcending my interiority by being exterior. Being hostage to the exterior amounts to having no fully safe shore where my spontaneity can act without being interrupted from outside.

There is another remarkable similarity between the externalism proposed by Kripke and Levinas's insistence that knowledge (cognitive contact) cannot replace the relation with the Other that a demand brings about – the role of faces and proper names as exterior to descriptions. The face of the Other, for Levinas, stands for something that is never fully encapsulated by a description, or by any kind of epistemic operation that extracts from the Other what can be put in my own terms. Making sure that what is said (*le dit*) never makes the saying (*le dire*) redundant, Levinas insists that what is said is always under the spell of the act of saying – of the act of addressing someone. Instead of talking about faces, Kripke gives prior importance to the way proper names work. Proper names, like faces, are exterior to efforts to describe and to any cognitive contact. Just like the Other that addresses me and is not a description, the proper name is not fully reducible to the descriptions I associate with it. To be sure, Kripke claims that there could be a (necessary) truth about terms for which we have a fixed reference through a description, although that truth can be entirely different from that description. At least in cases such as *Hesperus* or the cloud *Morning Glory*, there could be descriptions that prove both necessarily true and very different from 'the evening star' or 'a low-level solitary atmospheric wave'. Levinas would rather have the Other preserved in infinity, which for him means preserved outside any delimitation. Nevertheless, in both cases the fixed reference or the fixed interlocutor who addresses me transcends my current descriptions. It is beyond any cognitive process. It is exterior. In both cases, it affects my thinking from outside.

## Proximity

Proximity concerns what is almost the same, but not quite. It could be a species of the genre 'almost', if indeed that is a genre of the order of the other. When we depart from sameness, proximity is our sole guide, and in that sense it is a projection of sameness on to the other. Friendship is often thought of as a figure of proximity: Aristotle thought friends were one soul in two bodies, and Montaigne thought friends have everything in common and that responsibilities between them are no longer felt as such. Bojana Kunst understands friendship as a departure from the sameness of my identity or the idiocy of my own endeavours: in short, as an interruption. It is through those who are in proximity that I find my neighbourhood.

> I can only cease to be an idiot if I find somebody who is like me, who is almost the same. What we have here is a kind of a paradox: I cannot find who I am only with myself, yet I can find who I am with somebody who is almost like me [. . .][81]

Proximity points towards the minimal exterior – towards what is slightly out there. A small variation, and in that sense what comes at a small distance. Proximity is the interiority next door. Friendship, as Kunst and others notice, is both an actual form of proximity and a consequence of it. Proximity is both a requisite and an expression of friendship. It is as if there were friendship before friendship – as if the actualisation of friendship were itself an act of friendship. Friendship helps make clear that proximity is both a state and an event; it is an event prefigured in a state – or rather, in other events.

Indexicals are about what is near: this, that and the Other are close to me, located around where I am, found from the position I occupy. Proximity contrasts with a view from nowhere. It is what makes anything situated. The horizon of an interiority is constituted by an indexical environment from which what is real appears; I am the centre of the environment, but as a centre, I cannot dispense with what is in my proximity. Proximity – what is nearby, close, in the (indexical) neighbourhood – constitutes an interiority. The notion of proximity (*proximité*) is central in Levinas's *Otherwise than Being*. There, it is articulated with the notions of substitution and recurrence. Proximity points at whoever comes after me, the one who will follow me and in that sense will substitute me. The Other is in my proximity because it is the Other that substitutes for me, the Other that steps into my shoes. In general, proximity is a condition for substitution: one can replace wine more easily with grape juice than with peach juice; someone with my same background and experiences can replace me in a decision-making meeting; lilac can be used to replace purple better than brown. Similarly, the Other in proximity could be having the piece of bread I am eating. Substitution is also the starting point of Levinas's conception of a subjectivity not as identity, but as recurrence: I am eventually substituted by the Other in the sense that I act for the Other, and then I start a journey back to what I was.[82] There is no agenda of mine pushing through a substitution and a recurrence – only a drive towards the Other

The Other is present in me in a proximity that triggers a responsibility: the scope of what I care for is not my own body, but my proximity. A subjectivity is not oriented towards itself but towards what is close. The position in which it is situated is not structured as a centre in which there is a self and a periphery where an (indexical) environment circumscribes the centre. On the one hand, there is no (substantive) identity in the centre closed off from what is in its proximity. On the other, there is always a returning point where the centre of the subjectivity is available. More than a governing capital, this centre is more like a refuge. The middle point between the two poles is what makes subjectivity a recurrence: it is not a position separated from what there is in the proximity, but a place to return to. In that sense, it is maybe like a homeland one returns to with a different mind after the journey, rather than being itself an identity. The movements of a subjectivity within the space in its proximity are those of incomplete return. Proximity is a constitutive part of a subjectivity. Further, subjectivity requires proximity; subjectivity becomes hostage to proximity. The plot of being called by the Other and being substituted – and eventually recurring to where I was, which has now become different from my point of departure – takes place in the proximity. Since indexicalism understands an interiority along the lines of how Levinas conceives of a subjectivity, the indexical environment is what is in my proximity.

Proximity is alien to description. It is not a family, a tribe, a physical neighbourhood that is in the vicinity – it cannot be described in substantive terms. Friendship is an approximation. What is nearby is precisely what happens to be nearby; attempting a description of proximity dismantles proximity.[83] The presence of the Other in my environment is not something that engages with my thinking and would open what is outside to my sovereignty. Rather, the Other towards whom 'the question is addressed does not belong to the intelligible sphere to be explored. He stands in proximity.'[84] Proximity does not require thematisation or any sort of structured thinking; it precedes thinking in the sense that it is the point of departure for thought. The exterior is present in the proximity precisely because it precedes every engagement in a sovereign effort of addressing a theme – it is the environment from which thinking obtains its focus. Levinas writes that the essential point of his thesis is that 'proximity is not any kind of conjunction of themes, is not a structure formed by their superposition'.[85] What is in proximity is not an object, but part of the open structure of subjectivity. The subject is not a closed individual, but a point of departure for substitutions that take place in her proximity. Levinas claims that subjectivity appears to thinking as a pronoun – typically a 'me' or a 'mine'.[86] Proximity – indexical environment – is where subjectivity becomes what it is. The notion of interiority in indexicalism has a similar structure: interiorities have addresses, points of departure, and what is in their proximity forms an environment from which deictic operations are brought to the fore. Interiorities are situated, tied to engagements; they are never hovering everywhere. They are always somewhere.

Precisely because *proximité* is not structured in terms of the substantive description of a position, Levinas understands it as *anarchic*. Proximity is not family connections, nor is it familiarity – it is an anarchic force that can be tied to anything nearby.[87] Proximity has to do with vulnerability to surroundings as much as it has to do with responsibility, and the scope of my responsibility is not determined by a substantive description. Levinas makes it clear that proximity is not like disorder, where a different order could be found if the effort of thematisation – the engagement in substantive descriptions – were sufficiently pursued. Proximity is indifferent to thematisation and often runs counter to it. My proximal surroundings are not determined by any substantive description of my position; they are composed of what appeals to me, what has the capacity to be present in an environment that is neither of my making nor alien to my subjectivity.

Here again, we recall the ontological argument of *Totality and Infinity*: what is exterior imposes itself as such within my proximity. The exterior inside proximity comes from no determined place. The anarchy of *proximité* is the unpredictability of contact; spatial contiguity introduces an element that is forcibly exterior to any organised structure. It is this contiguity that is invoked in the notion of proximity, but Levinas considers that substitution is behind contiguity, including spatial contiguity – my neighbour is the one who follows me. He wonders whether contiguity itself could be intelligible without a sense of substitution and therefore of justice.[88] This anarchic sense of justice is one that evokes responsibility for what is within the reach of my indexicals – for what is close enough to be pointed at. It is anarchic because there are many technologies of contact and many spaces of contiguity. Levinas takes this anarchic justice, which gives rise to contiguity, to be human. That means no other, non-human subjectivity enjoys proximity. Later I will discuss these restrictions imposed by Levinas; what matters now is to be clear that the anarchy of proximity brings in substitution, and therefore the responsibility a subjectivity senses for what is around it. Indexicalism takes interiorities to be placed in an environment and to respond to it. The anarchy of proximity, however, makes sure nothing can be predicted concerning the entrenchment of any interiority: they just happen to be close together.

Heidegger opposes proximity (*Nähe*) to that which knows no distance in his *Einblick in das was ist* ('Insight Into That Which Is'). These Bremen lectures expose the opposition and the gradual replacement of proximity by *Ge-Stell*, which can be translated as 'frame' or 'device', or in Andrew Mitchell's translation, 'positionality'.[89] While proximity is related to attending to the pace of events, positionality is a state where what is around becomes at one's disposal. Positionality dismisses all distances, though this brings no nearness. *Nähe* is about a presence that is not forced; it's about not placing something on a map but waiting until it makes itself present. It is akin to having something on one's horizon. In contrast, positionality, like a device, exposes and produces objects, placing them in standing reserve. The distinction between proximity and positionality lies in the way things make themselves present – in proximity they present themselves of their own accord. Positionality extracts things from proximity and makes them available to be viewed, as if in a showcase. It is as if it places things outside a neighbourhood to expose them such that they could be seen from nowhere.

Positionality is indeed similar to thematisation: Heidegger described the gradual passage from proximity to *Ge-Stell* using the difference between *physis* and *thesis*. The former is understood as bringing-here-forth – it is the opening of something closed from itself and therefore like letting something become present of its own accord. *Thesis*, in contrast, arranges a presence in a position. A stone present by *physis* is arranged into a staircase and its steps by *thesis*. Here we see how *thesis* disguises itself by trying to present things as if they were present in the *physis* way: as if they were in view, exposed, out there of their own accord. Hence, the project behind positionality is to place things in fixed addresses, formulated as much as possible in *de dicto* form. While positionality is a conscription, proximity guards things by allowing them to conceal, to retreat and to withdraw from exposure. Heidegger also describes the passage from proximity to positionality as the turning of the world into a *Ge-Stell*. This places the world in danger because things in the world become persecuted, followed in order to be exposed, to be presented against the grain. The effort of thematisation is therefore a betrayal of proximity, a departure from a state in which things are guarded and present themselves of their own accord.[90] *Thesis* conscripts them and places them in a state of exposure where they are available to be seen, to be presented from anywhere, and are not near to anything in particular.

Heidegger's account of proximity has some similarities with Levinas's. Above all, he also contrasts proximity with what is available to a view from nowhere, where distances are abolished and asymmetrical relations vanish. However, thematisation (or *thesis*) is not, for Levinas, a betrayal of proximity – it is precisely where proximity shows its presence and its strength, mostly because Levinas sees in thematisation the effort of saying (*dire*) and therefore of a *diaphonía* that makes the Other present. For him, to say that there is an indexical structure behind thematisation where there is an inescapable dialogue is not to claim that the *dit* could possibly cease to exist. Thematisation is the locus where the Other and its asymmetrical relation to me are present. Surely, *thesis* does not get detached from *dire* such that it could be the truth-bearer of a totality – the said never exhausts the saying. The relation between them, though, is not one of contrast or of passage, in which *thesis* is gradually replacing proximity; rather *thesis* is always accompanied by an underlying structure of proximities that is not often explicit. In other words, the Other is present in the way thematisation takes place; Levinas holds that there is no Other if there is no effort to claim something – it is one's thinking that makes one hostage to the Other. The asymmetrical relations between the different indexicals cannot be separated from the efforts in language to thematise – rather than a friction between *thesis* and proximity, there is a complementarity in which the latter expresses itself in the former. Proximity, in the form of saying, requires something being said: something that expresses a claim, and which at the same time is hostage to a structure in which there is an exterior element that makes it inescapably corrigible. Language is a realm of vulnerability; everything is ultimately responsive to an interrupting interlocutor. This account of language, where indexicality is always implicitly present but does not stand without claims about something, is one of the cornerstones of how the Other affects a subjectivity from outside. Further, the idea that the Other cannot be present but through claims that implicitly refer to dialogue and *diaphonía* anticipates some central tenets of Derrida's deconstruction.[91] Although not focused on writing, Levinas espouses the idea that there is a plurality of interlocutors in any act involving language; what is thought or said has an underlying structure of dialogue that is typically expressed in claims.[92]

Levinas agrees with Heidegger that proximity is an exposure to being.[93] This is so because proximity exposes the Other – and the indexical structure underlying what is thought and said. The exposure to being, however, doesn't dispense with thematisation – *thesis* is not the opposite of proximity but rather it is where proximity is expressed. Further, Levinas understands experience itself, and the sensible in general, in terms of proximity. While the content of perception – the outcome of an experience – has a form akin to something said, the sensible, where experience takes place, lies in proximity. Proximity is a relation with the Other, a relation that spells vulnerability and can be described in terms of fruition and wound.[94] Sensibility is proximity, it is where things are presented to the perceiver – as Wahl once wrote, perceptual experience is not about explanation but about presentation.[95] The Other is presented through sensibility; it is the moment when something exterior makes itself present in one's indexical environment. As we will see in Chapter 3, our constant perception of something entails that we are permanently open to what is exterior.

By connecting sensibility and proximity – and therefore the

presentation of the Other – Levinas hints at a conception of sensibilia as engaged in contact. It is through exercises of sensibility that indexical environments gain their contents. But they cannot do so indifferently to what is said in experience. Here again we cannot strip the saying from the said: we cannot strip the presentation of something in an indexical environment from what is presented. The indexical structure in the sensible doesn't have a content of its own. The sensible presents the Other with a content, with something said: there is no sensible without exercises of sensibility. Chapter 3 will present a somewhat more detailed conception of sensibility as exposure to the Other. The exposure reveals a deictic structure where what is exterior becomes present. This is what the sensible is capable of doing through proximity. There is no such thing as a proximal *content* separated from what is thematised; the saying comes with the said. But through proximity, the sensible exposes the indexicals that underlie what is said. In any case, considered in terms of proximity, the sensible as contact is not restricted to the organs of sensibility. Rather, it expands to wherever contact takes place, even beyond the limits of human sensibilia.

## Object-oriented

It is instructive to compare indexicalism with recent developments such as object-oriented philosophy. Graham Harman contends that objects relate to each other in a way that resembles the descriptions Heidegger gives of the *physis* and of the *Nähe*: they make themselves present as much as they withdraw. They are not simply what is made present to us, but there is a realm of their own in which their presence escapes any perception or sensual quality and takes place of their own accord. He makes use of the distinction between the *vorhanden* and *zuhanden* that Heidegger introduces much earlier.[96] While the latter indicates a coupling of objects independently of any framework of making something apparent, the former is like a broken tool that requires the introduction of something like a theory or a practice of mending. When the tool is working, there is a coupling with it that disappears when it breaks and one needs to do something about what went wrong. The contrast is similar to that between the world where *physis* takes place on the one hand (*zuhanden*) and *Ge-Stell* – positionality – that replaces worldly relations with relations within a cartography, within a prefigured space. Importantly, both theory and practice require positionality, a thetic framework that arranges objects in a conscription. There are the available sensual objects, by which Harman means objects available to or in contact with any other object, and there are the withdrawn real objects, present but not available. The distinction between real and sensual objects comes together with that between real and sensual qualities to form a quadruple structure that is common to any actual existent.[97] The four elements are independent from each other in the sense that they can be perceived on their own; together they compose any object and, *a fortiori*, anything that exists.

The presence of real objects (and qualities) commits Harman to the idea of a limitation: nothing is capable of grasping reality as it is. Access is finite, there is an element associated with proximity – and with what is *zuhanden* – which escapes any experience, any sensual contact. Real objects (and qualities) are situated; they make themselves present not because they are available but because they are in proximity. A central feature of Harman's account is that he conceives of real objects and qualities as noticeable in connection to the inevitably partial exposition of their sensual correlates; they escape like *noumena*, except that they are things-in-themselves beyond the access of any other object. There is a hidden, withdrawing, escaping in-itself in each object, and it is not accessible by any other object. Harman makes the Kantian transcendental distinction between phenomena and things-in-themselves into a general feature of any object. There is an ultimate component of any existent that is never shown, and this element beyond the reach of any access is all-pervasive, as '[e]ven inanimate objects fail to grasp each other as they are in themselves', he writes.[98] '[F]initude', as a consequence, 'is not just a local specter haunting the human subject, but a structural feature of relations in general including non-human ones.'[99]

Harman's object-oriented ontology, just like monadological metaphysics, is adamant in its commitment to the rejection of the bifurcation between the human and non-human realities. Just like indexicalism, his approach attempts to displace the human from centre stage in philosophy – his is a general account of the object that would make no exception for the human subject. Further, Harman incorporates the idea that reality is intrinsically tied to exteriority: the real object is the Other to perception. It is what escapes any attempt to access, a leftover that cannot be assimilated to any sameness.[100] The real object is present while inaccessible, like the Other that makes itself present in a deictic operation. There are elements of externality to the very (quadruple) structure of any object. Any object is in itself other to any other – this otherness is precisely the in-itself that escapes the access of anything else. Harman understands exteriority in terms of real objects that escape contact and make themselves present while being alien – it is as if a horizon where looms the inaccessible were always part of any territory. The Other has a mapped place in his quadruple structure of any object. However, by giving it that place, Harman turns the Other into a substantive; it is as if there were a position in the cartography of the object where otherness lies, a position that can be described, albeit not accessed, through a substantive description independent of any deixis. His objects can be described as having absolute withdrawn dimensions, irrespective of any other object that attempts to access them and therefore independent of any deictic operation. Real objects are like Heideggerian proximity in that they are coupled and yet not viewed or sensed as objects in a way that would position them and remove them from their proximal state. But by understanding proximity independently of any deixis, Harman positions the real object independently of its situation; it is an inaccessible feature viewed from nowhere. Once exteriority is viewed as reality that can be viewed from nowhere, it stops being exterior in the sense that it is not exterior to anything in particular. As a consequence, there are senses in which Harman's object-oriented ontology turns exteriority into totality.

Certainly, Harman rejects the idea that a complete description of the external world is possible. Real objects (and qualities) are inexorably elusive and ensure that no complete description can be given, not even a description from the view from nowhere. Secrecy and inaccessibility are features of the furniture of the universe. Similarly, Harman's ontology clearly makes room for interiority, as each object has an interior life independent of any connection with the totality formed by everything. Each object is capable of perceiving no less than being available to the perception of the others. Just like a monadological metaphysics, his object-oriented ontology is committed to the interiority of what exists and of perception as making the world what it is through agency. And further, more so than monadological metaphysics, Harman postulates the Other – understood in terms of real objects – as a genuine feature of the furniture of the universe. Still, if totality is understood in terms of the postulation of neutral terms – and through a structural symmetry between the different existents – Harman's object-oriented ontology, by turning the Other into a substantive real object, ends up conceiving of exteriority in terms of totality. The withdrawn structure present in the other object is symmetrically postulated in any object: any object is like an alter ego, like an image of the same object. The quadruple structure is therefore a common denominator or a neutral predication applied to any object that can be seen from nowhere: the world is a world of objects with withdrawn parts. Harman's commitment to the (paradoxico-metaphysical) desideratum of exteriority – in the form of a real object that escapes access – is at least mitigated by some adherence to the idea of totality in these senses. His objects are viewed from nowhere and analysed in terms of a neutral common structure through which objects enjoy symmetrical relations with each other. As a consequence, real objects remove the deictic sting of the Other by flattening everything with substantives. What is exterior to an object becomes the substantive mirror image of the subject who perceives – and as such, the substantive object is not close to or far from any subject.

Harman's object-orientation perhaps illustrates a more general tension between the exterior and the real, a tension expressed in taking the external world to be a reality independent of both what is internal and what is external. Often the very idea of reality appears as hypostasis of the deictic exteriority; it is no more than a tamed surrogate of otherness. Harman seems to present reality as exteriority spiced up with a hidden dose of totality. In contrast with Harman, Tristan Garcia proposes an object-oriented philosophy that postulates no real object. He introduces his position as a contrast with two alternatives: a view according to which a thing is defined in terms of a substratum independent of any of its predicates (events, states of affairs, qualities and relations), and a view which understands the being of a thing as distributed throughout a bundle of its predicates. While the former promotes the hypostasis of the peculiarity of a thing – the thing-in-itself – the latter understands that peculiarity in terms of the discernible differences from anything else. What makes a thing what it is is therefore either its (indiscernible) ingredient that constitutes an in-itself independently of anything else, or the vector of its predicates. The contrast between these two models is a contrast between the postulation of an in-itself – like a real object – on the one hand and the vectors of being coming from elsewhere.

In *Immaterialism*, Harman contrasts his object-oriented ontology with Latour's actor-network theory using the case of the VOC (the Verenigde Oost-Indische Compagnie, the Dutch East India Company). While the approach espoused by Latour – in line with monadological metaphysics – understood the VOC in terms of its actions and relations, its operations, alliances, characters and sponsors, Harman's object-orientation postulates a real VOC underlying all the actions and relations the company was involved in. Harman hence defends the virtue of the first approach considered by Garcia against the second, endorsed by Latour. He argues that a real object – an in-itself – is what best explains the trajectory of a thing and the history of the VOC in particular. Garcia would reject both views on the VOC and on things in general, since he advocates instead a third view that postulates a peculiarity of a thing as such without appealing to an in-itself. He agrees with the second view when it comes to departing from the postulation of an in-itself: a thing has to have something outside it, and it is nothing except in contrast with something other than itself. But he also agrees that a thing is not only its contrast with everything else; it is not only what is discernible. He then introduces a third view that contrasts with the other two in a way that is especially interesting for my indexicalism. His view is that a thing is like a territory and what makes it what it is is its borders, which divide what is inside the thing from what the thing is inside. The border is a contrast between the external and the internal that traces the peculiarity of the thing. To be sure, the border itself is drawn by the predicates in the vectors that make something discernible – it is the bundle of predicates that distinguishes the thing from anything else. But just as in a nation or state, the border is not only what draws it; the border between Germany and France is to a great extent independent of the history of the wars that has placed it where it is. The border itself is what makes the thing what it is: a thing, Garcia writes, is like the difference between content and container. It is like an immaterial bag. Anything could be the content of a bag; things are made of nothing but their borders. There are no things in themselves, only contrasts.[101]

This independence between the drawing of the border and the border itself is what Garcia calls *de-determination*.[102] It follows from a crucial distinction between *objects* placed among others and *things* that are only placed within their containing universe. Although Garcia in *Forme et objet* presents things before he presents objects, Cogburn, in his book on Garcia, reckons that the best exposition of his system would be to start with objects and then move to things.[103] Objects are determined by their predications, their relations, their qualities, their potentialities, the events they are part of. From an objective point of view, there are objects and their predicates that determine objects; there are objects giving an identity to others. From a formal point of view, there are things and the universe around them; things are defined by their borders, drawn by objects and predicates, but they are de-determined – they carry on independently of the history of their borders.

I understand this movement of de-determination in terms analogous to those used by Kripke and other theorists of direct reference to distinguish between a true description and a fixation of reference. Consider the cats in the example from Putnam mentioned above. The borders of the kind *cat* – considered as a thing and not an object – were determined by descriptions such as 'cats are animals'; such descriptions can be false and still fix the reference of the kind *cat*. That is because when the word 'cat' is introduced, it carves out the thing *cat* and distinguishes it from anything else in the universe that contains it. The cat is considered, from a formal point of view, independently of the truth of the descriptions that determined its borders; a thing is therefore determined in order to be what it is and de-determined to be considered formally within its containing universe. There is a formal reality independent of the objects that bring being to a thing, and this formal reality is not an in-itself, but a difference between the internal and the external. Similarly, in order to fix the reference of something, it is not enough to make sure there is a difference – say, between what is and what is not a cat. To fix a reference is not to point at a substratum that subsists in itself or to a first substance in the way Aristotle conceived of his *ousia prote*. Importantly, there is nothing substantive that makes a thing what it is; a thing is what results from the de-determination that is made possible through the effort of determining objects. A thing is an object removed from the realm of objects and placed on its own in an environment composed only of its containing universe. De-determination produces a difference, and not anything in-itself: it produces a border. The border is not merely a line drawn; rather, it fixes a region that is circumscribed by what is discernible. The description of cats as animals not only states something in its attributive use, but also does the referential job of pointing at parts of the world. Every determination comes with a de-determination – there is no object that cannot be viewed as a thing.

Garcia's object-oriented philosophy, and its notion of de-determination, are closer to indexicalism than Harman's. In particular, it is through other objects that things become what they are; there is nothing substantial underlying them. Further, his criticisms of the in-itself and of compactness – being without borders – are part of a thorough exorcism of the assumptions of totality in metaphysics. The very idea of totality entails a content with no containing universe. Totalities have no borders, and thus they cannot be things. The universe associated with a thing, in contrast, is no totality, for it is both infinite and indefinite; in fact, a universe is as relative to a border as its circumscribed thing. There is no universe but a universe for a thing.

Garcia's system nevertheless falls short of indexicalism. Though the formal characterisation of a thing – and its universe – does not appeal to anything substantive, it is still not indexical. While things are de-determined, and therefore relative to the positions they are made to occupy among objects, things are understood independently of these objects. It is as if de-determination deprives objects not only of their subservience to the truth of descriptions but also of the deictic character of the borders that constitute things. The formal image of a thing and its universe preserves an element of the substantive; Garcia's de-determination is still somehow *de dicto*, for the operations that keep the border in place are removed from any formal consideration. Although the border between France and Germany is independent of the history of the two countries, it is only with respect to countries and citizens (and merchandise, taxes, the jurisprudence of laws, etc.) that the border exists. Borders are not substantive; they cannot subsist without deictic operations, operations that take the form of this and that, here and there, same and other. Garcia defines things in terms of their borders, but some of the indexical character of borders that enables de-determination – and that enables reference independent of the truth of any description – ends up dismissed, as the formal account of things conceals their constitutive deictic operations. Still, the formal account enables the rest of the world to be contrasted with the thing in terms of its universe, infinite and indefinite. From the point of view of the thing, the formal account makes explicit its relation to its surroundings, a relation where exteriority is crucial.

### Tentacular Thinking

Donna Haraway envisages a model of thinking that contrasts with that of seeing things from above, from no perspective, from nowhere. She is inspired by the sensibility of tentacular beings that spread their extremities in their environments. She is inspired by a spider that lives in her area, *Pimoa cthulhu*, and that gets 'her specific name from denizens of the depths, from the abyssal and elemental entities, called chthonic'. The spider inspires Haraway to conclude that 'nobody lives everywhere; everybody lives somewhere. Nothing is connected to everything; everything is connected to something.'[104] The spider reacts to its situation within the bounds of what reaches its tentacles; *tentacles* comes from the same root as *temptations* and *tentative*. Tentacular sensibilia inspire Haraway to conceive tentacular thinking: a thinking that never recoils from engaging in panoramic appreciations of how things are around it. Tentacular thinking is tied to its ground and can be described in indexicalist terms – it is bound to deictic capacities. According to indexicalism, this is not because it is limited or confined or incapable of going beyond a limit, but rather because there is nothing non-deictic to be grasped.

An indexicalist, tentacular metaphysics contrasts with what Benjamin Noys labels *drone metaphysics*.[105] Akin to a theological drive towards security, drone metaphysics postulates a travelling eye of God capable of distancing itself from everything. The authority of a drone image is a result of a metaphysics in which the non-deictic grounds and explains away any *de re* thought. Tentacular metaphysics is what indexicalism intends to suggest: it postulates that there is nothing beyond the deictic, while there is always a deictic beyond. To a great extent, tentacular metaphysics is the claim that a view from nowhere is not really available. The radio transmission arranged by Antonin Artaud in 1943, *Pour en finir avec le jugement de Dieu*, brought forward several issues to do with a view from nowhere.[106] Artaud denounces a frame of mind according to which there is a God judging each gesture based on how things are supposed to be. God's judgement is present in each functioning that could be deemed correct, appropriate or adequate. Artaud associates God's judgement with the idea that there are organs and that they are order devices meant to be used in specific ways. He attacks these organs as devices that have a way to be used properly. They come with a judgement – a judgement one can describe as based on their proper functions. Yet as Deleuze and Guattari understand it, his war on organs is actually a war on organism.[107] The war is on a properly used assemblage of organs: it is against an organised totality. Deleuze and Guattari want to make sure one can still recover the organs if they are understood to be always assembled in different ways.

The organism, though, invokes a ready-made totality that unifies the organs. It hints at the (Lacanian notion of a) big Other that, like a shared fiction, orients the action of everyone; the organism is what watches and judges every working organ in its movements. Even though Deleuze and Guattari are often understood as making Artaud a voice for immanence, they are equally setting him against a unity that connects together all multiplicity (the war against the organism is a battle for the irreducible multiplicity, referred to by them as $n-1$). They would rather have a disassembled multiplicity forming no totality; a body without organs is an open field for coexistence that does not attend to a judgement embodying a normativity oriented by a totality. Jacques Lacan describes the assumption of the big Other in terms of a symbolic aggregate of all the others.[108] This big Other becomes the one we report to when we expose who we are; it is the Other to whom we entrust our identity. The big Other is the symbolic audience to which we report, which therefore can see everything and judge the appropriateness of each organ in an organism. Yet the big Other does not necessarily entail an all-encompassing or coherent (transcendence-free) totality.

In his characterisation of the current state of culture and habits as the age of capitalist realism,[109] Mark Fisher presents a big Other which is decentralised and hardly an object of full-blown belief, but still thoroughly operative. Fisher describes how capitalist realism has slowly developed from the late-capitalist postmodern ideology articulated by Jameson on the basis of Lyotard's description of a growing disbelief in great narratives. Capitalist realism is an acute and distinguishable intensification of postmodernity characterised by the absence both of any alternative narrative of what life could be without capitalism, and of any special connection whatsoever with modernity as a privileged project. Capitalist realism features public relations and spinning as the basis of a shared mentality that maintains a big Other, a working common fiction that is the basis of social life. Fisher argues that the capitalist realist big Other is not tied to a coherent view sanctioned by an authority, but rather is composed of various unconnected pieces that are still quite different from what actually takes place – it is a purportedly objective image fed by everyone. Hence, there is a false story that each company and each public-sector institution tells itself, as appearances have to be constantly maintained. Fisher writes that one

> important dimension of the big Other is that it does not know everything. It is this constitutive ignorance of the big Other that allows public relations to function. Indeed the big Other could be defined as the consumer of PR and propaganda, the virtual figure which is required to believe even when no individual can.[110]

The totality that the capitalist realist big Other articulates is one of make-believe. Fisher mentions the case of Gerald Ratner, who described 'the inexpensive jewelry his shop sold as "crap" in an after dinner speech', causing a monumental loss for his company – and lost his job.[111] Customers might previously have been aware of what he revealed, but the big Other didn't know and was not meant to be informed. This big Other works very much in the same way as Žižek's Stalin, for whom denouncing disagreement as lethal is more lethal than disagreement. As a shared fiction independent of anyone's beliefs, the big Other is a reality in the Lacanian sense, deprived of anything real, in the also-Lacanian sense that there is nothing external about it. The big Other is in here, while what is exterior is out there.

The big Other is meant to provide a fake exteriority: the pressure coming from this supposedly big force is not exterior because the big Other is nothing but a fictional character that cannot deviate from the descriptions that determine it. The big Other is not a real Other – it is a fictional character fully dependent on prescribing descriptions. It is not an Other capable of challenging what is thought about it. According to Fisher, the struggle against belief in grand narratives has turned out to be a cleansing device that establishes that there is no alternative. There remains one big Other commanding no great degree of belief, as capitalist realism requires no great commitment, but only a conviction that there is no other game in town. Nobody needs to wholeheartedly believe propaganda; a slight inclination to prefer its narrative is good enough for a consumer, just as bare compliance with a rule is good enough for a functional precarious worker. However, the different scripts that are played for the big Other – that of a consumer, a precarious worker, an auditor of one's own job or a faithful employee as much as of a good parent, a family member and a law-abiding citizen – create a mosaic that solely constitutes the big Other. The capitalist realist big Other is no priest caring for the religious soundness of each attitude; protocols for the adequate way to play each role are good enough, and the roles are many. There is no need for an all-encompassing organism or totality that orders everything. The big Other as an ersatz exteriority shows that there is more to ontotheology than the affirmation of a totality. Organs, functional bits and bobs, scripts, *Ge-Stell*.

The big Other is a character of the *Metaphysik* Heidegger intended to find ways to overcome. In any form, it is an appropriate model for a sideways-on view, and for the idea that everything can be exposed – that nothing can resist being a showcase available to inspection. The big Other is a character that produces the narrative and the reader of the *official version* of things. This official version is as different from reality as the world for Heidegger contrasts with *Ge-Stell*: they are the same, 'but the same is never the equivalent. [. . . They are] set against one another.'[112] The protocols of a big Other – even when no ordered totality is in place – take over what there is and conceal whatever is not made available to be seen. The big Other is the commissioner executing the persecution of being that puts it in constant danger, according to Heidegger's image.[113]

While total exposure is one of the tricks of the big Other, it is enough for the reader of the official version to have no more than a complete view of each existing thing, no matter how integrated they are. The big Other is the one who sees what is there to be seen – what is made available to be seen – and therefore makes what there is be permanently shown, even though occasionally hidden by circumstances. Making the big Other coincide with reality, stressing that they are the same and dismissing their contrast, is the gesture of ontotheology. It is the forgetting or concealment of being as what escapes any metaphysical protocol. It amounts to the claim that being hidden is an accidental part of reality while being exposed and open to view is essential to it, even when it is impossible to bring something to the view of anyone. The big Other is the reader of an official version that doesn't admit that anything is concealed except circumstantially. More than a commitment to (transcendence-free) totality, the big Other is a character in substantivism. The eye judging from outside is also fully known and therefore fully present. The big Other – as the judgement of God – is also the opposite of the Great Outdoors.

As totality contrasts with exteriority – and the view from nowhere with reality that is not all open to view – the Great Outdoors contrasts with what affords full exposure. The Great Outdoors is precisely what is other, beyond, outside, and not a window for the indoors to be seen. If the big Other deals in the expected procedure – and the ontotheologically described events – the Great Outdoors points outwards; it is the unexpected, the out of reach. The Great Outdoors is what is not already present in the indoors and not a complement of what is already known. It is outdoors because it is beyond the very reach of a judgement of God. The Great Outdoors is eerie and weird and cruel in the sense of Artaud; it is oblivious to God and the organs. It is nothing that can be thought in terms of substantives. It strikes us because it is out there. Being out there is not being part of a totality or something like a big Other judging what is indoors. To think about it is neither to reaffirm a limit beyond which nothing can trespass, nor to project what is indoors outwards. It is rather to concentrate on the outdoors as such, on the Other, on what is genuinely out there and can only barely be pointed to. What is out there can do no more to any judgement – or any cognitive claim – than interrupt it. The Great Outdoors is not a balcony or a garden; it never comes in. But it situates us where we are: it affects us merely by being out there.

## Notes

1. Levinas, *Otherwise than Being*, p. 25.
2. Rephrasing would amount to being able to point to what exists and to what does not. Replacing is suggested by Gilles Deleuze when discussing the importance of intensity in 'What Is an Event?', the chapter on Alfred Whitehead in his book *The Fold*. See Deleuze, *The Fold*, p. 77.
3. The distinction between *de re* and *de dicto* beliefs was introduced in Willard van Orman Quine's 'Quantifiers and Propositional Attitudes'. Quine's distinction expresses the difference between two kinds of belief attribution: one requires the presence of things with which the believer is in relation, while the other is independent of any relation whatsoever. The latter, *de dicto* belief attribution, deals with descriptions that are endorsed by the believer. The former, *de*

*re* belief attribution, is about something that is presented to the believer. As much as there are different, opposing ways of expanding and applying the distinction, it is reasonably safe to say that content attributed *de re* is situated. *De dicto* content is somehow in the air, non-situated, and requires no relation between the believer and anything else, while *de re* content requires a position – it is a situated content.

4. The phrase 'furniture of the universe' became famous with an image Hilary Putnam offers in his 'Models and Reality'. There he provides arguments, based on Löwenheim-Skolem results, against what he understood as the metaphysical realist quest for a sole model of reality. He concludes: 'The search for the "furniture of the universe" will have ended with the discovery that the universe is not a furnished room' (Putnam, 'Models and Reality', p. 481). In what follows, I will come to agree with the idea that the universe is not a furnished room – but for reasons very different from those that motivated Putnam's subsequent positions after abandoning metaphysical realism.

5. These three different perils point at some sort of recoil from the idea that there is something external – or that there is something external accessible to us: the Great Outdoors. The peril of idealism is that anything external is replaced by an ersatz inside me. The peril of subjectivism is to take anything external as being, to some extent, at the mercy of my subjective activity. The peril of correlationism is to have to accept that only a correlation with what is external is available to me; see Meillassoux, *After Finitude*. More on correlationism below.

6. Thomas Nagel, who made the phrase 'view from nowhere' popular in his book of that name, argued that an objective view of reality is possible even though ultimately incomplete. He struggled to make sense of a view that is not tied to any subjective position or perspective. His is a substantivist metaphysics. See Nagel, *The View From Nowhere*.

7. These ideas were sketched in Bensusan, 'Towards an Indexicalist Paradoxico-Metaphysics'.

8. Cogburn, *Garcian Meditations*.

9. Cogburn, *Garcian Meditations*, pp. 8–9.

10. See below for more on exteriority, on the view from nowhere and on the Other contrasted with what makes me the other for another.

11. Levinas holds that the relation is asymmetrical because the same is not the other of the other.

12. See Levinas, *Totality and Infinity*, p. 196. The Other, for him, appears to be a subjectivity before any effort to think, or in general before any act of intentionality. The presence of an external element presents a subjectivity as oriented – and positioned, situated – before any engagement or any act of intentionality.
13. See, for instance, the opening pages of section II in Levinas, *Totality and Infinity*. There, he presents a contrast between the metaphysical desire that makes one relate with the Other and the attempt to provide a substantive account of anything.
14. See Whitehead, *Science and the Modern World*, p. 52, and *Process and Reality*, pp. 7–8.
15. See Harman, *Towards Speculative Realism*; Harman, *Immaterialism*; Garcia, *Form and Object*; Dolphijn and van der Tuin, *New Materialism: Interviews and Cartographies*; Coole and Frost, *New Materialisms*.
16. Eduardo Viveiros de Castro understands the body as the basis for perspectives that are observer-relative; see Viveiros de Castro, 'Perspectivismo e multinaturalismo na América Indígena'.
17. This is my translation of the phrase '*un contact nu et aveugle avec l'Autre*'. See Wahl, *Traité de Métaphysique*, p. 702. Wahl is not only an interlocutor of Levinas's attention to the Other, but also an immediate precursor of his stance in metaphysics. Wahl's suspicion that Hegelian dialectics ushers in totality, in an inevitable move, influenced not only Levinas in his departure from the existing accounts of alterity, but also Deleuze in his rejection of the prevalence of identity over difference.
18. Aristotle, *Categories and De Interpretatione*.
19. Levinas, *Existence and Existents*, p. 82.
20. For more details on the social character of existence in monadological metaphysics, see Bensusan, *Being Up for Grabs*, ch. 3, and Bensusan and Alves de Freitas, *A diáspora da agência*.
21. I find a monadology in Leibniz's mature texts, those published from 1706 onwards. The key ideas of his monadological system are found in *Theodicy*, the 'Monadology' and 'The Principles of Nature and Grace' (see *The Philosophical Works of Leibnitz*).
22. For an analysis of the common features of all monadologies, see Bensusan, *Being Up for Grabs*, ch. 3, and Bensusan and Alves de Freitas, *A diáspora da agência*, pp. 93–108.
23. For a presentation of these systems as monadological based on features common to any monadology, see Bensusan and Alves de Freitas, *A diáspora da agência*, pp. 109–224. See also chiefly Tarde,

*Monadology and Sociology*; Whitehead, *Process and Reality*; and Latour, 'Irreductions'. These are the three texts that present most clearly the (neo-)monadological elements in these authors' thinking. Notice that while Tarde and Latour state that they are proposing monadologies, Whitehead has a more complex and nuanced relation with Leibniz that can be better appreciated from his *Adventures of Ideas*. Still, his philosophy of organism is a reformed monadology, and on several occasions he pointed to the general similarities and the specific differences between his and Leibniz's systems. The role of God and pre-established harmony, which he rejects, are central differences – see Whitehead, *Science and the Modern World*, ch. 11, and Whitehead, *Adventures of Ideas*.

24. Whitehead, *Modes of Thought*, p. 152.
25. Latour, 'Irreductions', 1.2.3. This is similar to indexicalist interiorities: they cannot be counted independently of deictic operations. Latour's claim here amounts to a rejection of the view from nowhere.
26. This is the example given in Leibniz's correspondence with Arnauld; Leibniz, *Leibniz–Arnauld Correspondence*.
27. Levinas, *Totality and Infinity*, p. 55.
28. Whitehead, *The Concept of Nature*, p. 70.
29. Whitehead, *The Concept of Nature*, p. 71.
30. Levinas, *Totality and Infinity*, p. 58.
31. Levinas, *Totality and Infinity*, p. 54, and Levinas, *Otherwise than Being*, pp. 113, 195 n. 18. While there is no limit to what I can require of myself, it is criminal to require more of others than their due.
32. McDowell, *Mind and World*, p. 34.
33. Husserl, *Cartesian Meditations*.
34. Levinas, *Time and the Other*, p. 83. He repeats the formula in several places.
35. Levinas, *Otherwise than Being*, pp. 50, 68–9, 98–129.
36. Levinas, *Otherwise than Being*, ch. 4. I will draw on ideas such as substitution and recurrence – that no subject is ever identical to oneself – to build the (indexicalist) notion of an interrupted process.
37. Cogburn, *Garcian Meditations*, p. 71.
38. Derrida, *Of Grammatology*, pp. 58–9.
39. Perry, 'The Problem of the Essential Indexical'.
40. Perry, 'The Problem of the Essential Indexical', pp. 19–20.
41. Perry, 'The Problem of the Essential Indexical', p. 20.
42. Perry, 'The Problem of the Essential Indexical', p. 20.

43. See Donnellan, 'Reference and Definite Descriptions'; Kaplan, 'Demonstratives'; Wettstein, *The Magic Prism*; Putnam, 'The Meaning of "Meaning"'; and Kripke, *Naming and Necessity*.
44. Wettstein, *The Magic Prism*, p. 75.
45. Kripke, *Naming and Necessity*, pp. 122ff.
46. Just as indexicalism can be read as an explicitly metaphysical (and anti-metaphysical) doctrine extracted from Levinas's philosophy of the Other, it can also be seen as drawing explicitly metaphysical (and anti-metaphysical) consequences from ideas in the philosophy of language. Manuel de Pinedo and I have coined, in an unpublished conference paper, the phrase 'linguistic turn of 360 degrees' to express how attention to language can shed light on metaphysical issues.
47. Donnellan, 'Reference and Definite Descriptions'. Kripke, in 'Speaker's Reference and Semantic Reference', rejects Donnellan's aim of criticising Russell's theory of definite descriptions through his distinction between attributive and referential use of a description and ends up rejecting Donnellan's distinction in favour of one between semantic reference and speaker's reference. He also makes clear that although Donnellan's distinction resembles the *de re*/*de dicto* distinction, it is an altogether different distinction.
48. Perry, 'The Problem of the Essential Indexical', p. 20.
49. Sextus Empiricus, *Outlines of Scepticism*.
50. Kaplan, 'Demonstratives'.
51. Kripke, *Naming and Necessity*, p. 114.
52. McTaggart, 'The Unreality of Time'.
53. See Whitehead, *The Concept of Nature*, p. 70.
54. Fine, 'Tense and Reality'.
55. These three alternatives concerning reality and tense – drop neutrality, drop the absolute character of reality or drop coherence – can be applied to other discussions as well. Fine shows how, for example, discussions on the reality of possible worlds and on the appropriateness of first-person descriptions have a similar structure.
56. I expand Fine's cubist *über-reality* to a broader stance on objects and perspectives in Bensusan, 'The Cubist Object'. In Bensusan, *Being Up for Grabs*, ch. 3, I explore the nature of his fragments.
57. David Lewis proposed that modal reality is itself indexical in *On the Plurality of Worlds*. The actual world is real only to the extent that it is the one, among infinite others, where we are. Lewis, like Leibniz, posits worldly individuals who enjoy no trans-world identity. His indexicalist move is bounded by his modal realism:

when he holds that all possible worlds equally exist, he seems to posit something akin to a transcendence-free totality visible from nowhere.
58. Deleuze, *The Fold*, pp. 81–2.
59. Levinas, *Time and the Other*.
60. de Sousa, *Horizonte e Complementaridade*.
61. Heidegger, *The Beginning of Western Philosophy*.
62. Severino, *The Essence of Nihilism*, pp. 1–35.
63. It is only due to a fixed standing location that something passes or takes place; it is something similar to the Doppler effect, where speed is itself indexical to the measuring point. I explored the general import of the Doppler effect for metaphysics in Bensusan, *Being Up for Grabs*, chs 1, 2 and 6.
64. To be sure, a view from the space outside the planet is not a view from nowhere. Maps, in fact, are not totalities; they have borders outside of which nothing is pictured.
65. Barad, *Meeting the Universe Halfway*, p. 19.
66. Heraclitus, *Fragments*, fr. 3.
67. Wittgenstein, *Remarks on the Foundations of Mathematics*, p. 38.
68. Whitehead, *The Concept of Nature*, p. 79.
69. Quine, 'Carnap and Logical Truth', p. 374.
70. Wittgenstein, *Philosophical Investigations*, § 95.
71. Whitehead, *Process and Reality*, p. 44.
72. Putnam, 'The Meaning of "Meaning"'.
73. Wittgenstein, *Philosophical Investigations*.
74. Levinas, *Totality and Infinity*, pp. 53–81.
75. Levinas, *Otherwise than Being*, ch. 1.
76. Levinas, *Totality and Infinity*, pp. 71–2.
77. Levinas, *Otherwise than Being*, p. 10.
78. 'Demand' is a possible translation of Levinas's word *demande*, the one adopted by Alphonso Lingis. While the verb *demander* can be translated as 'to ask', in this book I sometimes use 'demand' as the corresponding noun.
79. Levinas, *Totality and Infinity*, pp. 37–8.
80. See Chapter 3 below.
81. Kunst, 'Nearness', p. 22.
82. Levinas indicates that consciousness is the place one comes back to in this journey, 'the very locus of the reverting of the facticity of individuation' (*Otherwise than Being*, p. 83). It is, therefore, the place where one recovers from the contact with what is external.
83. Levinas, *Otherwise than Being*, p. 94.

76 Indexicalism

84. Levinas, *Otherwise than Being*, p. 25.
85. Levinas, *Otherwise than Being*, pp. 93–4.
86. Levinas, *Otherwise than Being*, p. 85.
87. The idea that proximity is not tied to anything substantive affords an interesting reading of Deleuze and Guattari's *Anti-Oedipus*. There, families appear as a target of subjective effort that requires an operation – the Oedipus operation – to reinforce and maintain: one is geared to be oriented towards one's family. This subjective effort, however, is clearly not only erotic energy and focus but also a sense of responsibility and vulnerability that could be best described in terms of proximity. We will see later that there are several points of contact between Levinas's rejection of a substantive complete description of what there is and the notions around Deleuze's (and Guattari's) plane of immanence.
88. Levinas, *Otherwise than Being*, p. 81.
89. Heidegger, *Bremen and Freiburg Lectures*, p. xi (Translator's Foreword).
90. This is why in the last of the four Bremen lectures, the one entitled '*Die Kehre*' ('The Turn'), Heidegger envisages the possibility of retreating from *thesis* and returning to *physis* by some sort of engaged forgetfulness where one loses the grip of what is thematised. See Heidegger, *Bremen and Freiburg Lectures*, pp. 64–75.
91. Derrida, *Of Grammatology*.
92. Levinas, *Totality and Infinity*, pp. 69–70. He credits Plato for the idea that thought is never a chain of impersonal true reports but always assumes interpersonal relations (*Totality and Infinity*, pp. 71–2).
93. Levinas, *Otherwise than Being*, pp. 80–1.
94. Levinas, *Otherwise than Being*, pp. 62–3, 100. In *Totality and Infinity*, Levinas has a different account of the sensible, and it is less clear that it connects with what he calls proximity in *Otherwise than Being*.
95. Wahl, *Vers le concret*, p. 30.
96. Heidegger, *Being and Time*, pp. 62–7.
97. Harman, *Towards Speculative Realism*.
98. Harman, *Quentin Meillassoux*, p. 4.
99. Harman, *Quentin Meillassoux*.
100. Peter Gratton remarks that Levinas's influence on Harman's object-oriented ontology was perhaps greater than that of Heidegger (Gratton, *Speculative Realism*, p. 7).
101. Garcia, *Form and Object*, pp. 70–1.

102. Garcia, *Form and Object*, p. 89.
103. Cogburn, *Garcian Meditations*.
104. Haraway, *Staying with the Trouble*, p. 31.
105. Noys, 'Drone Metaphysics'.
106. Artaud, *To Have Done With the Judgement of God*.
107. Deleuze and Guattari, *A Thousand Plateaus*.
108. Lacan and Miller, *The Seminar of Jacques Lacan*.
109. Fisher, *Capitalist Realism*.
110. Fisher, *Capitalist Realism*, p. 44.
111. Fisher, *Capitalist Realism*, p. 47.
112. Heidegger, *Bremen and Freiburg Lectures*, p. 49.
113. Heidegger, *Bremen and Freiburg Lectures*, pp. 51–2.

# 2

# The Metaphysics of the Others

*What is attractive about conversations is right there: in the other being truly an other, and in his thoughts being unfathomable to his interlocutor [...] I [...] have to face the superior unity of collective creation.*

Cesar Aira[1]

## The Others

Indexicalism can now be described as the claim that deictic operations are the building blocks of what is real. They compose interiorities where the Great Outdoors makes an impact without ceasing to be exterior. Since exteriority can never be fully neutralised in a totality, the only possible metaphysics is one that paradoxically accounts for the impossibility of metaphysics. Indexicalism inherits from Levinas a stance towards the Other. It extends it to the Outdoors, transcending any interiority which is available to any standing location. The deixis of indexicalism is therefore cosmological: it includes not only humans and human societies but also whatever traffics in indexicals. It proposes a picture of the non-human as partaking in the exercise of being situated. It embraces this deictic common ground, ensuring that each standing location is transcended by its outer, its others, its beyond, its strange and its unexpected.

A central element of an indexicalist position is the transcending Other. We have seen that indexicalism gains its plausibility by combining arguments for different kinds against totality – both against any access to a complete view, and against the intelligibility of a non-situated viewpoint that would neutralise exteriority and render barren any contact with what is outside – with remarks on the pervasive nature of situatedness when we consider tense, proximity, measurements, demonstratives and many of the implicitly *de re* elements that make thought what it is. Indexicalism is a way to preserve exteriority against every attempt to neutralise it, by finding it in the building blocks of what exists even at the cost of inviting a measure of paradox into the main picture. No matter how far or deep you look, claims indexicalism, exteriority does not collapse into something else that could be viewed from nowhere. That is because there is a transcending Other, there is an exterior, there is something beyond.

Once exteriority is judged to be its main concern, metaphysics – in its only possible branch, paradoxico-metaphysics – is geared towards the others. Indexicalism aims to cluster together the Other – as conceived by Levinas in terms of the human who can address me and not only refuse but also contest my thoughts and actions – the others – as conceived in the monadological way as alien units of agency – and the Great Outdoors. We can consider these figures of the exterior; the others, in general, are what lie on the outer side of a border. These figures are at the centre of any metaphysical quest; the metaphysics of the others is a department of indexicalism. It is an attention to the others as a deictic operation that inserts exteriority into a standing location. This chapter elaborates on this approach to the Great Outdoors: the extension of Levinas's Other beyond the human, the reorientation of process philosophy towards genuine exteriority, the constraining of speculation so that it is not geared towards totality.

It is usual to distinguish other humans from the vast expanses associated with the Great Outdoors. We often claim that other humans can influence one's own thought in a way the Great Outdoors itself cannot, or that the Great Outdoors is such that other humans are not part of it – or rather, that we can be alone in the Great Outdoors without the company of other humans. The usual image seems to be a variation of the triangle Donald Davidson explicitly stated when talking about three varieties of knowledge: me, other humans, the external world.[2] The metaphysics of the others rejects the distinction between the second and the third vertices. The Other that is my fellow human is also the Great Outdoors – the distinction between the human and the non-human alien is not metaphysically salient. The Great Outdoors is approached as composed by any others, by the exterior, by what is beyond.

The metaphysics of the others follows in the footsteps of Levinas, bearing in mind that the others for him do not include the

Outdoors. Nevertheless, his approach to the metaphysics of the others is a blueprint that can be revised to focus on the very fabric of exteriority by way of alterity. This revision will ultimately lead to a conception of perceptual experience that is in line with the pan-perceptualist image of the world embraced by Whitehead, who thought whatever was concrete – any actual entity – was endowed with a sensorium, a capacity to affect and be affected. Coexistence is therefore an issue for sensibility. Perceiving for Whitehead is also an act of creation, and therefore it is through sensoria that novelty arises. What interests the metaphysics of the others is that the others should be capable of novelty; the exterior forms no totality. In fact, Whitehead exorcises from his metaphysical view the tenets of what he sees as morbid stabilities in which inhibition and sheer repetition of existing patterns block the way to adventure. Accordingly, he intends to distance his image of the world from that of a 'barren tautological absolute'.[3] Claiming that process is the main character, he holds that there is 'no totality which is the harmony of all perfections'; furthermore, he continues, there are 'always "others", which might have been and are not'.[4] Process is not driven by imperfection, but rather by an openness to what can still come. Whitehead writes that 'it belongs to the essence of each occasion of experience that it is concerned with an otherness transcending itself'.[5] The others are experienced with a measure of concern that counterbalances the striving for self-enjoyment. Concern is directed towards the rest of the world.[6] Indeed, Latour, in a Whiteheadian move, suggests that we replace 'matters of fact' as a way to describe what is settled in the world with 'matters of concern'.[7] Whitehead's attention to the others, partly because of his (neo-)monadological leanings, counterbalances his detailed description of the inner working of perception; the others are as much the focus of his metaphysics as the inner and the indoors. The Great Outdoors is a place crowded with actual entities where each agent aims at reaching self-enjoyment.

The metaphysics of the others is therefore the double endeavour of extending the Levinasian Other to the Great Outdoors and reforming the perception-based process philosophy proposed by Whitehead to make room for a transcending Other, that is, a transcending Great Outdoors. Rendering the metaphysics of the others as perception-cum-transcendence, however, is the task of the next chapter. This one will concentrate on the idea of a metaphysics of the others and how it compares with similar enterprises. It focuses on how the outer impacts the inner and on the metaphysics around this impact. This is a chapter on the *physis* of the others.[8]

## The *Physis* of the Others

The others, taken in the general way I am proposing here, have a *physis* – a way of doing things that is their own. Their innate character entails that they challenge any complete view of them. The Greek concept of *physis* is perhaps appropriate, as it points towards the coming to the fore of anything – in a usage that differs from that of Aristotle and Simplicius, who contrasted *physis* (normally translated as 'nature') with *tekhné*. The others come to the fore by introducing exteriority into something. It is almost as if they have a function; but instead of being ingredients, they are disrupters. In a series of lectures in Brussels, Anna Tsing presented in simple terms the task of giving the best possible account of the world in a way that would include others, and other accounts of the world.[9] She presented a double injunction to be satisfied: 1) to give an account of the world using the best of one's capacities and 2) to leave space within that account for other, different accounts.

The friction between one's best account and a different one coming from outside is the origin of *diaphonía*. Levinas finds, in the existence of an alternative approach to anything, a trace of the Other; one can profit from the alternative approach to better one's own, but one is equally called upon to do justice to the alternative approach. Therefore he sets out two uses of the alternative approaches to what one thinks: one can restrict one's own spontaneity in order to achieve a better way of thinking – which would be a technical improvement to one's thinking – and one can restrict one's own spontaneity to do justice to the Other. In the latter case, one is moved not by a drive towards truth, but by a desire to take into account the concerns of the Other – even when they are not fully shared by one's own way of thinking. Issues concerning how to deploy sovereignty and spontaneity in one's thinking are always tainted by issues of justice towards the Other.[10] Both approaches appear when we confront any state of affairs in the Great Outdoors – there is an appeal to justice coming from Outdoors.

As a consequence, to consider any topic is to set the stage for disagreement. Thinking deals in multiplicities. Whenever our opinions are in conflict with states of affairs, we can also say that we have to manage a *diaphonía*. We sometimes face situations in which we ought to give up our opinion in order to do justice to the state of affairs. When we consider the Great Outdoors, however, we seldom deal solely with a single other. It is not that the opinion of my opponent is to be adopted because she has some kind of priority, being Other: for there is also justice to be done to the others who are the topic of the controversy. I am called upon to do justice to the sun and the Earth when discussing the views of Galileo. There are cases in which not all of the others involved can be accommodated. We cannot always surrender to the others since the administration of justice is what is asked for when we attend to many different others – which is the case when we exercise conceptual capacities (or make theories). Sometimes, a recalcitrant state of affairs has to be tolerated because we cannot accommodate it with all the others. The metaphysics of the others postulates that recalcitrance is inevitable. As a consequence, *diaphonía* is seldom fully dissolved.

Tsing holds that we should attend to both points (1) and (2) mentioned above. To attend to (1) only would entail the commitment to a complete view shaped by my sovereignty, and that would leave no space for anything beyond it. To satisfy only (2) is to recoil to a quietist abstention or a Pyrrhonic *ataraxia* or suspension of judgement in which there is no effort at building a picture or theory. But when we satisfy both (1) and (2), we leave space for the others while giving an account of them. Tsing's injunction expresses what is at stake in a metaphysics of the others: to account for reality in its exterior dimension, while acknowledging the others that are exterior. To attend to both is something akin to being dogmatic while engaging in an *epokhé* at the same time, to use the terms of Sextus Empiricus. Sextus's *epokhé* was recommended when no decision could possibly be made concerning one or other of two voices, so that any choice would be ultimately arbitrary and slide into dogmatism. Sextus's suspension of judgement claims that the best thing to be done in these situations is to circumvent the need for a decision, either by refusing to follow one of the voices or by simply following the appearances in each case.[11] Sextus was convinced that one cannot do both things simultaneously, for that would involve entertaining two incompatible attitudes towards the issue – and, in fact, entertaining two attitudes towards the others.[12] To attend to both (1) and (2) is to deal with the others both as *a subject* (or a topic) and as something one is *subject to* (an opponent or an antagonist). Tsing urges attention to the others, guided by both truth and by justice: to give an account of them with them.

Her injunction shows that the metaphysics of the others ventures into a paradox inherited from indexicalism. Its task is to give a maximally general account of reality, such that genuine others – and genuinely other maximally general accounts of reality – are possible. Since the others are infinite – no less than the Other and the Great Outdoors – a metaphysics of the others never reaches a transcendence-free totality. More than a landscape of what is there to be contemplated in a total view, the metaphysics of the others is like a discovery plot in which the covered area is constantly expanding. By leaving space for different accounts, one's account is never complete, yet it should aim at completion as well as being open to interruption. What emerges is an ongoing, interrupted account that paradoxically takes into consideration what comes from outside even when no voice is fully heard. Such is the *physis* of the others.

The metaphysics of the others is a consequence of indexicalism: it is situated among others and deals in what looms on the horizon. The proximity of the others spells an appeal that can appear in the form of a trace of exteriority. The language of the others – the only public language we have available for thought and action – is a language of responses; it is a language suited for dialogue, for addressing an interlocutor. It is a language crafted for saying more than what needs to be said, as Levinas puts it. Satisfying Tsing's double injunction leads to something close to a conversation in which interlocutors bring in different accounts while appealing, interrupting and asking for responses. Just as in conversations, not all claims are explicitly made; not all voices are simultaneously heard. They rarely cease speaking.

The metaphysics of the others is a conversational metaphysics. Like any conversation, it is open and situated; every previous assumption can be revised and reconsidered. Every interlocutor can bring others to the forum, explicitly or not. When it comes to claiming something, a conversation is often inefficient. Nothing gets said once and for all. A conversation is not said to be paradoxical when described as taking place between speakers, but if it is described as the speaker (or the author) itself ('a conversation said this and that . . .') it is paradoxically often placing opinions in parallel. Often, conversations are not seen as authors, even though they lead the development of a topic in a way outside the control of any interlocutor.[13] In this sense, they can be compared with Haraway's string figures.[14] Conversations are sympoietic: they are jointly created. Also, conversations are often taken to be (heuristic) means of achieving the goal of stating something: they are too open-ended to be our best way to deal with a topic. If the metaphysics of the others is something similar, its outcome is closer to a brainstorm than to a final report.

Moreover, the metaphysics of the others is like a conversation with the Great Outdoors and its many (and perhaps uncountable) others. Conversing with the non-human is much of what is at stake in perception, as we will see below. The interplay of concepts and sensible intuitions forms an open dialogue where, often enough, no final word emerges. If the metaphysics of the others is a broad conversation, it is one in which a new interlocutor is always expected.

### Perspectivism

From its inception, anthropology has been dealing with the others (Marco Antonio Valentim has even been pursuing the idea that it should be renamed *xenology*). Its theoretical and practical efforts have been focused on how to respond to the stranger and how to make the contact with someone different be more meaningful, if not insightful. It has developed ways of approaching the others such that they have an impact on one's worldview, either by changing it or by making its insufficiency explicit. Anthropology has typically dealt with the human others, first with people from different places – having different cultures – and then with people in proximity, who always display enough dissimilarity to be treated as others as well.

Recent developments in anthropology have investigated different ways of portraying and relating to the non-human. These efforts, which are sometimes paradoxically referred to as an 'anthropology of nature', seek to identify and contrast different attitudes concerning the inorganic and various species of living beings. This is not simply about how the non-human is viewed or represented, but also about how it has established ties with human populations and is part of the maintenance of their social networks. The picture prevalent among modern people – derived from a bifurcation between what is natural and what is social – is that there is a physicality common to both humans and non-humans and an interiority that is exclusive to humans and varies with ethnic and cultural traits. As a consequence, there is a single nature common to everything, while cultural diversity between different human groups is still to be expected.

Philippe Descola calls this modern disposition towards the non-human 'naturalism', and opposes it to three other attitudes.[15] One of those, animism, is in direct contrast with naturalism, as it posits interiority to be spread among humans and non-humans and physicality to be what varies between different populations. The same interiority is to be found in, say, humans and jaguars, although their bodies are importantly different. Non-human populations enjoy as many social ties as human ones, and make alliances and cut deals as frequently as people, albeit often by other means. Animism tends towards a multinaturalism as much as naturalism tends towards a multiculturalism. As there are varieties of naturalism, there are different forms of animism associated with different groups; among the differences are those concerning the way different animisms conceive of the common interiority that they find in humans and animals, some plants and some artefacts. In any case, animist groups, which are spread throughout the Americas but also found in north-eastern Asia and some Pacific Islands, form social ties that are clearly and explicitly not limited to humans. Attention to animisms as something other than a different culture – and requiring more of an 'ontography' than ethnographies – paved the way for an approach in anthropology that John Hartigan labelled 'Aesop's anthropology': theorising culture and society across species lines.[16] Anthropological focus on animist groups, especially in the lower Amazon area, along with other non-naturalist groups with different dispositions towards the non-human, prompted a multispecies view in which interiority and the social ties it forms are considered beyond the boundaries of the human. The anthropological gaze, with its attention to the friction with otherness, is directed beyond humans – and contact between people and animals, say, is understood in terms of connections between interiorities.

Among animist Amerindian groups, at least some adopt a conception of interiority that is common to everyone as deictic. Drawing on ideas from anthropologists of the lower Amazon, such as Kaj Århem's insightful work, Tania Stolze Lima and Eduardo Viveiros de Castro have developed the idea of a central perspectival quality in these groups' thought.[17] Descola himself remarks that the view that interiorities are perspectival is open to every animist group, although not all animists would be perspectivists.[18] Viveiros de Castro uses the term *perspectivism* to describe the way some groups from the lower Amazon relate both to human and non-human populations, postulating what he calls in the title of his article a cosmological deixis. He holds that there is a widespread belief across the Americas, upon which 'horticulturalists do not differ much from circumpolar hunters', that at least some animals – in general, those that are ecologically close and engage in daily contact with humans – have an underlying human spirit that gives them a perspective on their surroundings.[19] Viveiros de Castro remarks that this amounts to adopting a theory 'according to which the universe is populated by extra-human intentionalities endowed with their own perspectives'.[20] Perspectivism understands that what is common between intentionalities across species is deixis, and his description of, say, blood being beer for a jaguar has much in common with the indexicalist claim that thought – and reality – is not ultimately *de dicto*, and that deictic features are widely spread.

Viveiros de Castro notes an antinomy between two powerful and contrasting research intuitions concerned with the Amerindian population. First, there is the idea that Amerindian communities are ethnocentric, a generally accepted idea that dates back to Lévi-Strauss: each community considers other peoples non-human (or less than human). They draw a line between the human and the non-human precisely at the borders of their group. Second, there is the most recently documented animic mode of the Amerindians, according to which idea they conceive of a great number of entities as intrinsically human and as establishing social relations analogous to those between humans. Instead of solving the antinomy by choosing between the older and the most recently uncovered pole, Viveiros de Castro proposes that they 'apprehend the same phenomena from different angles'; in fact, the opposition between the two poles derives from a 'substantivist conceptualization of Nature and Culture [. . .] which is not applicable to Amerindian cosmologies'.[21] He proceeds to remark that Amerindian words that translate as 'human being' function 'less as nouns than as pronouns'.[22] They indicate the position of the subject, and Viveiros de Castro describes these names as pointing at a perspective and not referring to a substantive. These groups don't refer to themselves with a substantive or a community name; most ethnonyms are the result of interactions with ethnographers and come from other groups that refer to them by the name. 'Ethnonyms', Viveiros de Castro writes, 'are names of third parties; they belong to the category of "they" not to the category of "we".'[23] He infers that whatever possesses a soul is a subject with a point of view, and that 'Amerindian souls, be they human or animal, are these indexical categories, cosmological deictics' that call for 'animist psychology or substantialist ontology'.[24] He remarks that 'terms such as *wari* [. . .] *dene* [. . .] or *masa* [. . .] mean people but can be used for – and therefore used by – very different classes of beings'.[25] They can be used by humans referring to humans, but also by peccaries self-referring to peccaries, or jaguars somehow pointing at themselves. Under this deictic light, animism is not a projection of human qualities on to animals, but a resolute denial of substantive metaphysics in favour of an indexicalism in which both humans and non-humans enjoy positioned relations towards each other and everything else. Viveiros de Castro summarises this conclusion in terms of the classical distinction targeted by any anthropology of nature: 'culture is the subject's nature'.[26] 'Humanity' is to be understood as a general name for any subject, or in the terms of this book, for an interiority capable of deictic operations.

The contrast between multinaturalism and multiculturalism is itself informative about deixis and interiorities. Multinaturalism is the idea that both humans and non-humans are engaged in the same deictic operations with respect to their surroundings. They have different natures but similar deictic capacities. What these deictic capacities target is different: what for us is blood, is beer for the jaguar; a muddy puddle is for the tapirs a ceremonial house. Viveiros de Castro emphasises that while Amerindian thought stresses these deictic relations with the surroundings, multiculturalist relativism understands perspectives as partial viewpoints on an otherwise inaccessible totality.[27] The core of multiculturalism is that there is an ontological totality beyond any subject's grasp, something alien to any interiority and accessible only from the point of view of nowhere. Multinaturalism, in contrast, posits a commonality in the indexical structure. Viveiros de Castro writes that 'body and soul, just like nature and culture, do not correspond to substantives, self-subsistent entities or ontological provinces, but rather to pronouns or phenomenological perspectives'.[28] Body and soul are stances of interiorities; they are standing locations. Bodies, under multinaturalism, can have different natures and yet share the same deictic operations.

Multinaturalism, together with the idea that non-human populations with social ties to human groups can be found across different species, ushers in an anthropology that cannot stop at any human border. This multispecies turn, or animal turn – or more broadly, posthuman turn – brought about by researches into the anthropology of nature (and by the reflections of Elizabeth Povinelli and Anna Tsing) points towards an engagement of anthropology with 'general claims about the way the world is', in the words of Eduardo Kohn.[29]

Kohn is adamant about bringing ontology back into the anthropological picture, by taking into account social connections and perspectives beyond the human real:

> an anthropology beyond the human is perforce an ontological one. That is, taking nonhumans seriously makes it impossible to confine our anthropological inquiries to an epistemological concern for how it is that humans, at some particular time or in some particular place, go about making sense of them. As an ontological endeavor this kind of anthropology places us in a special position to rethink the sorts of concepts we use and to develop new ones.[30]

The effort of anthropology is to attain a view of the relations between humans and non-humans by looking at how different societies establish social relations with what surrounds them. Anthropology becomes a social study of what is around a human population, and therefore a social study of reality in the sense of the (positioned) society of reality. Kohn writes:

> This search for a better way to attend to our relations to that which lies beyond the human, especially that part of the world beyond the human that is alive, forces us to make ontological claims—claims, that is, about the nature of reality. That, for example, jaguars in some way or other represent the world demands a general explanation that takes into account certain insights about the way the world is—insights that are garnered from attention to engagements with nonhumans and that are thus not fully circumscribed by any particular human system of understanding them.[31]

This anthropological attention to representations of jaguars in connection to their human neighbours shifts the content of the discipline from the category of human sciences to that of metaphysics. Perhaps there is no such thing as a human science, and efforts in these directions were failed attempts to segment out knowledge of humans from information concerning their surroundings. In any case, the posthuman turn in anthropology clearly qualifies it to become a department of metaphysics. Further, Viveiros de Castro understands perspectivism to be an appropriate anthropological method: a method of interacting with the native's deixis.[32]

Seen in this light, anthropology indeed becomes closer to indexicalism in its focus on interiorities than to a specialised science that concentrates on one side of a divide between stable and indifferent nature on the one hand, and humanity, with its shifting politics and cultures, on the other. The divide places anthropology within a bifurcated totality. The posthuman turn drives it back to the metaphysical drawing board – the board where the metaphysics of the others lies.

### The Metaphysics of the Others in the Age of the Correlate

Quentin Meillassoux criticised the prevalent tendency in philosophy since the eighteenth century not to move beyond what there is *for-us* towards what is absolute – either in the form of absolute beings or of absolute principles.[33] He calls this tendency *correlationism*, and the philosophical epoch inaugurated by Kant's critiques *the age of the correlate*. By stopping short of the absolute, philosophy confined itself to a preoccupation that could not go beyond the correlation between us and the world. In the age of the correlate, the dispute between subjectivists and their opponents became a controversy concerning whether the correlation is a construction of our own, or whether it reaches all there is to be reached. Similarly, the debate between realists and idealists was mostly placed within the borders of correlation. The questions therefore became something like: given our concepts and the practices in which they are embedded, is it possible for us to conceive of a world completely different from the way our thinking is geared to proceed? Or do we, and our intentional states, experience the independence of what is presented to us?

This age was inaugurated by Kantian weak correlationism,

which holds that *knowledge* and *experience* are confined to our correlation with how things are. Kant's view still makes room for *thought* to go beyond correlation, though this is rendered impossible by strong correlationism. Kant introduced the idea of transcendental philosophy by asking questions concerning what makes the correlation stand – what makes our knowledge within its limits universal and necessary? It is as if in the age of the correlate, our correlation with the world is always the main protagonist and we cannot step outside it. Studying the correlation is not an endeavour like the ones carried out by (pre-critical) metaphysicians. The right way to proceed is, instead, to assume the correlation and wonder what makes it the way it is. This entails, for example, assuming that transcendental subjects – capable of making empirical judgements by using categories, concepts and norms, just like us – are somehow present whenever the correlation is in place. The challenge to correlationism was therefore twofold: it involved 1) questioning our ability to step beyond those limits and 2) wondering whether *our* correlation could somehow be discarded – and the centrality of the human ways put aside.[34]

Meillassoux felt the need to engage in this challenge. His attention was primarily focused on (1). His discomfort – which he shared with speculative realism – was with the fact that we accept the limit on our knowledge and thought. With this discomfort came an epic proposition: that we overcome these age-old limitations and venture into what is deemed to be outside the proper realm for philosophy. This led to looking back at the history of the current age to find blocked paths, forbidden ways of thinking that were now open to the daring. To be sure, it was not simply an issue of boldness; to overcome correlationism would also require that its history and its rationale be considered, as well as its lessons learned.

Meillassoux is convinced that one widespread tendency in the age of the correlate – that of considering the correlation itself to be absolute – is misguided. Correlationism, whether weak or strong, simply accepted that we are confined in the correlation, while some metaphysicians simply ignored the correlationist move and proceeded with pre-critical metaphysics. While these two alternatives are to be steadfastly discarded if the goal is to overcome correlation, and not to accept it or dismiss it, a third tendency – that of holding that the correlation was itself absolute – is to be rejected for its failure to take the lessons of correlationism seriously. In

*Après la finitude*, Meillassoux calls this tendency *the metaphysics of subjectivity*, and ascribes to it several post-Kantian philosophers, whom he describes as having learned only half of Kant's lesson.[35] Kant's correlationist message, according to Meillassoux, was that the correlation was inevitable – at least as the starting point of our rapport with what is outside – but not necessary. In other words, the correlation is not something we can circumvent; it is factual in the sense that it is not grounded in any necessity, but is simply a matter of fact. We are stuck with our correlation – even if we manage to go beyond it, it is a point of departure – but it is thoroughly contingent. The metaphysics of subjectivity accepts that correlation is an inevitable point of departure, but takes it to be absolute and therefore not contingent. Meillassoux is adamant that this is not the way forward: it arrives at an absolute, but only by admitting that the facticity of correlation is here to stay.

Yet the metaphysics of subjectivity is attractive for two intertwined reasons. First, it understands correlation as a genuine metaphysical discovery and not only a barrier to our otherwise absolute knowledge. It can posit correlation as a component in the furniture of the universe, and it is what makes the universe thinkable or knowable or experienceable in general. Second, it pictures the correlation as being other than ours, as something out there. Subjectivity can then be presented as a way out of the predicament of correlationism: there is subjectivity in the world, and therefore we are not confined within it, but rather revealing an item in the furniture of the universe. Meillassoux finds the metaphysics of subjectivity in philosophers as distinct as Hegel and his followers on the one side, and Nietzsche, Bergson, Whitehead and their admirers Deleuze and Latour on the other. The distinction between these two groups points towards two quite different ways of understanding correlation as absolute. According to the first, correlation is the mediation that opens the world through concepts – there is no more than one correlation, the one brought about by concepts and accessible to us through the work of reflection on experience. According to the second, there are multiple correlations everywhere, not only our correlation with the river but also that of the lake with the river – while there is no river-in-itself, there is a river-for-us as much as a river-for-the-mountain. While in one case our correlation is absolute – because conceptual mediation is what makes things visible – in the other what is absolute is the plurality of entangled correlations. In both cases, the correlation is absolute in the sense that it is not a veil that could, at least in principle, be removed – there is nothing beyond it.

Meillassoux finds instructive the failure of the metaphysics of subjectivity to assimilate the lesson that correlation is factual. He reckons that facticity is about the gap between what something is and what something appears to be – things can be completely different from how they appear. Not taking the facticity of the correlation into consideration entails a commitment to the transparency of the world. This commitment shows itself both in the insistence that ultimately concepts are not misleading in any sense, and in the rejection of the bifurcation between the experience something has of an actuality and that actuality itself. Hence, what the metaphysics of subjectivity rejects is the occultation of reality: that there is something structurally hidden, concealed or veiled in it. The contingency of correlation is precisely what paves the way for occultation: reality could be completely different from the way it appears, either in our own or any other correlation. If what is shown in correlations is not necessarily true, there is something in reality that resists being shown. When the metaphysics of subjectivity claims that there is nothing beyond the correlation(s), it accepts that there is no holdover of reality beyond what is accessible. Although neither of the two types of metaphysics of subjectivity holds that any subject can access reality once and for all, both are committed to the structural transparency of reality. According to Meillassoux, this is because correlation is thought to be absolute.

Now, indexicalism, in its attention to deixis including the exterior, gives birth to the metaphysics of the others. As a criticism of metaphysics in general, this could be seen as a variation on correlationism. It is via deictic operations that any interiority accesses the world through proximity; what is absolute about deixis involves the borders between the inner and the outer, the around and the away from, the within and the beyond. Levinas himself can be seen in two different ways. Either he is a weak correlationist, since it is in what makes theoretical thinking possible that the Other appears – knowing is intrinsically hostage to the Other – and not in (ontological) knowledge itself. Or he is a strong correlationist, since no total view of things can even be conceived.[36] However, Levinasian correlationism is utterly odd, for it engages directly with exteriority, or with the outdoors. Theoretical thinking depends on the absolute character of the Other; if there is a correlation, it brings about exteriority itself. The refusal of a total view is, for Levinas, the refusal of finitude. A Levinasian correlation can only be incomplete because it reveals infinity in the Other. In that sense too it prefigures indexicalism: it crosses the border towards metaphysics only in the same gesture that makes it impossible.

Once its criticism of metaphysics becomes itself a (paradoxical) metaphysics, indexicalism holds that there are deictic operations that are not reducible to substantives. As a metaphysics, this can be compared with the two types of metaphysics of subjectivity mentioned above. We can compare the metaphysics of the others with the likes of Hegel if we replace concepts with indexicals, and we can compare it with the likes of Whitehead if we understand correlation in terms of the application of deictic operators. Interestingly, the appeal to deixis makes it possible for correlations to be multiple while sharing a common structure that is not grounded in predicates. Certainly, indexicalism takes any standing location to be contingent on where the interiority is, since any connection with the exterior is situated. But deixis itself is absolute. And certainly, it cannot be pared down by a view from nowhere that would be different from any correlation, proving that there is something beyond any of them. So in a sense, if we take deixis to compose a correlation, it is deemed absolute. However, due to its own nature, it does not follow that reality is transparent. In fact, reality is constituted by exteriority, by a transcending element (outer, beyond, Outdoors) that is not fully accessible – like what looms on the horizon without being fully presented. If indexicalism is a sort of metaphysics of subjectivity, it is a strange sort, for absolute deixis makes nothing transparent in reality.

Meillassoux has his own way of overcoming correlationism, which is different from the other alternatives he mentions. He intends to seize that which is beyond what is *for-us*. Rejecting any metaphysics of subjectivity, he rejects what is *without-us* in the sense of being *for-the-others* and settles for what is *in-itself* or *for-nobody* (or rather, *for-nothing*). It is not enough to embrace what is *without-us* by being *for-someone-else* (or *for-something-else*) – the absolute that is hidden behind any (factual) correlation is *for-nothingness*. Meillassoux seeks this *for-nothingness* precisely in the relation between occultation and facticity. He claims that the absolute is what makes occultation possible, and the absolute is the facticity of everything, the necessity of contingency. In other words, what is absolute is that reality eludes, so that therefore there could be anything behind the scenes. Stated differently, what is absolute is the contingent character of everything. If it is a bad speculative move to make correlation absolute, it is a wise speculative step to find grounds in the non-transparency of reality to consider contingency itself absolute. The metaphysics of subjectivity in its many varieties finds the absolute by taking as a premise the surest thing in the age of the correlate – the correlation itself. Given that the absolute cannot be contingent, Meillassoux then takes contingency as a premise to reach the absolute facticity of everything. The ubiquity of contingency is itself a problem for the claim that reality is transparent: everything could be very different from how it appears; it is as if contingency erodes any supposed absolute character of correlation if that character entails the transparency of reality.

By confronting correlation and the absolute, Meillassoux contrasts the speculative procedure that starts from the known correlation and arrives at the pervasive nature of correlation with the speculative procedure that departs from the accepted idea that something is always hidden in a correlation, and concludes that everything is contingent. In both cases, the speculative method is in play: one begins with a well-known or accepted phenomenon and goes beyond it by taking it as an example of something broader. Speculation, like the flight of an aeroplane in the image Whitehead presents, starts from a runway of certitude and ends with a less certain and more general view from above, beyond what is established.[37] Whitehead is also adamant that the better the point of departure, the broader the view one reaches. Speculation is a jump towards the unknown that can be corrected afterwards but has no reason to proceed with restraint.

Meillassoux's speculative conclusion is that what is absolute and non-correlative (and not only non-human) is the principle that everything is contingent – except the principle itself, of course. It is this principle that is manifested in the misleading character of any appearance. Correlation itself is an example of the intrinsic link between facticity and reality; nothing is transparent, everything could be something else. Being absolute, the principle is neutral: it is independent of any perspective, standing location or situation, and is taken to be *for-nothingness*. Through the principle, something absolute can be thought (and known). According to the absolute (and neutral) principle, everything is under its scope; nothing escapes this hyper-chaos.[38]

This principle that enables a total view is, for Meillassoux, the right antidote to the predicaments of the age of the correlate. Breaking with the finitude issued by the correlation, one reaches beyond the limits towards a view that is neutral with respect to any subject, and total in the sense that it sees everything from nowhere. Meillassoux thinks that the opposite of finitude is a total image of reality in which everything is available to speculative eyes. It is as if once one is beyond the level of correlations, one finds a viewpoint without a standpoint and spots things directly from the Great Outdoors. Such a view from nowhere is strictly speaking not a view from above or outside, but a view from the outside of the outside. (Things for-nothingness cannot be accessible but from a view from nowhere.) For such a view, there is no asymmetry left, no nearness; everything is equally exposed, as in a showcase where what matters is the general collection and not any item in particular. An absolute principle with total scope – that pertains to everything except itself – is the right way to avoid finitude, according to Meillassoux. Once the principle is accepted, one can say that everything is as contingent as our correlation. Through speculation, one projects the same on to the unknown – or reduces the Other to the Same, in Levinas's apt phrase.[39] In fact, speculation proceeds through specular steps, by means of mirrors, whereby what is already seen is projected on to the unseen. There is an element of enumerative induction in speculation: it can reach a totality by means of a projection from a sample that acts as a premise. For Meillassoux, there is nothing blocking his principle from having anything else within its scope. His speculative move leads him towards a totality, in which a principle has everything else in its scope. The principle entails that any appearance is deceitful and exposes how things for-nothingness are – they are contingent and, in this case, one cannot be deceived by them. Being absolute, contingency is transparent – it is the transparency to end every transparency, the transparency that ensures that everything else is concealed by its appearances.

The speculative method, however, is blind to the possibility that exteriority is a better antidote to finitude than totality. What confines us to a correlation is not the lack of a total, sideways-on view, but rather a neutralisation of what is exterior. Such a neutralisation amounts to a perceived indifference to what transcends, to what is outer or beyond. Finitude is an incapacity to realise that the Great Outdoors is already fully available on the very borders of our interiority.

From the point of view of the metaphysics of the others, it is precisely totality that prevents any access to the infinite, which lies in what is beyond. The infinite is the unlimited, the unbound that borders an interiority from outside. It lies in the Great Outdoors that is the opposite of totality – totality is no more than finitude expanded when asymmetry is minimised to make room for specular relations. If a total view is available, there is no Other, no transcendence, no situatedness and – just as unattractive as correlationism – no Great Outdoors. To avoid correlationism through an absolute that produces a view from nowhere is to move from a restricted finitude to a broader one – from limitation to full confinement. In contrast, the metaphysics of the others holds that access to the world is always incomplete, not because of our finitude, but because the Great Outdoors cannot be anything but infinite.

Meillassoux is clear that not even a God could exorcise the principle of facticity.[40] He escapes finitude to reach a totality where interiorities and the external world are equally confined. To be sure, totality is also committed to transparency – if everything can be placed in a showcase, then nothing can be concealed – as in Heidegger's image, everything is under persecution. In the case of the total scope of the principle of facticity, at least the contingency of everything is transparent (as much as its capacity to hide behind its appearance). The total image that supposedly replaces finitude cannot cope with the infinite of exteriority and the occultation that follows. From the point of view of exteriority, Meillassoux's move is to surrender to a broader finitude by neutralising the external world and placing the Great Outdoors inside an expanded version of our confinement.

## After Speculation

Harman's object-oriented ontology, like Meillassoux's recommendation of the principle of facticity and the metaphysics of subjectivity, relies on speculation. His point of departure, as we saw earlier, is concealment: the withdrawal of all objects into a secret realm. His rejection of correlationism is closer to option (2) than option (1) above, as it emphasises that concealment is not something our correlation promotes, but rather a general feature of every relation between any two objects. His position also resembles the metaphysics of subjectivity because it makes a feature of correlation – occultation – the basis for a speculative jump towards a general account of objects that makes room for hidden real objects. Here, the speculative move leads to a totality that is no showcase, but rather one in which there are hidden elements in every object. Just as in indexicalism, reality is not transparent. As we saw earlier, however, exteriority plays a role here only in a totality of objects. Just as with Meillassoux's speculative universal contingency, speculation leads to a totality, and the perceived lack of transparency of all objects for-us becomes a certain lack of transparency in the general structure of objects.

Indexicalism entails that whatever exists is entangled with deixis. It is a paradoxical claim because it is about how everything is, and yet it makes transcendence-free totalities impossible. As a claim about what there is, it contrasts both with correlationism and with any attempt to overcome it through a mere exercise of speculation. If correlationism is to be avoided – and indexicalism avoids it, insofar as it is more than a simple criticism of metaphysics – it is due to its blindness to the outer side of a border. Correlationism is finitude because it cannot face the outer as infinite, as a beyond that can never properly be reached. The idea that it can be fully reached leads to the quest for a totality that proves to be the very mirror image – perhaps the specular image – of correlationism. The indexicalist way out of the predicament is to consider the Great Outdoors as an insistent character of a (paradoxico-)metaphysics, never fully accounted for, and in this sense never fully present. It is not only what lies beyond the border, but also what drives us across the horizon.

The contrast between totality and exteriority spells difficulty for speculation. Speculation proceeds through projecting more of the same, like a mirror, which cannot reveal anything but what is already there. It is somehow related to totality but also includes transparency – the transparency of what is reflected in mirrors. Speculative transparency leads to totality, if its tendency towards an exorcism of the very idea of an exterior is not corrected. Speculative realism puts forward the issue of how the secret – the concealed, the hidden – is reflected in the mirror. It deals in a contrast between the transparency of speculation and the concealment that is postulated in reality. It is about the specular itself: how is it possible that what is concealed has its image reflected everywhere? It is as if the specular procedure – and the transparency associated with it – could reflect the blind spots that cannot be seen but leave hints in mirrors. Reflected in such a mirror, withdrawal becomes a procedure that is exposed in its attempt to conceal.

Both Meillassoux and Harman use the speculative method to reach total images from what is not transparent in reality. In both cases, there is a tendency towards substantives – hyper-chaos in one case, the real object in the other. In contrast, indexicalism postulates that there is something exterior to any conception of the world. It starts out with deictic operations leading to interiorities, units that are capable of transcendence. The outside, the outer, the Outdoors, the Other are components of a reality that is more like a horizon than something that can be mapped. Reality is therefore not only incomplete, but incompletable. As a consequence, indexicalism is realist about deixis and combines this with the realism found in the criticism of metaphysics. It is not a realism that proposes a totality to cope with what is occult, but one that finds reality in the ever-transcending exterior that makes a total view impossible. It is the realism of an open reality.

As such, it cannot resort to unrestrained speculation. Indexicalist commitment to exteriority makes horizons a more important metaphor than mirrors. As a consequence, it reflects no blind spots, but only acknowledges them as what bounds the mirror from outside. By contrast with speculative realism, indexicalism does not try to accommodate the occult in a total view of reality, but places the blind spot outside the scope of the mirror. There is no reflected image of the secret; a mirror cannot reflect what is outside the field of vision even if this field is extended by the mirror. What is beyond the mirror looms on the horizon in the sense that it cannot be shown but still can be pointed to, just as we point to the exterior from within.

Speculation has to be counterbalanced by an attention to exteriority. The effort to project the Same on to the Other is not the last word in metaphysics. Levinas called this effort ontology, understood as the effort to bring everything to a common ground by removing alterity. The ontologist is in the business of surprising what exists in order to bring its strangeness to the neutral shore of a concept.[41] To turn the stranger into a concept is to attempt to accommodate what is outer with a substantive description. Levinas rejects the idea that ontology, understood this way, can be a first philosophy – it is not much more than pure violence as it places truth before justice to the Other. Rather, as criticism should precede dogmatism, metaphysics should precede ontology.[42] Metaphysics, for Levinas, is a study of transcendence – the metaphysician and the Other are separated and form no totality.[43] Taking precedence in metaphysics is the priority of the Other as Other, not of a mirror image, but rather as a figure of transcendence that shapes my borders. The idea of the priority of the others is informative here: speculation, like ontology, should be combined with a respect for exteriority, and furthermore, it should be bound by it.

Indexicalism, and its metaphysics of the others, operates therefore in a post-speculative register. It proceeds in a speculative manner when it moves from my interiority – and my being transcended by the Other – to a broader image of deictic operations and an outer border open to the Great Outdoors. This speculative step, however, leads to no transcendence-free totality; indeed, it yields a paradoxical totality that can only be shaped like the horizon – with a beyond that is included among the deictic operators that provide the paradoxical furniture to a paradoxical universe. The paradoxical aspect follows from a speculation bounded by its starting point, deixis, which already includes the elements of its transcendence.

## The Priority of the Others

The metaphysics of the others is metaphysical only to the extent that its obsession with the exterior – the external world, the outer, the Great Outdoors – can precede any attempt to reach a total view. The metaphysics – or ontotheology – that Heidegger wanted to overcome through a renewed interest in the blossoming (and veiling) of being is a similar project in the sense that it entails the relevance of horizons. Levinas viewed metaphysics as the attention to transcendence: to keep the exterior separated and not replace it with inclusion.[44] In the metaphysics of the others, Levinas's *métaphysique* has to act as a prolegomenon to every *Metaphysik* that Heidegger wants to overcome. Because the totality it reaches cannot be other than paradoxical, the *métaphysikal* enterprise is to study transcendence in general, or rather to show that a totality formed by tools for transcendence itself has the capacity to be transcended.

Levinas takes the Other to be the source of transcendence. The drive towards the exterior is something that disrupts the indoors;

metaphysical desire – a component of Levinas's conception of subjectivity in *Totality and Infinity*[45] – is a drive towards the Other, the outer, that is not guided by any goal and not part of any agenda.[46] As such, metaphysics is asymmetric and one-sided – it is a response to the outer, and surely not a mutual relation with it. The attraction of totality is akin to that of ontology, of the neutrality and anonymity of being. In 1935 Levinas had already diagnosed *ontologism* as the fundamental dogma to be avoided; there is more to reality than just being.[47] It would be like the final realm, the ultimate domain, and it is precisely this element of the parricide of Parmenides that Levinas endorses: there should be something other than being. Breaking with the dominion of being over all reality is to make space for something beyond it; for Levinas, it is not to embrace nothingness but to make room for an exterior Other that brings alteration to everything that exists, an alteration from the outside.[48]

Ontologism is the claim that nothing, not even the others, has priority over what there is. It is the claim that being has no exterior borders, and therefore nothing beyond it can be real. If ontologism is right, there is no ultimate recalcitrance and no unresolvable *diaphonía*. As a consequence, there is no metaphysics of the others. Ontologism is a reason to dismiss any interruption.

It is interesting to return briefly to Plato's *Sophist* where the Stranger proposes, together with the parricides, a departure from ontologism.[49] While proposing his five greater kinds – Same, Other, Rest, Movement and Being – the Stranger convinces Theaetetus that we cannot oppose Movement and Rest without the notion of Sameness, and that Sameness cannot be the same as Being, as not all that is is the same.[50] Sameness is not the same as Being, so Being ought to be another element in the set of kinds that constitutes everything. Further, they conclude that the Other should also be one of these kinds. It is through the notion of the Other that nothingness would be able to be conceived, as that which is completely other than Being. But the Stranger not only introduces the Other into the picture of the world, he also talks about its pervasiveness in everything that is. This is why what is not – what is Other than Being – has to be counted among the many things that exist and Parmenides is to be disobeyed.[51] The Stranger states that the Other 'traverse[s] all things and mutually interpenetrate[s], so that the other partakes of being'.[52] The parricide promoted by Plato is not a step towards flooding being with non-being, but rather towards understanding non-being as a consequence of a friction between Being and the Other: the Other being primary to non-being and positioned at the same fundamental level as Being. The five greater kinds are all at the same fundamental level, and Plato's Stranger-led non-ontologist picture puts ontology on a level with dynamics, statics, the metaphysics of the other, and the metaphysics of sameness as its constitutive and fundamental elements of reality.

In an indexicalist interpretation, they are five groups of deixis, and the metaphysics of the other – or rather of the others – is the cornerstone where all are made incomplete. In contrast, Levinas suggests that being always comes in substantive form. In his earlier works at least, being is always plural, because existents precede existence and for every existence there is a hypostasis.[53] Although each being is tied to a substantive, they all can evade it.[54] Evasion shows that there is an external border that can be crossed. Indexicalism would rather emphasise the evasion route, the structure of exteriority, as each being is understood as a unit of transcendence. Indeed, transcendence is an evasion from one's standing location – a response to a demand from the others that could take the form of a curiosity.

No interiority is immune to its outer bounds, and none is fully dependent on them.

According to the Stranger, the five kinds engage in interplay through a *dynamis koinonias*: a power to have communion, or a will to interfere, or a capacity to relate. The interplay could be considered a capacity to affect – no kind is immune to the others, but they are all equally ready to act together – if to affect is not always to promote a change. This capacity to interfere while remaining external can be understood in terms of an ability to respond. Each kind may be asked for (something) by the others, and each can respond. It is important to notice that here, demands and responses dwell not in necessity – like deontic necessity terms such as 'command' or 'request' – but rather belong to the realm of appeals, petitions and pleas. This cannot be understood in terms of a request or a command – that would make each kind ruled by the others – or in terms of a causal or somehow necessary drive that would make each kind determined by another kind. Instead, no kind is grounded in any other. This is what makes them external to each other and still capable of being interrupted by any of the others. The five kinds can be affected from outside only if a demand is made and a chosen response is given – neither an inclination nor an imperative would make the kinds both external to each other and capable of interplaying with what is beyond. Each kind can be interrupted, as in a conversation. Interruption paves the way for the interplay that brings about what is real. Each kind has an unbounded capacity for interruption that is never put to rest by a given decision; each can come to any door that can be knocked on. The interruption, in this sense, is infinite.

The metaphysics of the others, as a response to Tsing's injunction, is a sort of readiness for interruption. As such, it is driven by exterior forces that, being never-ending, ensure that recalcitrance is here to stay. Since it is a paradoxico-metaphysics, *diaphonía* is closer to propagating *dialetheas* than to being eradicated and replaced by a final representation of reality. If interruption is a methodological kernel within the metaphysics of the others, perhaps it can be compared with speculation. At first glance, one might think that the metaphysics of the others proceeds by successive interrupted speculative moves. Perhaps speculation itself is bounded by interruption. This is perhaps a reasonable image. Nonetheless, it stresses too heavily the active element in proceeding towards the outer border. It is almost as if the interiority has an agenda to go outwards. Clearly, the capacity to relate gears the interiority towards the outer – and this is what Levinas understands with evasion from being. But interruption is not merely an eagerness to evade. It is rather what prompts a need to respond. The speculative gesture is itself a response to an interruption. Interruption breaks the (speculative) mirror, introducing something else which is not merely a projection of the same. Each interruption can be followed by a new speculative move – by a new mirror. The emerging image is of a mosaic of mirrors, each placed where the previous one was broken; the outcome is like a patchwork wall that never ceases to be broken and eventually mended again. Since transcendence is what moves interiorities towards the outer, the others in their interruption are what prompt the theoretical activity. The lure of feeling that Whitehead ascribes to theories – as much as to books, music or concepts – is primarily occasioned by what interrupts.[55] Whitehead himself hints in this direction when he briefly considers the vocabulary of *recipients* and *provokers* to describe experience.[56] The others are the starting point of an expansion which is, from the point of view of the metaphysics of the others, asymmetrical. They force me into an affective state. The capacity to respond is embedded in each interiority and amounts to a drive outwards. To respond is to face the others – to create a way to deal with what they ask for.

The problem with the image of the interrupted speculative move is that there is no such thing as uninterrupted speculation. The patchwork wall is in fact fractal, and each piece of mirror repeats the previous interruptions that shaped it. Thinking itself means navigating among interruptions.

## The Interrupted Nexus

As a metaphysics of coexistence, the metaphysics of the others can be compared with monadologies and existing process philosophy. Monadologies (and neo-monadologies) assume there is a plurality of agencies that coexist, each pursuing its own agenda. In Leibniz, there is no exteriority and the others are inside a monad as much as they are inside a contingently chosen – and already fully determined – world. Perception of something other is nothing more than perception of something internal to a monad. In more recent (neo-)monadologies, that character of determination disappears, as the coexistence of the infinitely many units of action is not organised *a priori*, but rather is hostage to all sorts of negotiations in a *cosmorealpolitik*. Combined with process philosophy, as in Whitehead (and Latour), these negotiations become the open ground where order, institutions and concrescences gain shape. There is nothing beyond process; it is through the association of agents that any nexus emerges. Here, coexistence is an open prospect, and events are not bound by any concrete determination – abstractions are potentialities available to actual entities in their perceptive processes, which generate concrescence. The open process is limited only by the goals of the different units of action. Each one of them, as seen earlier, is associated with an agenda tied to its sense of satisfaction, and informed by self-enjoyment. They pursue their aims and associate with others in an open way limited only by their sense of accomplishment – Whitehead, no less than Leibniz, was adamant in recognising a degree of final cause for everything.

An indexicalist interiority, in contrast, is not substantive; as such, there are local and open tensions within each one. The tension between the internal and the outer – between self and the others – takes place within a deictic environment and therefore within an interiority. This is where Levinas's account of subjectivity as recurrence comes into the picture.[57] To be oneself is to be recurrently oneself, not always so. One is constantly displaced from anything inner towards the outer. The indexical structure is always present; a subject is never defined without reference to the others, but this reference cannot be described in terms of a substantive structure – the others don't have a fixed role for a subjectivity. Instead, they persecute it, tempt it, attract it. Levinas considers that there is no solidarity with the others without being persecuted by the others.[58] Not quite an identity in itself, a subjectivity is described in terms of the proximity of the others. To conceive of subjectivity as recurrence – as opposed to self-identity – enables a picture of interiority as a neighbourhood, an address that contains both a location and its proximity.[59] The traces of the Other in a subjectivity make subjectivity into an indexical labyrinth where the external and the internal are entangled. The Other is present in the space between each piece of bread and my mouth, between each formulated goal for my self-enjoyment and its actualisation. The Other can replace me; this is why indexicalism pictures an interiority not as an oriented unit, but as a complex deictic environment. Levinas stresses the force of substitution: to act for the Other as the result of an appeal is not something that has limits, and the Other appears in proximity with an anarchic force that can disturb the goals of any subjectivity from any side.[60] The appeal to responsibility brings an anarchic force that erodes the structures of any self.[61] A metaphysics of the others understands any interiority as hostage to its exteriority: far from being a substantive with a goal, it is understood as a location surrounded by what is beyond it and that can make claims on it.

Comparing the metaphysics of the others with a metaphysics of subjectivity in general – and in particular one that postulates more than one correlation – is instructive. In the former, metaphysics deals with each unit of subjectivity for which all the others are external: there is no total, drone-like view that would bring together all the interiorities in their struggles and connections with the outer together in a sideways-on view. Exteriority, in this case, means absence of transparency. The metaphysics of subjectivity, on the other hand, can offer a general picture of everything in terms of the friction between many units of action.

Granted, Whitehead's totality is an open one, contrasting with a barren tautological absolute, in his terms. In fact, it is becoming clear that Whitehead is less of a foe than an important influence both on indexicalism (with his notion of *locus standi* and his attention to the event) and on the metaphysics of the others (with his insistence on the open solidarity between actualities). Still, however, he assumes a third-person view of the assembled subjectivities striving to build association and breaking concrescences into new pieces, each piece oriented towards its goal. Because a metaphysics of subjectivity – and its speculative ground – is a picture of a transparent universe, it is open both to an increasingly detailed process of construction and to an increasingly broad view. Whitehead's own broad view is transient, constantly being renegotiated and shaped by the solidarity between all drops of experience; it is nevertheless a global view, and it is shaped by the goals pursued by each actuality. Indexicalism holds, by contrast, that the world is a (paradoxical) assemblage of standing locations. Partly as a consequence of its picture of interiorities, the metaphysics of the others also contrasts with Whiteheadian process philosophy in terms of how the solidarity between all existents is to be considered.

Whitehead understands each actuality, by definition, to be linked into the solidarity of all things. There is an interdependence between all actual entities because each connection between them involves the help of everyone else, and according to the ontological principle, everything is to be explained in terms of actual entities.[62] The principle is to be applied to actual entities themselves, so they are explained in terms of other actual entities in a circular fashion due to the solidarity between all entities. Since the general picture is one of (metaphysical) transparency, there is nothing in the actual entity that eludes this interdependence of all entities. There is nothing hidden in each unit – transparency means that the entire life of an actual entity is exposed to the rest of the universe. Interdependence, the solidarity of all actual entities, is such that there is no room for anything external to transparency. Whitehead's solidarity entails impersonality. There is no special character to any actuality: his standing locations are addresses with respect to all the others at once.

In contrast, the metaphysics of the others emphasises that a standing location is more a point of view (or a point of measurement) than a point on a plane. Indexicalism makes contrasts such as *inner and outer* central. An interiority is vulnerable to all the others, and vulnerability has a capacity to respond, a *dynamis koinonias*. The interplay between them is not on any level describable from an impersonal point of view. The metaphysics of the others posits demands and responses in the interaction of an interiority with what is outside. A demand is not a requirement, but neither is it a mere possibility, potentiality, or disposition. It is a different kind of metaphysical connection; it is an interruption, and something is asked for. In any case, there is no interdependence in the same manner as in the solidarity of actualities endorsed by Whitehead. Levinas cares about the freedom of those that can transcend, and freedom is tied to satisfaction.[63] This is why he claims that there is no transcendence without separation; just as religion requires a dose of atheism, since one cannot choose to believe in God if one is fully in the hands of God, without being separated from the Other there is no transcendence. One cannot be in the hands of the Other by necessity – being hostage to the Other means that the Other can interrupt at any point with an appeal.[64] Truth, Levinas claims, is to be found in the Other, but by those who are independent and separated from the Other; the distance is only crossed by a demand brought about by an interruption followed by a response.[65]

Indexicalism inherits a great deal of Levinas's conception of subjectivity as a house. A (neo-)monadological house is fully exposed to the outside. It can be represented by the houses built by Hreinn Fridfinnsson in the 1970s, where the internal accoutrements – dressing tables, wallpaper, bookshelves – were moved outdoors. Levinas insists that the distinction between the inner and the outer is crucial for a house to be both a shelter for someone specific and an instance of hospitality. The interiority formed by the house is important; without it, my relation with the Other would be transparent to the rest of the world, and we would be in a totality.[66] A house is also a shelter from the impersonal. Separated from the rest of the universe, it can accept an appeal from outside and allow the Other in. But it can refuse, and this is where interruption meets hospitality. The connection to the outside is not compulsory and carries no necessity: it is about appeals. An appeal is modally very different from a necessity, but with comparable metaphysical credentials. When there is an appeal – and a response – something different from an interdependence visible from anywhere takes place. The appeal is an interruption. There is an interference in the process that does not boil down to a conflict of agendas, but is a genuine constituent of the inner life of an existent. Exteriority is constitutive.

In order to compare the monadological subjectivity with that defended by Levinas – and partly inherited by indexicalism – it is interesting to look again at Husserl's foray into monadology in the fifth of his *Cartesian Meditations*.[67] Levinas is quite influenced by this work of Husserl, a series of lectures delivered at the Sorbonne in 1929, in which he makes clear in what sense transcendental phenomenology invents a first-person philosophy that contrasts with the neutrality of the transcendental subject in Kant. Levinas adopts this first-person approach as one of his points of departure. Husserl's main transcendental tenet is the inseparable correlation between the intentional act and its content – between the act of thinking, say, and what is thought about – a correlation that reveals nothing either about the world or about the thinking subject beyond the correlation.[68] The intentional act is a transcendental experience.[69] This experience is personal, indeed first-personal: there is nothing in it beyond the intentional concentration of my own acts. It is a foundational experience in which I can see nothing but my own cogitations. But this inseparable correlation is utterly indifferent to any other, unless as a content of my intentional acts. I cannot go beyond my intentional acts; there is no me beyond them. This is where Husserl diagnoses the danger of a transcendental solipsism according to which there could be other empirical subjects, but I am deemed to be alone with my intentional acts in the experiences that make any empirical subject possible. Anything external comes to me only through my intentional acts.

Husserl invokes a monadological reasoning to rescue his transcendental phenomenology from solipsism. This is where Levinas parts company with him. Husserl believes that at some intermediary point in a transcendental story involving intentional acts and an ego also understood in terms of intentional acts, it must become evident that aside from the ego of my first-personal experience, there are others: *alter egos*. Alter egos are conceived in the ego's image and likeness. The alter ego hosts intentional acts as I do – different ones, of course – and is as excluded from the intentional acts outside its realm as I am. The alter ego has cogitations about my ego as much as I have cogitations about my alter ego. There is a symmetry: I am the alter ego of my alter ego. Putting together ego and alter ego, there is a totality of egos that can be envisaged, even though a view from nowhere has limited space in the resolutely first-personal approach to philosophy that Husserl espouses.

Husserl's alter ego is discovered by my own ego; the alter ego is shown and verified in my cogitations. It is fair to describe the gesture Husserl describes from the ego to the alter ego as rehearsing a speculative move. Husserl argues that my intentional act forming an *ego cogito* can appear to me as an example of something else that I find in the alter ego; both my ego and the alter ego are instances of the same structure that my cogitations indirectly reveal. Here again, it seems that the reality beyond the correlation is really a mirror image of the known starting point that I find in my cogitations. The alter ego resembles the ego in which I am confined in my cogitations; it is equally confined in the same way as I am. The speculative gesture expands confinement instead of reaching beyond it. In contrast, Levinas would advocate that the Other transcends the Same, that it cannot be something as neutral as my ego is – not something that is as much an instance of a subject as the alter ego.

Hence, Levinas disagrees with Husserl's resorting to monadology, and in particular with his accommodation of the Other as an alter ego. To begin with, he insists that the Other is not another ego, but rather what I am not.[70] The Other is not a parallel self but someone who interferes in my subjectivity: not by being a theme of my cogitations, but as an exterior element to which I am hostage to the point of what Levinas described as recurrence, where I can no longer be guided by my agenda, but rather by my responses to the demands of the Other. Levinas rejects the idea that the starting point of my discovery of the Other could be my own cogitations; this implies that freedom precedes justice and responsibility.[71] The Other is not a result of my sovereignty but rather a transcendental condition for my spontaneity. Responsibility for the Other is what grounds my freedom, and not the other way around. The Other is a third person – an *il-eté* – inside my intentional acts, which are hostage to what the exterior asks. It is not quite that my cogitations depend on the Other because the Other is fully brought in and made present in them, but rather that they are hostage to the Other. My cogitations are vulnerable to the exterior, in a limitless way. Levinas thinks Husserl ends up doing violence to the Other by attempting to keep transcendental phenomenology – and its emphasis on first-personal uninterrupted intentional acts – immune to solipsism. Levinas's portrayal would instead be that intentional acts are fully vulnerable to interruptions, and the Other is neither something internally present in a subjectivity, nor present in the parallel life of an alter ego kept far enough away to make sure I am immune to interruptions.

Levinas's rejection of Husserl's account of the Other as an alter ego and of his monadological path away from solipsism might lead to a general criticism of the monadological understanding of subjectivity. It is true that Whitehead's interdependence between actual entities yields no egology in the sense that Husserl finds in his transcendental phenomenology; the focus is not on my own grounding experience, but rather on the experiential character of everything. In no non-phenomenological monadology is experience described in first-personal terms. Husserl's monadology is unique in its transcendental preoccupations that posit the personal as a condition of possibility for the impersonal – and this is what attracted Levinas to phenomenology. But monadological thinking cannot conceive of the others as anything different from alter egos; they are instances of experience that intersect only to the extent that they carry on their own endeavours amidst each other. Monadological subjectivity is, in this sense, based on identity and not on recurrence – an existent is always a self, itself, even when it is an alter self. Subjectivity is substantive.

By contrast, indexicalism conceives of subjectivity as hostage to its borders – being non-substantive, it is not much more than that: a border with the exterior. Levinas connects the kind of relation he advocates with what is exterior to the personal. In line with Heidegger, he pictures the impersonal as neutral, akin to totality and to a view from nowhere, because it is incapable of response.[72] When the personal is converted into the indexical – and exteriority is made into the central metaphysical concern – a plurality that takes the form of interruption emerges in the picture. Subjectivity is separated from the exterior and yet hostage to it – it is affected by an appeal but has no necessity to satisfy any demand. Interruption is indeed broader than the scope of demands in terms of what is asked for in a particular circumstance.

Beyond cases in which something is explicitly asked for, an interruption can be a change in the course of action guided by one's agenda. It is a change promoted by what is exterior: not as an imposition, but as an appeal. In this sense, interruption lies in the space of asking for something. It brings about no compulsory response, but it prompts a response. Such is the *physis* of interruption: tied to the *physis* of the others.

To take interruption in a metaphysically serious way is also to take metaphysics to be driven by the capacity of what is outdoors to interfere. Metaphysics is itself vulnerable to interruption. In any case, the interrupted nexus of each actual entity by the Other is what makes each agent's agenda hostage to what is exterior. The interruption coming from the Other drives the agent away from an agenda. If monadological agents are driven towards satisfaction, agents in a metaphysics of the others are subject to interruption. The metaphysics of the others can be described as an interruption to the metaphysics of subjectivity: an interruption to transparency but also to the agenda formed by the nexus attached to each subject. Agents can no longer trigger process by being oriented by their nexûs when in the company of the others; this solidarity is broken by something that is asked, and that may not be intelligible within one's nexus. The Other makes subjectivity capable of substitution – a subject can give up being itself for being another. Subjectivity becomes a space of possible replacement in which everything can take a different direction, including identity. If monadological coexistence depends on interdependence, a metaphysics of the others depends on the capacity to interrupt identity itself. In fact, I understand the metaphysics of the others to be a result of Levinas interrupting Whitehead.

The metaphysics of the others is also an interruption of transparency. Levinas's appeal to infinity brings transcendence to the scope of coexistence. Infinity cannot be transparent; it cannot all be visible at once. Harman's object-oriented philosophy amends Whiteheadian and Latourian process philosophy by positing real objects that are withdrawn from what is manifested in qualities and relations. Objects transcend their interactions and appearances. They host a singularity in themselves; real objects can withdraw into a singular realm alien to every interaction. Here we can compare the contrast between indexicalism and object-oriented ontology with the one between Levinas's singularity of the Other and Kierkegaard's singularity of the self. Kierkegaard posits a subject that is never fully manifested, neither in any description of her relations nor in any of her interactions with other subjects. There is something in me, according to Kierkegaard, that resists any system: a *sui generis* element that makes any neutral picture of what exists incomplete, since what I am escapes any systematic approach. Levinas writes that what is the same is 'essentially identification within the diverse, or history, or system'. He continues: 'It is not I who resist the system, as Kierkegaard thought; it is the other.'[73] The Other is what escapes any effort to systematise; an ontology of the Other is impossible – there is no quadruple theory, no substantive account. The infinite in the Other is part of what makes the Other leave a mark on my image of the world, and makes it incomplete. The Other brings in interruption: the metaphysics of the others is the interrupted nexus.

## Process Metaphysics of the Others

Process philosophy is central to the enterprise of developing a metaphysics of the others. A focused attention to what it is reveals why that is – why interruptions and demands are ingredients of a genuine process philosophy. Charles Sanders Peirce provides a good general understanding of what a process philosophy looks like.[74] A minimal condition for process philosophy is to repeal what Peirce calls necessitarianism: the claim that 'the state of things existing at any time, together with some immutable laws, completely determines the state of things in every other time'.[75] Necessitarianism is understood as the thesis that everything follows by necessity from what was set once and for all, given some immutable laws. In other words, necessitarianism is the view that reality was produced (by necessity) in one stroke. It holds that everything that is can be condensed into an arguably finite – if almost recursively enumerable – set of laws and initial states that is, in important senses, smaller than the world that depends on it in turn. Peirce writes that 'the instantaneous state of a system of particles' is defined by a number that 'remains the same at all times', and therefore, 'the intrinsic complexity of the system is the same at all times'.[76] In any form, necessitarianism is the view that there is no genuine diversity, novelty or surprise, and Peirce endeavours to oppose it. This is how he responds to his imagined opponent:

> you think all the arbitrary specifications of the universe were introduced in one dose, in the beginning, if there was a beginning, and the variety and complication of nature has always been just as much as it is now. But I, for my part, think that the diversification, the specification, has been continuously taking place.[77]

He then proceeds to provide reasons for his claim, which include the advantages of postulating 'pure spontaneity of life as a character of the universe' that explains both the irregularities and the uniformity of nature.[78] Peirce believes such spontaneity can be inferred from 'broad and ubiquitous facts' and that 'there is probably in nature some agency by which the complexity and diversity of things can be increased'.[79] He contends that, faced with the irregularity and the diversity of the universe, the necessitarian can either deny that they are genuine, and hope to show that ultimately everything is regular and explainable in terms of a single overarching necessity; failing that, the necessitarian can posit unexplainable irregular elements. The latter claim is what drove the Epicureans to posit *clinamina*, those swerves in the determined and necessary orbit of any atom that allow novelty (and diversity) to take place. Peirce, like many before him – including Leibniz in his controversy with Pierre Bayle – understands the postulation of unexplainable events such as random swerves to be a drawback of the system.[80] In contrast, his hypothesis according to which variety comes from spontaneity can provide enough explanation for both regularities and novelties, both order and exception.

Peirce's opposition to necessitarianism, and his effort to spell out an alternative, reflect the kind of atmosphere in which the need for process philosophy is felt. A similar atmosphere appears in John Dewey's argument that human experience has to be conceived as akin to a nature that is wistful and pathetic, turbulent and passionate, and in Jean Wahl's opinion that there is always some sort of conflict in the concrete.[81] The drive towards process philosophy can arise from the idea that reality doesn't spring from a single plan (and from its unexplainable exceptions).[82] This is why Peirce's debate on necessitarianism is a good starting point to make explicit what constitutes a process philosophy. Necessitarianism is often presented as a consequence of a broader claim that reality was conceived in one go; one commander, one commencement: a single *arché*. Call it *arché*-ism. Process philosophy posits a plurality of *archés* fully in action in their coexistence, leaving no room for necessitarianism. Monadological process philosophy considers the plurality of *archés* in coexistence in terms of aims, associations or networks. Different Whiteheadian actual entities obey no immutable law and can be reduced to no single principle of command and commencement. There is a plurality of nexûs, a plurality of plots of concrescence that coexist and continuously produce diversification and specification.

Interrupted nexûs enable a composition of reality in which each interiority interacts with the others, and at the same time responds to the demands coming from outside by changing the course of action in the agenda. The Whiteheadian image of solidarity between actual entities that attempt to pursue their own aims and attain their satisfaction is replaced with one in which interiorities have their agendas interrupted by what is asked from outside. Still, indexicalism – built on Levinasian subjectivity – is itself a process philosophy: the outdoors affects each unit of action and therefore interruption composes reality. Arché-ism is countered by the anarchic character of proximity, and necessitarianism is contrasted by the freedom grounded on the situated interiority and on infinite responsibility. Freedom is what makes responsibility possible – it is through a vulnerable sovereignty that I can be responsible given an interruption, given something that is asked for by the Other. Freedom, as Levinas writes, is a discovery of responsibility and therefore of the absence of freedom.[83] Infinite responsibility cannot affect an action unless it is autonomous – to the heteronomy following interruption is added the autonomy of the response. The response can take several different forms, and nothing but situated considerations informs the decision. There is no ultimate necessity; decisions that are made under infinite responsibility shape coexistence and continuously produce diversification and specification.

The metaphysics of the others can be thought of as an effort towards a description of how reality is a process guided by the others. In this sense, it is a process philosophy. Furthermore, its process can also be considered in terms of a conversation, in which there are interruptions, demands and responses. A conversation never follows ultimate laws of necessity or derives from an interdependence between agents. Instead, it requires vulnerability to what is claimed and a capacity to respond, a *dynamis koinonias*. This capacity to respond paves the way for a kind of cosmopolitics in which negotiation knows no limit: nothing is beyond politics.[84] The cosmopolitics of interruption is such that each interiority is vulnerable to the demands of the Other; it claims that exteriority has demands that require responses, appeal to responsibility and are capable of interrupting. Interruption disrupts what was previously going on and makes sure process is ongoing.

Everything is part of a cosmic, unending conversation, and everything is subject to interruption. The metaphysics of the others is an exterior-oriented cosmopolitics. It assumes that anything exterior to the situated interiority that is the departing point counts as other. What triggers the interrupted nexus is precisely that there are others all around – and not merely within – other humans. In order for this infinite conversation to go beyond the exchange of words in language by humans, it has to extend towards the Great Outdoors.

Ursula K. LeGuin's poem 'The Marrow' focuses on what can hear the word of a stone:

> There was a word inside a stone.
> I tried to pry it clear,
> mallet and chisel, pick and gad,
> until the stone was dropping blood,
> but still I could not hear
> the word the stone had said.
>
> I threw it down beside the road
> among a thousand stones
> and as I turned away it cried
> the word aloud within my ear
> and the marrow of my bones
> heard, and replied.[85]

Rather than a big, all-encompassing conversation between ears and stones and the marrow of the bones, I would suggest the image of parallel and equally cosmic but segmented conversations, all subject to interruption from outside. The Great Outdoors is a conglomerate of others, each ready to engage in a personal, specific, situated conversation.

## Robinsonology and Transcendental Xenology

Extracting lessons from a novel by Michel Tournier about the others, Deleuze suggests a topic which easily turns into a branch of metaphysics: he calls it *robinsonade*, though it could also be called robinsonology – the study of a world without others.[86] Robinsonology has different philosophical incarnations, from solipsism to arche-fossils, from the origin of life to the inhabited universe. Deleuze reads Tournier's novel as being about Robinson Crusoe's immigration from a society of humans to a society of elements. Deleuze finds in the novel an unfolding of the structural role the others play – not simply an ingredient of perception but rather of what makes any ingredient effective. The others play the transcendental role of enabling every category of perception to be applied. In a gesture similar to that of Levinas, Deleuze begins by portraying the others as separated from the Great Outdoors – without them, the Great Outdoors cannot be viewed or experienced in the same way. He reckons that it is precisely this schism that makes it possible for the others to be a distinct transcendental structure. Robinsonology in general is about this schism; there should be parts of the world that are not my companions – that do not inhabit the world as much as I do – in order for me to be able to be isolated. Robinsonology appears as a branch of metaphysics lying between the study of the aggregate of what exists and the study of what does not exist; its presupposition is that when I am on my own, I am not yet surrounded by nothing. Within the metaphysics of the others, an adapted robinsonology could take two forms: 1) the study of what it would be like to have no outdoors at all and 2) the study of the absence of some others in a world still filled with other others, assuming no prior distinction between fellow others and the Great Outdoors. Pursuing (1) in an indexicalist manner would mean that there could be no isolated existent: if one is on one's own, nothing has a position. On the other hand, because (2) is possible, the metaphysics of the others can draw lessons from a robinsonology that presupposes the schism.

Tournier's Robinson is moved by his steps towards progressively becoming a citizen of an otherwise inhabited island, and not by a careful reproduction of the past he left behind. In the novel, Robinson switches from interacting with human others to non-human others. What emerges is a different kind of interiority, no longer defined by its borders with the human world beyond, but rather feeling the pressure of elements in its exterior. A first feature of Tournier's robinsonology is that without others, there is no interruption. The fact that somebody else could appear is enough to make anything at the margins of one's perception capable of becoming central. The other interrupts to reorganise a matrix of importance – without the others, that matrix runs unchallenged. The role of the others is therefore to interrupt. Without them, speculation runs amok in the sense that it proceeds all the way towards a totality.[87] Tournier also emphasises that the others create possibility; without them things cannot be thought otherwise, there is no more than one line of thought. But Tournier also emphasises that an uninhabited world is a world of elements where everything is hostile, and night reigns over any place outside my perception. In a world without the nuances created by fellow inhabitants, being naked is a luxury no one can afford. A lone inhabitant of a world is one who experiences no proximity. Deleuze summarises the predicament by writing that there would be nothing but unreachable distances and absolute differences, or viewed the other way, unbearable repetitions and extensions superposed.[88] The others bring about a necessary structure for perception – there would be no perception without them. This amounts to saying that there is no perception of the uninhabited; because there is no alternative line and no interruption, there can be no definite content. Deleuze writes that the terrified face is not like the terrifying object that is perceived, but it expresses it and therefore produces it. In my perception of what is around – and in the facial expressions that perception shapes – I am hostage to the others that create alternatives and ultimately correct me. An inhabited world provides habits and a normalcy; it is against the background of habits that the odd and the surprising are perceived as such. Tournier's Robinson saga is one of rehabituation in an environment that is rather different from that of human societies. Eventually a different perception comes about, which is also grounded in habit and contrastive in nature.

Wittgenstein's remarks on private language and internal content are also themselves an exercise in robinsonology.[89] No examination of the activities of an isolated subject, no matter how thorough, can reveal any content – much as no detailed inspection of a packet of butter reveals its rise in price.[90] But here is where Deleuze's robinsonology becomes particularly interesting for the metaphysics of the others. He sees in Tournier's Robinson the seed of a different thought altogether, a thought that dwells in the elements and is hostage in its very content to the sun and its shadows, to the cycles of the land and to Speranza (the island) itself. It is as if the intersubjectivity that a public (human) language offers could be found in the Great Outdoors. If the private language remarks of Wittgenstein point towards a robinsonology that presupposes the schism between the others and the Great Outdoors, Deleuze is hinting at a different approach: one is not indefinitely isolated on a desert island. One finds company. Something different from thoughtlessness takes place.[91] He sees Tournier as describing how Robinson switches off from his previous standards of community and is no longer distinct from objects.[92] One inhabitant is just like no inhabitant: the desert island is still desert after Robinson arrives. Or, rather, it is as inhabited as before. For Robinson, a new type of company – and of intersubjectivity – is inaugurated. It is as if Tournier is mapping the road to bridge the schism in order to find in the Great Outdoors, beyond any human other, the ingredients of a new structure of intelligibility. In this new structure there are not multiple subjects facing objects, but rather a subject merged with a plurality of objects. The company Robinson finds can be substantive or indexical – objects or others. This is the limit of Tournier's robinsonology: there are no emerging legitimate others capable of interrupting lines of thought – rather, it is as if the isolated subject is merged with substantives of different kinds. The robinsonology of a metaphysics of the others will favour the idea that others will always eventually appear: there is no non-inhabited island, and in a sense, no less inhabited island.

However, Tournier's movement as pictured by Deleuze is what matters most here. The movement is from a human exterior to the Great Outdoors; this is crucial to the metaphysics of the others. It is crucial for his Robinson that other others can be found. The novel is therefore also an exercise in xenology, in the sense of a quest for other others. Robinson needs new transcendental conditions, new transcendental structures, to carry on in his new environment; his saga concerns a transcendental switch. This is the movement needed from Levinas to the metaphysics of the others or from the Other to the Great Outdoors. Tournier's Robinson on Speranza finds himself with no Other to perform the transcendental task of making his freedom and thought possible – he has to forge himself another transcendental xenology. His saga is one in which he becomes genuinely capable of being interrupted – refused and contested – by non-human others. Non-human interruption is what takes place with D. H. Lawrence in his poem 'Snake'. The poisonous snake arrives first in the source of water and eyes him as he hesitantly throws a stick in the animal's direction. Derrida considers the poem to be a response to a comment once made by Levinas about the face of a snake.[93] In the poem, meeting the face of the snake abruptly changes the train of thought Lawrence is following; he becomes deeply ashamed of his action. After arguing that cats have no faces – they have miens, but faces only appear in humans – J. M. Coetzee's Elizabeth Costello claims that when she found a pregnant stray cat in the village of San Juan, where cats were hunted by humans, she decided that she would side against her tribe of hunters and with the cats at whatever cost.[94] This decision, which took no calculation into consideration, drives her away from being sensible and reasonable to the point of castrating the cats she begins to feed. Her stance towards them is grounded in something other than reason. Similarly, G. H.'s whole perspective on life is changed after meeting a cockroach in Clarice Lispector's novel *The Passion According to G. H.*[95] In all these cases, the xenological movement is oriented towards animals that can detect humans, and more to the point, gaze at them. The movement that the metaphysics of the others requires is greater; it posits that we respond to whatever is in the Great Outdoors. A relation to the exterior is to be primarily one of response. Lawrence's snake, Coetzee's cats and Lispector's cockroaches change the course of events by affecting the pursuit of previous goals; the metaphysics of the others goes further in taking anything in the Great Outdoors as capable of interrupting and asking for a response. The xenology of the Great Outdoors is one in which habits and interruptions are built on exteriority, proximity and substitution; interiority is surrounded by the infinite beyond.

## From the Other to the Great Outdoors

Levinas often assumes the absolute Other to be the other human that appears to me as a voice coming from a face. The voice is one I can understand, and is therefore a voice that can ask me for something I can recognise. The alien that matters is neither eerie nor awkward to the point of non-recognition, or rather of *misrecognition*, to use Derrida's term. Levinas seems often to distinguish between what could be under my power and what is beyond it. Levinas's analysis of labour – including being served by other non-human existents – exempts it from any violence.[96] A lot seems to hinge on the claim that the non-human can refuse my possession, but it cannot contest me in the way human others can do 'and accordingly can consecrate it'.[97] The difference between *refusing* and *contesting* is perhaps one of those instances Descola describes in which we use different language to describe what ought to be different simply because humans and non-humans ought to be doing different things (other animals mate but do not have relationships, they communicate but do not talk, they eat but do not dine, etc.).[98] Perhaps there is no distinction between refusing and contesting but that the latter is not usually attributed to non-human animals. On the face of it, the substantive 'human' seems to intrude into Levinas's thought about otherness and exteriority. (To be sure, there could be a less substantive interpretation of the difference between refusing and contesting, but I assume that Levinas is not hinting at an underlying indexical distinction.) Often, he seems to envisage his Other as presenting an immediately recognisable face which appears human (and masculine).[99] He ascribes animals and plants to a biological domain that is an extension of being – his doctrine of the existential crack in every existent is not applied to the organic. As a consequence, he leaves the non-human world untouched by his criticism of the ontologist presuppositions about the imperialism of the same over the Other. Concerning things, he takes them as 'those that never present themselves personally'.[100] Things are described as lacking identity in a way that would not make them Other, but simply means towards ends.[101]

This is where Levinas seems to be blocked from what the non-human other can ask. It is also where Whitehead interrupts him. Levinas's exteriority seems confined to the human – and his metaphysics does not cover the full scope of the general xenology that the metaphysics of the others pursues. The enlargement of this scope – as in the saga of Tournier's Robinson – is central to the present task. This Whiteheadian interruption can be made in different ways. What matters is to make sense of the appeal of the Great Outdoors as enabling a response that dwells in its infinity and maintains its exteriority.

Silvia Benso, in her book *The Face of Things*, attempts to extend the Levinasian Other by extending the notion of face beyond human features. She intends to broaden the notion of face so that it covers the appearances with which anything presents itself. Interestingly, she turns precisely to Heidegger's contrast between things and objects in the context of his opposition between *Nähe* and *Ge-Stell*.[102] Heidegger holds that things are gatherings, elements or places that connect different events together. As such, they present themselves of their own will through a concernful approach.[103] In contrast with taking things as objects (*Gegenstände*), which would mean they become present by being a standing reserve at something else's disposal, as things they unveil and conceal themselves out of their own interest. They decide of their own accord when and where to show their faces. The idea is that a face is no more than a presentation or a manifestation of something. Along these lines, and stretching Heidegger's reading of phenomenon as manifestation, phenomenology could become a prosopology, a study of faces. Whatever appears must show its face.

Certainly there are similarities between Levinas and Heidegger, especially in their relation to Husserl. Both philosophers look into what is underneath intentional acts. Both hold that intentionality ought to be somehow grounded. Benso's solution to expand the Other beyond the human is reminiscent of the transcendental realism Levinas shares with Heidegger. The issue – understood by Husserl as the influence that anything but the sovereignty of my *solus ipse* has on my thoughts and perceptions[104] – is indeed tackled by Heidegger through his account of phenomenology.[105] Heidegger takes phenomena to be what things manifest to us, what they make available. Phenomenology, as a return to things themselves, is taken as an encounter with things via the appearances through which they make themselves present. The appearances, the phenomena, are the lures things offer us in order to affect our cogitations. The appearances are, in this sense, the face through which things present themselves; thinking relates to things through their appearances. Heidegger grants that phenomenology is not about how to access things but about how things access us – how they make themselves present by showing something to our thoughts and perceptions. Perhaps short of a prosopology, it is a study of what is shown (and what is concealed in the showing). Benso reads this stance towards Husserl's transcendental realism as pointing towards a convergence with what Levinas claims about the transcendence of the Other – that responsibility in the form of obsession precedes my cogitations and my spontaneity.[106] (Obsession with what is outer is what leads to the substitution of myself for the Other – I act for the Other – in the way of thinking that Levinas presents in *Otherwise than Being*.) The face of the Other interrupts me just like the appearances of things do – the phenomenon has to do with a protagonism in showing something to the perceiver, not a passivity in sensing. Benso holds that to appear is to have a face, and therefore the very notion of face can extend the Levinasian Other beyond the human scope: if the Other has a face, everything with a face can be a genuine Other.

Benso's suggestion does have some shortcomings. First, the notion of face she ends up espousing is too broad. Perhaps it comes close to that of a thing in the neighbourhood (*in der Nähe*) which is neither sufficient nor even necessary for Levinas's *proximité*, as we saw earlier. Speculative prosopology is maybe not enough for a sound general xenology. Levinas's account of a face makes it more than a simple manifestation. The face of the Other in Levinas has two distinct features: a voice and a gaze. The voice enables a saying, a *dire*, that is irreducible to something that is said – the voice introduces the personal, the language of addressing and appealing. The gaze is both an appeal and an indication of a vulnerable body. It is clear that similar features can be found (perhaps speculatively) away from the human face, but they seem to be more than what must be present in any manifestation, more than what it takes for a thing to present itself of its own accord. Second, Heidegger embraces the ontologism Levinas wants to exorcise. Heidegger's *Ding* is taken to be both manifesting and concealing its being. It is described as what he calls 'a dispensation of being', in an ontological register. Levinas intends the Other to be a departure from the ontologism he finds prevalent in Heidegger, and – as we saw – which he longs to exorcise as a general metaphysical project connected to exteriority. Levinas's notion of substitution is conceived as a way out of being, as in an evasion to the exterior. There is no infinity beyond being in Heidegger's thing. Third, Levinas conceives the Other from within the act of thinking and saying – the Other brings in responsibility. The Other interrupts the intentional act because content is itself grounded in a *diaphonía*. Heidegger's thing is closer to *physis* – and to *zuhanden* – than to thematisation, to *thesis*. Levinas believes the Other is closely tied to any thematisation; a contentful approach to anything is hostage to the Other. There is no separate realm of the Other, as exteriority leaves its traces everywhere. To be sure, things can be said to leave their marks on objects, on thematisation – but they can somehow be separated from *thesis* to the extent that we can separate the world (or *Nähe*) from *Ge-Stell*.

Benso's emphasis on things in their capacity to interrupt and be responded to moves in the right direction. She builds an ethics of things based on the impact of their presence in front of us. She understands things as carrying genuine appeals and therefore provoking an openness towards them. The attention to things is considered in terms of tenderness, understood in contrast with possession and in line with Heidegger's concernful approach. Benso writes that 'tenderness is passivity, patience, susceptibility to what is other than itself and the subject in which it is experienced'.[107]

Tenderness provides inspiration; it lures in not only a cluster of sensations, but also an understanding of what is other than oneself. Tenderness, she claims, is a metaphysical horizon.[108] It is a horizon oblivious to universality, and Benso contrasts it with the violence and aggression that she associates with ontology.[109] Tenderness is situated, directed to singularities and guided by a claim to responsibility. In that sense it is also perseverant, as it sticks to an aim that is not guided by an agenda, but by a need to respond. Benso's tenderness is triggered by something singular that calls for attention, breaks with the habitual, demands engagement. It is an appropriate dimension of the attitude the Great Outdoors has to be able to command if it is composed by genuine others. Tenderness is a focus on the singularity of an encounter, away from the impersonal, away from concerns about what can be universalised. In this sense, it points in the direction that the metaphysics of the others privileges: towards the outer, with its unforeseen possibilities.

Derrida also meant to extend the gist of Levinasian gesture, and deployed several related strategies to do so. A vantage point from which to consider the operations Derrida performs on Levinas's concerns with exteriority is the notion of the supplement.[110] The supplement contrasts with the total or full presence of something: if the presence is complete, no addition can in fact make any addition, for nothing brought from the exterior can make any difference. There is nothing to be gained from the exterior – this is the paradox of addition.[111] To make room for a supplement is to remove a degree of completeness so that coupling with whatever comes from outside is possible. (Derrida's examples involve the incompleteness of nature that makes culture important, the insufficiency of origin that makes history relevant, the lack in a body that demands other bodies.) In the framework of complementation, a presence is contrasted by an absence – the origin, the *arkhé*, contains everything that originates within it. The idea of a lack in general makes sense in the framework of complementation: when totality is not yet reached, something is lacking. Full presence makes the exterior indifferent; there is nothing that could make any difference. If I am fully present, the other has to be absent, or at least absent for me – unless the other is interdependent with me and a part of me that makes me complete. It is the supplement that brings about exteriority, for within this framework, something absent can be neither a redundancy nor a complement that brings about totality. From the point of view of supplement, adding promotes a transformation, and therefore anything supplemented is neither indifferent to nor necessarily connected to its supplement. In a relation of supplementation, the *relata* are neither independent nor interdependent; a supplemented item is neither fully present as a determination nor absent. The logic of the supplement is anathema to an all-encompassing, complete view of reality; there is always something to come that will supplement what is viewed. The notion of the supplement also makes clearer how assuming a totality is a way to make any existing item fully present in that totality; any item is fully present if it is in its total environment. This is what happens to monadologies like Leibniz's; it is the world of a monad that makes it fully present. Whitehead's attempt to avoid an all-encompassing whole that would make actual entities barren while maintaining the idea of a solidarity of all existents would benefit from the logic of the supplement. This is perhaps another way of saying that Whitehead's process philosophy needs to be interrupted by Levinas's exteriority.[112]

The supplement makes sense of the Other as infinite; neither I nor the Other are fully present: me being fully present would make the Other absent, and the Other being fully present would mean completeness. The Other appears as a trace. This is why Levinas holds that I am separated from but not indifferent to the Other, and this is how a *dynamis koinonias* dwells in supplements. The logic of the supplement makes sense both of the transcendence brought about by exteriority and of the separation from the outside that prevents interdependence (and totality). The supplement, for Derrida, is another name for the trace and also another name for *différance*, which is the act of bringing about identity and signification. Both identity and signification are relative to what is around them and supplements them – they are thoroughly situated because they are hostage to what could come to supplement their presences, which are never completed. Identity and signification are both hostage to exteriority, without holding a necessary connection to anything that may be added to them. The logic of the supplement therefore is the logic of exteriority: it is the supplement that interrupts and fuels process. Hence, the interrupted nexus could also be the supplemented nexus. Reality emerges as never fully present; it is always up for grabs in the sense that additions to it will not eventually make it complete, but rather will continuously revamp it. The furniture of the universe cannot be anything but the supplementation of the universe, and this is why the outer, the beyond or the Other cannot constitute anything but paradoxical furniture. If talk of the furniture of the universe is not a passport to a total view of reality, it should allow paradoxes related to self-transcendent totalities. Transcending what seems to be a totality is what a supplement does.

The supplement also helps with understanding substitution in Levinas: to be substituted by the Other is to be supplemented and eventually to return to the state of insufficient presence. It is precisely this insufficient presence that brings in the obsession with the other – the obsession to evade one's own being. Because of this insufficiency, subjectivity is always hostage to the others. Subjectivity is separated from yet not indifferent to what is outside it. The notion of the supplement can help with understanding substitution within a general indexicalist framework of the metaphysics of the others. An interiority, determined by its borders, is no full presence but can be supplemented by what comes into contact with it. Since supplementation transforms what is supplemented, the interiority is affected by the outdoors. Proximity – which also entails no full presence – provides supplementation and substitution. Due to an operation we will look at soon, an interiority is affected by the outdoors and acts on its behalf. Such an operation makes sure the interiority is open to supplements and can therefore be resituated by being affected by what is beyond.

In general, the logic of the supplement is adequate to deal with exteriority, and therefore with the Great Outdoors. A reality open to supplementation is one in which transcendence is a guide and anything outer can engage in substitution. An account of subjectivity that makes it stop short of full-blown identity like Levinas's can be expanded into an account of indexically defined interiority that can always be supplemented. The relation through which the Great Outdoors can affect me is not one between full presences. The Great Outdoors affects me because I can always be supplemented; my presence is never full, and I am (by Levinasian obsession) eager to attend to what is outer. The me before the Great Outdoors is constantly being supplemented by the others outside. Similarly, the Great Outdoors is in the proximity, albeit never fully present.

The supplement is also connected to hospitality. To be less than fully present is to be open to what comes from outside. In his seminar on hostility and hospitality, Derrida reflects on the nature of a law of hospitality.¹¹³ Derrida understands hospitality as a response to an arrival. The law of hospitality points towards an unbounded willingness to receive what arrives. It is, to some extent, an extension of Levinas's concern with the personal Other for whom I am infinitely responsible. It is this law of hospitality that gives priority to the snake in the water, the source of D. H. Lawrence's poem. This law is unconditional, and in that sense incapable of determining what actually happens by itself. There is a tension between the law of hospitality and the laws of hospitality, which are the laws of the land, including immigration and importation as much as the usual practices of hosting and welcoming.¹¹⁴ The law needs the laws to command, although it is impossible for the laws to express the unbounded nature of the law. Further, satisfying the laws of hospitality is not enough to make one hospitable – that is, to follow the law of hospitality. One could, for example, be polite. But politeness itself is not hospitality, and yet one cannot be both impolite and hospitable. This tension is central to hospitality: it requires respecting the laws and somehow transgressing them. The law of hospitality concerns the supplement: it is an openness to the infinite beyond, and at the same time it is about the surprising, unruly and unscheduled character of interruption.

Hospitality is also an issue that Levinas tackles in *Totality and Infinity*. He claims that when one has a house and is therefore separated from the others, one enjoys a freedom that entails infinite responsibility. This amounts to saying that with a house one feels the pull of Derrida's law of hospitality. Both Jabès and Klossowski are greatly concerned with the unbounded character of genuine hospitality. In *Le livre de l'hospitalité*, Jabès considers hospitality to go beyond responsibility, which itself goes beyond solidarity. The host, he writes, asks the guest to forget everything else in order to be nothing but a guest. Klossowski's Octave in *Les lois de l'hospitalité* has an open door to whoever appears on the horizon; he works hard to keep curiosity unconstrained.¹¹⁵ Hospitality is an openness towards what is exterior – Derrida's law of hospitality, along with curiosity and tenderness, points at how exteriority invites engagement. They articulate a drive towards the others in ways concerned with the framework of the supplement. I am supplemented by the outdoors because it affects me; the laws of hospitality, curiosity and tenderness are symptoms of a less-than-full presence. Engagement with the exterior, from the point of view of the supplement, is not only interdependence, but is also a consequence of insufficient presence. The pull is not towards completion but towards supplementation.

The framework of the supplement is indeed appropriate for dealing with exteriority and is broad enough to enable any other to interrupt a nexus. In general, it portrays interiorities as insufficient presences pulled towards the supplement in the Great Outdoors. Supplement interrupts and inflects a change in the agenda. Even fleshed out in terms of hospitality – and further in terms of curiosity and tenderness – the framework of the supplement is too abstract if compared with the effort Levinas makes to provide for a phenomenology of encountering the Other. Notions such as obsession, substitution, recursion, the call of a face, enjoyment and the proximity of the other attempt to describe exteriority in more concrete terms – in terms of what is involved in the very movement of supplementing the interiority. Something more along these lines is in order if the Great Outdoors is to be seen as an exteriority that supplements. To extend the Levinasian other beyond the human face, we need an account of how the Great Outdoors interrupts.

## Perception and Supplement

The answer I would like to recommend is straightforward: it is through perception that the Great Outdoors interrupts a nexus. The others that compose a genuine exteriority are those perceived from the outer side of the sensorial interface between what is inside and what is outside. Perceptual experience provides constant supplements. The very image of a perceiving subjectivity is of a house with an open view; perception is the very locus of hospitality in the interiority, as this is where an openness towards the exterior lies. In its capacity to disrupt what is habitual and alter an agenda, perception is interruption. Perceptual experience is precisely where nexûs are at stake, and with ingredients such as curiosity and tenderness, it is a broad symptom of insufficient presence. As we will see, Whitehead's analysis of perception that finds it beyond human (or animal) sensoria helps us understand the impacts of the others in terms of exercises in receptivity. The next chapter elaborates a detailed version of the account of receptivity as hospitality – and of perceptual experience as the place where interruption occurs.

Levinas understands sovereignty and spontaneity as what make possible an infinite responsibility towards the others. The freedom inside the house is what enables the host to exercise unbounded hospitality. This is how perception of what is outside a nexus can bend the agenda in an indeterminate manner. What is perceived changes one's course of action, one's intentions and eventually one's overall preferences. To be sure, perception in the organic is also connected to self-preservation and to maintenance. There is a cybernetically negative circuit in the organic that involves being able to receive salient signals from the environment in order both to reinforce existing features and to adapt to different circumstances. Such cybernetics are part of the general relation that an organism has with the surrounding environment – one of mutual creation or sympoiesis, but also one where a certain equilibrium is at times reached and preserved.[116] This cybernegative element in perception is what can be taken as the habitual: the habits that define a house, a place of residence. In contrast to the house, which Tournier's Robinson needs to build for himself on Speranza, there can be perceptual disruption. When others interrupt, they can be accommodated in the circuit if sufficient revision can be provided. But revision is only one possible follow-up to perceptual disruption, along with, for example, substitution – the path taken by Elizabeth Costello when meeting the pregnant stray cat in San Juan. The hospitality that Jabès takes to go beyond responsibility is unbounded, in the sense that the perceiver can go to any lengths to respond to a perceptual call. This is the cyberpositive element in perception that goes side by side with maintenance and self-preservation. There is no clear border between the cybernegative and the cyberpositive elements in perception because there is no fully present division between the two. Depending on what is supplemented in perception, the border can change. The usual perceptual operations can be interrupted. Precisely because interruption can come at any moment, there can be no safe perceptual circuit involving elements outdoors. The environment nearby provides sustenance to perceptual systems, but whenever engaged through perceptual acts, the Great Outdoors can provide a supplement.

As a supplement, perception hinges on the possibility of substitution. Something I perceive can lead me astray, all the way towards something other than attention to my well-being – a scream in the sea can lead me to change the direction of my homebound boat. When I perceive, I am separated from what is being perceived but also respond to it. My response can take any shape because there is no limit to hospitality: what is perceived is outer, indexically defined as what is beyond and not substantively defined like a determinate class of requirements. Perception, broadly speaking, is tied to responsibility; it is involvement with the others. There is a sense in which I make myself hostage when I open my eyes.

## Notes

1. Aira, *The Conversations*, p. 42.
2. Davidson, 'Three Varieties of Knowledge'.
3. Whitehead, *Modes of Thought*, p. 93.
4. Whitehead, *Adventures of Ideas*, p. 276.
5. Whitehead, *Adventures of Ideas*, p. 180.
6. Whitehead, *Adventures of Ideas*, p. 268. See also Shaviro, *The Universe of Things*. Whitehead mentions the Quakers when he deems that concern is a decisive force in guiding action. Despite this, among his ideals – truth, beauty, adventure, peace – no room is left for sanctity.
7. Latour, 'What Is the Style of Matters of Concern?'
8. Some of the ideas in this chapter have been rehearsed in Bensusan, 'O realismo especulativo e a metafísica dos outros'.
9. Lectures presented in September 2016 at the GECO research group at the Université Libre de Bruxelles. See also Tsing, *The Mushroom at the End of the World*.
10. Levinas, *Totality and Infinity*, pp. 82–101.
11. Sextus Empiricus, *Outline of Scepticism*.
12. In *Being Up for Grabs*, ch. 4, I explored what I called an ontology of doubts, which allow one to be convinced that one's own doubts are the best depiction of a given topic. In the present case, however, the attitudes are no longer incompatibly different.
13. Grice, *Studies in the Way of Words*.
14. Haraway, *Staying with the Trouble*, p. 35.
15. Descola, *Beyond Nature and Culture*.
16. See Hartigan Jr, *Aesop's Anthropology*.
17. See Århem, 'Ecosofia Masuna'; Lima, 'O dois e seu múltiplo'; and Viveiros de Castro, 'Cosmological Deixis and Amerindian Perspectivism'.
18. Descola, *Beyond Nature and Culture*, pp. 61–9.
19. Viveiros de Castro, 'Cosmological Deixis and Amerindian Perspectivism', p. 472.
20. Viveiros de Castro, 'Cosmological Deixis and Amerindian Perspectivism'. He reckons that while plants, artefacts and mete-

orological phenomena are often equally endowed with perspectives centred on their positions in the midst of things, the prototype of the (extra-human) Other for the American groups is the animal.
21. Viveiros de Castro, 'Cosmological Deixis and Amerindian Perspectivism', p. 476.
22. Viveiros de Castro, 'Cosmological Deixis and Amerindian Perspectivism', p. 476.
23. Viveiros de Castro, 'Cosmological Deixis and Amerindian Perspectivism', p. 476.
24. Viveiros de Castro, 'Cosmological Deixis and Amerindian Perspectivism', p. 476.
25. Viveiros de Castro, 'Cosmological Deixis and Amerindian Perspectivism', p. 477.
26. Viveiros de Castro, 'Cosmological Deixis and Amerindian Perspectivism', p. 477.
27. Viveiros de Castro, 'Cosmological Deixis and Amerindian Perspectivism', p. 478.
28. Viveiros de Castro, 'Cosmological Deixis and Amerindian Perspectivism', p. 481.
29. Kohn, *How Forests Think*, p. 10. See also Povinelli, *Geontologies*, and Tsing, *The Mushroom at the End of the World*.
30. Kohn, *How Forests Think*, p. 10.
31. Kohn, *How Forests Think*, p. 9.
32. Viveiros de Castro, 'O nativo relativo', and Viveiros de Castro, 'Perspectival Anthropology and the Method of Controlled Equivocations'.
33. Meillassoux, *After Finitude*.
34. For a similar analysis of the twofold character of the challenge to correlationism, see Cogburn, *Garcian Meditations*, pp. 153–4.
35. Meillassoux, *After Finitude*, p. 37.
36. Levinas, *Totality and Infinity*, p. 43.
37. Whitehead, *Process and Reality*, p. 5.
38. Meillassoux, *After Finitude*, p. 64.
39. Levinas, *Totality and Infinity*, p. 43.
40. Meillassoux, 'L'Inexistence divine', pp. 90–122.
41. Levinas, *Totality and Infinity*, pp. 43–4.
42. Levinas, *Totality and Infinity*, p. 43.
43. Levinas, *Totality and Infinity*, p. 35.
44. See the opening pages of Levinas, *Totality and Infinity*.
45. Levinas, *Totality and Infinity*, pp. 33–42.
46. This drive towards the exterior could be presented in terms of

a phenomenology of curiosity. Curiosity involves risks, and it is driven not only by a will to know, but also by a structural insufficiency in what one is. It could be compared with Levinas's notion of evasion – see Levinas, *On Escape*. For Levinas, evasion is the drive outwards, moved by an uneasiness with what one is, with what makes one a specific being. It is present in desire but never quenched by its satisfaction.

47. Levinas, *On Escape*, p. 71. See also Levinas, *Existence and Existents*, pp. 19–21, for example, where he disconnects being from the good and prepares to show how evil cannot consist in a lack of being.
48. For an analysis of Levinas's relation to Parmenides, see Benso, *The Face of Things*, pp. 7–12.
49. See Plato, *Sophist*, 258C–D, for an example.
50. Plato, *Sophist*, 250A–255E. There is much discussion concerning whether these five *megista gene* should be taken as five forms, in consonance with earlier dialogues of Plato (see, for instance, Bluck, *Plato's Sophist*, pp. 125–32). I will simply consider them as five kinds.
51. Plato, *Sophist*, 258C.
52. Plato, *Sophist*, 258D–259A.
53. Levinas, *Existence and Existents*, pp. 82, 98–9, for example. Apart from the existents, he acknowledges a 'there is' (*il y a*), which seems to play a different role in his early writings and in *Totality and Infinity*. In the early writings, it is connected with the phenomenology of insomnia in a way that makes clear that existence is a burden for each existent. See Levinas, *Existence and Existents*, pp. 26, 29–36.
54. Levinas, *On Escape*.
55. Whitehead, *Process and Reality*, pp. 184–9.
56. Whitehead, *Adventures of Ideas*, p. 176.
57. Levinas, *Otherwise than Being*, chs 3 and 4.
58. Levinas, *Otherwise than Being*, p. 102.
59. It seems that earlier in his conception of monads, Leibniz pictured a monad as having a point as its physical counterpart. The structure of predicates would then somehow be associated with a location in space – a geometrical point. Later, in the *Monadology*, Leibniz abandoned this idea and preferred monads to have no proper physical counterpart apart from the areas of matter where a monad is expressed. Indexicalism, in contrast, would limit the unit to the point but conceive it less as a geometrical point and more as a point of view.

60. Levinas, *Otherwise than Being*, p. 101.
61. Levinas, *Otherwise than Being*, p. 26.
62. Whitehead, *Process and Reality*, p. 19.
63. Levinas, *Proper Names*, p. 112.
64. Levinas, *Totality and Infinity*, pp. 53–60.
65. Levinas, *Totality and Infinity*, p. 62.
66. Levinas, *Totality and Infinity*, pp. 120–1.
67. Husserl, *Cartesian Meditations*, pp. 89–151.
68. Husserl, *Cartesian Meditations*, pp. 39–41. The 'inseparable correlation' is a perfect example of what Meillassoux calls correlationism. Husserl rejects the idea that the cogitations that the *ego cogitans* reveals could in any sense ground the conclusion that 'ergo sum', that a substantial ego exists.
69. Husserl, *Cartesian Meditations*, pp. 27–9.
70. He repeats the formula in roughly the same terms in *Existence and Existents*, p. 95, *Time and the Other*, p. 83, and *Totality and Infinity*, p. 13.
71. Levinas, *Otherwise than Being*, ch. 1.
72. Heidegger describes the impersonal as what involves no decision and no response. The impersonal is a 'who' that could be said to be 'nobody'. Heidegger's picture of the impersonal is that of a void in responsibility. See Heidegger, *Being and Time*, p. 120.
73. Levinas, *Totality and Infinity*, p. 40.
74. Peirce, 'The Doctrine of Necessity Examined'.
75. Peirce, 'The Doctrine of Necessity Examined', p. 323.
76. Peirce, 'The Doctrine of Necessity Examined', pp. 332–3.
77. Peirce, 'The Doctrine of Necessity Examined', p. 333.
78. Peirce, 'The Doctrine of Necessity Examined', p. 333.
79. Peirce, 'The Doctrine of Necessity Examined', p. 333.
80. Leibniz, *Theodicy*.
81. Dewey, *Experience and Nature*, p. 56, and Wahl, *Vers le concret*.
82. See Deleuze and Guattari, *A Thousand Plateaus*, ch. 10, where an image is presented of a plan and a plane (both written *plan* in French) that illustrates the gist of process philosophy: there is a sphere containing projects, scores, architectures and flowcharts, and another where they coexist in their implementation and have to compose with each other. The former sphere, the plan of organisation, hosts necessities but is not fully actual. The latter sphere, the plane of composition, is where plans meet each other.
83. Levinas, *Totality and Infinity*, p. 271.
84. Stengers, *Cosmopolitics I*.

85. LeGuin, *Finding My Elegy – New and Selected Poems*.
86. Deleuze, *The Logic of Sense*, pp. 301–20. Tournier's novel is *Vendredi ou les limbes du Pacifique*.
87. We can think of islands where everything is endemic to the extent that nothing disturbs a routine. In Bensusan, *Pacífico Sul*, Captain Cook is joined by his non-contemporary Alexius Meinong to find an island where everything that is written, spoken or thought in the rest of the world takes place. They soon find that the events around them are not interrupted by their arrival – nor are their steps on the island affected by what surrounds them. They discover a thoroughly inhabited island that is scarcely a place that can be inhabited. The only ordinary person they meet is Cynthia della Griva, who is neither a native, nor strictly speaking an inhabitant.
88. Deleuze, *The Logic of Sense*, p. 311.
89. Wittgenstein, *Philosophical Investigations*, §§ 256–307.
90. Wittgenstein, *Philosophical Investigations*, § 693.
91. Wittgenstein is unclear about what would happen to mental content without a public language (see *Philosophical Investigations*, § 304). In fact, it is likely that he embraces an expressivism according to which there is no state of affairs conveyed in the language of sensations. Deleuze's robinsonology shows that Wittgenstein's account of content contrasts with Deleuze's account of thought as much as strong correlationism contrasts with the metaphysics of subjectivity, in the distinction made by Meillassoux in *After Finitude*.
92. Deleuze, *The Logic of Sense*, p. 316.
93. See, for instance, Derrida, *The Beast and the Sovereign*, p. 237, for the various places where he comments on the interchange that led to Levinas's comment.
94. Coetzee, 'The Old Woman and the Cats'.
95. Lispector, *The Passion According to G.H.*
96. Levinas, *Totality and Infinity*, p. 160.
97. Levinas, *Totality and Infinity*, p. 38. See also Chapter 1 above.
98. Descola, *Beyond Nature and Culture*.
99. In this respect, see Irigaray, 'Questions to Emmanuel Levinas'. See also Benso, *The Face of Things*, p. 211. See also chapter 4 of Benso, *The Face of Things*. The Other that appeals to Levinas appears to be another human male subject. He seems to envisage the Other as at least best presented in a masculine face that, from his acknowledged heterosexual viewpoint, cannot slide into the corridors of self-collapsing intimacy (Levinas, *Totality and Infinity*, p. 264).

100. Levinas, *Difficult Freedom*, p. 8; see Benso, *The Face of Things*, p. 46.
101. Levinas, *Totality and Infinity*, p. 159.
102. See Chapter 1 above. Benso bases her notion of things on the Bremen Lectures; see Heidegger, *Bremen and Freiburg Lectures*.
103. 'Concernful approach' is the way Mitchell chooses to translate *angehenden Anspruchs* in Heidegger (see *Bremen and Freiburg Lectures*, p. 62, for example).
104. Husserl, *Cartesian Meditations*, p. 89.
105. Heidegger, *Being and Time*, § 7.
106. Levinas, *Otherwise than Being*, pp. 83–9.
107. Benso, *The Face of Things*, p. 166.
108. Benso, *The Face of Things*, p. 167.
109. Benso, *The Face of Things*, p. 174.
110. See, for instance, Derrida, *Of Grammatology*, pp. 141–57.
111. Derrida, *Of Grammatology*, p. 229.
112. For the possible connections between Whitehead and Derrida, see the unpublished works of Timothy Mooney, 'Deconstruction, Process and Openness' and 'Derrida and Whitehead'.
113. The seminar *Questions de responsabilité V: hostilité/hospitalité* was delivered in 1995–96 at the Ecole des hautes études en sciences sociales. See Derrida and Dufourmantelle, *Of Hospitality*.
114. Derrida and Dufourmantelle, *Of Hospitality*, pp. 66–79.
115. In the second novel of Pierre Klossowski's trilogy *Lois de l'hospitalité*, called *Roberte, ce soir*, Octave writes that he is in his house, anxious to see on the horizon the stranger who will arrive. Octave is prepared to go a long way to host any stranger who would appear at his front door. He also states that he has to have some laws of hospitality to make sure his curiosity is not displaced by suspicion and jealousy (pp. 109–13).
116. See, for instance, Plant and Land, 'Cyberpositive'.

# 3

# The Hospitality of Perception

*When it came this time, the monstrous, tortured howl ripped through everyone like a bullet. Instinctively, the optician moved his hand to protect his face. [. . .] What the hell was out there?*

*The howl mutated into an unbearable screeching. The optician felt his stomach knot. Something was roaring underneath the waves and whatever it was the optician had a gut feeling that when they found it, it would be truly terrible. [. . .]*

*Then, suddenly he saw it: 'Fish! I see three big fish there! Francesco – five o'clock!'*

*[. . .] The optician kept his eyes trained on the black dots he had seen bobbing on the water and tried to steady his mind. But his brain was arguing with his eyes. What kind of fish would be on the surface of the water, idiot? Come on, what kind of fish?*

*[. . .] He willed his eyes and brain to recognize and interpret the forms.*

*Galata drifted closer [. . .] The optician started. One of the black shapes he was watching lengthened, partly lifted up from the water and flopped down again into a ball. It disappeared, leaving a white froth of disturbed water.*

*Oh God, no. Please God, no.*

*'People!' Giulia screamed. 'There are people in the water!'*

*[. . .] The people in the water had all seen* Galata *now and they were churning the sea into a frenzy with their flailing arms and legs. Every time a wave collapsed, another black dot or head was revealed. The sea was littered with them.*

*[. . .] The optician recognized [. . .] the music of dying, the final dirge of the drowning, played out right in front of their boat. And through the chorus of voices he could pick out each individual soloist. Everyone was begging to be noticed.*

*The optician swallowed. How, he thought, how do I save them all?*

> [. . .] *Even before he jumped down from the cabin and back onto the deck, the optician had understood that he would have to choose who would live and who would die.*
>
> Emma Jane Kirby[1]

### Doors of Perception

They were not fish. Not this time around. They were in proximity and required a different attention because these others were not fish, but drowning humans around the *Galata*. The perception of drowning humans in the sea comes tied with a different set of requests to a human perceiver. As the object being perceived becomes clear, the request becomes more solid – the brain argues with the eye to be exempted from giving a response. But the refugee bodies are nearby; they are there around the boat, visible. This is where perception faces a crucial element of its nature: passivity. Once a perception settles in, there is no action that can dispel it – even though there are (sometimes costly) ways to avoid giving any response to it.

I claim that the metaphysics of the others has a governing role in perception. With perception, one is compelled to respond to others beyond one's reach and outside one's control, bringing together all the vulnerability of a deixis attached to a standing location. This chapter aims to flesh out the general metaphysics of the others presented so far. As I have said, the others in general appear through perceptual experience, and responding to them is an exercise in hospitality. Responding to the others – understood as receptivity as opposed to spontaneity, in Kantian terms – is what follows an interruption. In order to show how a metaphysics of perception is a department of the metaphysics of the others, I will refer to several recent discussions concerning experience and empirical thinking and incorporate them into my main theme. These discussions – mostly on how sensibility affects empirical thinking – will be no more than sketchily presented.

It is in perceptual experience that the others knock on doors. The general empiricist outlook I want to endorse is the one hinted at by Whitehead's pan-perceptualism, which makes the concrete align with the sensible. Whitehead takes the concrete to be what is capable of sensibility. This fallacy of misplaced concreteness is a plea to attend to actual entities. Concreteness is to be found in what is sensible – what is capable of feeling, or rather capable of being affected – but there are no privileged sensibilia that define the sensible; anything is sensible through some sensibilia, provided it is concrete. Only what is abstract cannot be (directly) sensed by anything.

Sensibility is often taken to require passivity. In perception, one has no agency over what is delivered. This amounts to saying, from an indexicalist point of view, that what is delivered in genuine sensibility comes from outside. Perception is an exercise in receptivity – which Kant contrasted with spontaneity, the internal workings of the mind. Heteronomy is mandatory for any content to be perceptive. This heteronomy of perception encouraged a classical version of empiricism according to which perceptual experience produced verdicts for thought. Sensibility constitutes a tribunal whereby the world can judge ideas, claims and theories. The idea of such a tribunal of experience gains purchase if we consider perceptual experience to be associated with specific sensibilia (and therefore consider experience to be less than what is concrete, and restricted to what goes through specific sensoria). In this case, human sensibilia also act as a jury for the adequacy of human thoughts.

Kant understood sensibility as the 'capacity for receiving representations (receptivity) through the mode in which we are affected by objects' or 'the receptivity of the mind for impressions, in so far as it is in some way affected'.[2] Sensibility is portrayed as a receptivity. For Kant, receptivity and spontaneity, which opposes it, are conjoined in the same forum. They are combined together indoors. Although receiving something requires some passivity, Kant does not portray it as an issue of being entirely at the mercy of what comes from outside; he understands receptivity as a *capacity*, and therefore as something that can be exercised. Further, he conceives receptivity as requiring preparation (and prefiguration) within the mind, as a capacity 'necessarily antecedes all intuitions of these objects [and] it is easily understood how the form of all phenomena can be given in the mind previous to all actual perceptions'.[3] Independently of his conception of such preparation – according to which ideas ought to be available in order for perception to take place – he diagnoses an important feature of receptivity: it is a capacity to be exercised from the inside. Sensibility, understood as receptivity, is a capacity to respond. It is not simply a matter of breaking in – rather, what is exposed to the senses is ushered in, met at the entrance, received.

A frequent tendency of classical empiricism is to minimise protagonism in receptivity. Senses are taken to be passive receptors, and normal adult human senses are deemed to work in much the same way as the sensoria of animals do (or the sensoria of infants, for that matter). Further, it is assumed that what they deliver is the same. The reason for this lies in an attempt to make (adult) human perceptual experience natural, accounted for in terms akin to efficient causation. In this picture, the senses are like channels, and the most that needs to be done on the inside is to leave these channels clear so that messages can be delivered. The insider has little more to do than accept the delivery as a *gift*. Because we receive the gift, according to this claim, we are capable of adjusting to the outer world; without the tribunal of experience, we would be confined to our own ruminations. We are freed from this confinement because our senses provide contents to us as gifts. Further, the classical empiricist story continues, to be objective means precisely to be driven by the verdicts of the senses. The world outside, according to this picture, does favours to our thinking, presenting us with gifts without which we would not be able to engage with anything exterior to our own thoughts. Sensibility brings some exteriority to thought because it has a measure of passivity. In a sense, this picture makes it clear that thinking is hostage to the outer world.

The debate Kant raises concerning sensibility concerns the nature of receptivity. To deal with the question of how it is possible that what comes in through the senses can make an impact on thought, Kant uncovers the faculties of receptivity. Classical empiricism holds that only a non-mediated delivery by the senses could ensure the required passivity. Kant, in his turn, insists that receptivity carries the right amount of passivity even if its contribution to the content of empirical thinking is indistinguishable. Kant's analysis of perception in terms of receptivity uncovers the moment of hospitality in empirical thought. The senses have to be responded to; they provide incitements – or traces – and not full presences. Their content is not already present because it has to be received. Making clear that receptivity involves a capacity, Kant paved the way to an understanding of the senses as bringing about interruptions as opposed to just throwing in ready-made content. In contrast, when receptivity is considered the action of receiving – the action that makes passivity possible – it is only through a response that a difference is made indoors. Receptivity as a faculty is what enables perceptual experience to be a supplement.

## Hospitality and the Given

Let us consider in more detail the contrast between the classical-empiricist ready-made sensorial content and the idea that senses require a receptivity in order to have genuine content. The former is a broad outlook based on classical empiricism, but can take several different shapes. The gist of it is that a ready-made content somehow impinges on thought through the senses. Such contents can be conceived in different ways: they can be impressions or sense data, and they can also be exterior objects. Furthermore, senses can be seen either as somehow representational or as stimuli in nerve endings that affect empirical thoughts.[4] In any case, the senses are taken to impose something for which thought can have no responsibility. This lack of responsibility is what guarantees the exterior character of what the senses deliver. Presented with a gift from outside, the perceiver is not accountable and can at most provide excuses or exculpations.[5] This gift is not fully exterior, though, because it impinges on thought. Verdicts from the senses on thought are like a friction between what is native in thinking, and the invaders that have been forced in through the senses. If there is no capacity in perception, what comes through the senses is not quite exterior; the senses simply let things in and therefore constitute no genuine gate. As a consequence, senses do not exercise hospitality. They provide no demand or appeal; they deliver impingements and not incitements.

Any view grounded in this precis of classical empiricism faces at least two problems. One is the problem of illusion, and the other is the problem of blind intuitions, the latter often referred to as the *myth of the Given*. The problem of illusion is that the senses can be unreliable. What looked like an oasis proves to be a mirage, the stick is actually not bent, the sky is not really blue. These illusions can be disconcerting, especially because the senses carry on delivering the erroneous messages even after they have been proved wrong.[6] This indifference of the senses to what is correct vindicates the claim that deliveries by the senses land in thought unaffected by the thinker – the astronomical convictions of the thinker simply do not matter, and the sky will continue to look blue. However, these illusions spoil the purported objectivity of what is delivered. Furthermore, the traditional Pyrrhonic issue of the *diaphonia* of appearance makes the deliverances somehow less univocal. It is enough to consider the aforementioned modes of Aenesidemus: according to the first three, things appear different to (other) animals, they appear different to different people and they appear different to the same person at different times and under different circumstances. The sceptical conclusion from these modes is that the senses cannot be trusted – there is no reason to take them as gateways to the outdoors, as they could be forging their own creations all along. The sceptical conclusion can begin to be countered by insisting that there is wheat amid the chaff. Anyhow, the variety of quality in sensibility still poses problems concerning what deliveries are to be trusted. Perhaps some senses are less clean than others, some receptions blurrier, some intuitions more misleading; one needs to be able to tell the gold from the pyrites. In other words, there should be a tribunal to judge the verdicts of the senses.

To be sure, this second tribunal can be avoided if we give up on the need to recognise correct perception. Disjunctivism is a way of understanding perception as involving good and bad cases that the perceiver can access without being able to discriminate between them.[7] The difficulty with illusion could be avoided if the genuine delivery is conceived as (metaphysically) different from the misleading one, even if the perceiver cannot recognise which is which. It might not matter whether the thinker at the doorstep can tell them apart. The perceiver is therefore not only hostage to the outdoors – which makes thought external – but also to the working of the gates. The problem of illusion makes clear that there is protagonism in the senses. The idea of the senses engaged in receptivity – or in hospitality – is to take this protagonism as a starting point.

Apart from the problem of illusion – and independently of the merits of the disjunctivist picture – the classical-empiricist doctrine of verdicts provided by the senses to a perceiver who is not accountable for the content of what is received has a problem with blind intuitions. In the Kantian slogan – intuitions without concepts are blind – what is left when we remove the product of conceptual capacity is something that is short of a full-blown message. Although it is unclear what an intuition that is blind would be, such intuitions surely carry no content. The so-called myth of the Given is about full presences: the gist of classical empiricism is that what is delivered by the senses is complete, to the extent that there is room for no supplementation. It can be seen as a variant of Derrida's problem of addition, for it is hard to see how what is sensed can affect what is thought. Sensible intuitions can be present without affecting thought if they are not genuinely received by thought – if thought is not duly supplemented by sense perception. Sensibility requires a receiving end to which something is delivered, and it is this internal end that it must affect. The trouble is that, even when they appropriately and transparently bring in a message from outside, the senses can be too quiet. If the deliveries of the senses are firings in nerve endings, for example, they can be heard by networks of nerve connections that respond to them – in a way similar to the stone heard by the marrow of the bones in LeGuin's poem earlier – but (empirical) thought would be deaf to them. If the senses deliver anything less than full-blown predication – such as 'is green' or 'is a cardinal' – it is unclear how they can be understood and therefore affect thought. The myth is attractive because it seems as if holding that the senses are part of the (internal) workings of thought amounts to loosening the purchase of the idea of a tribunal of experience. The risk of abandoning the myth is to miss what classical empiricism mostly intends to assure – without the myth, thought would be, in the persuasive words of McDowell, 'frictionless spinning in the void'.[8]

To postulate a capacity in sensitivity to avoid the myth of the Given risks losing the contact with what is outside that the senses are supposed to provide. The myth attacks precisely the image of the senses that classical empiricism cherishes – that through the senses, the outer becomes available. The fertility of the idea that the senses do the action of receiving – that they exercise hospitality – is that it makes it possible for perception to be affected by the exterior by responding to it. That is, perception works through incitements and not by impingements. It is involved with the exterior by receiving it – it is affected by the others because it is moved by them. To hold that receptivity is an episode of hospitality is to understand perceptual capacities as being geared by something like the Levinasian obsession with the Other.

The myth can be dismissed by rejecting the idea that the senses deal with the exterior through impingements on nerve endings provoking brain reactions, which amounts to dismissing any conversation with the stone other than that of the marrow of the bones. This would be to embrace the naturalist approach to the epistemology of perception, which grounds perception on supposedly adequate, physiologically described mechanisms.[9] Such a stance turns perception into a network of laws – the laws of hospitality would fully replace the law of hospitality. By contrast, the myth can be exorcised by embracing the idea that the senses are the doors of perception. The view that receptivity is hospitality entails that sensory intuitions need to be ushered in to be understood – perceptual acts are acts of responding. In this view, perceiving is as much an act of receiving as accepting and responding are. The receiver is endowed with a measure of responsibility. The claim of the metaphysics of the others concerning perception is that the doorstep complexities of receptivity are the very intricacies of hospitality.

To receive something, whether it be a gift or a guest, is to attend to a specificity. A gift is not purchased merchandise to fulfil a purpose, and a guest is not an insider. It must be possible to host or receive something outer. The empiricist claim can be presented in its general form: experience itself must be capable of altering the course of (empirical) thought. Experience is interruption. This is where empiricism (classical or otherwise, as we will see) closely approaches the metaphysics of the others. Empiricism in general challenges, in the name of something exterior, the idea of a totality immune to any attrition. Experience is what makes thinking less than immune – and so long as experience is never redundant, no thought is such that it cannot be supplemented.

Because thought can be interrupted from the exterior by the senses, the idea of a Given is tempting. The claim that receptivity is hospitality has to be a form of non-mythical empiricism, the kind of alternative that Wilfrid Sellars sought. Sellars characterised the myth as taking the deliveries of the senses as 'given', as ready-made ideas provided to empirical thought; it is mythical to take the deliveries of the senses as full-fledged episodes of thought.[10] According to Sellars, the myth consists in the conjunction of three mutually incompatible theses: 1) sensing red is enough to conclude that '$x$ is red'; 2) sensing red requires no inference and no recourse to other capacities; and 3) to conclude that '$x$ is P' requires the exercise of a capacity which is alien to (pure) sensibility.[11] The first thesis states that sensing means already having sensorial ideas ready to be thought (and to participate in empirical judgements); content is ready, and ready to be absorbed. According to Sellars it is hard, nevertheless, to deny the two other theses – that sensing itself is a mere exercise of working organs of perception, and that to make predications involving terms such as 'red', some non-sensorial abilities have to be deployed.[12] The resulting trilemma entails that believing in (1) while accepting (2) and (3) is mythical. The myth is that there is a sensorial item that is both delivered by the senses and a token for thought – a genuine piece of thought received in the ready format through the sensorial gate. There should be a way to replace (1) with something suitable while maintaining the central idea that thought responds to what is outer in perceptual experience.

Sellars's quest for an alternative way to make sure senses are connected to the exterior emphasises that senses are geared towards particulars. Receptivity, and not spontaneity, is triggered by situated sensorial inputs that defy full definitions in terms of general predicates. This feature of receptivity is central to the account of perception that follows from the metaphysics of the others. If receptivity is the hospitality of (empirical) thought, the issue concerns the ethics of delivery and is akin to what Levinas took as the danger of ontological thinking: how to accommodate a particular coming from outside without making it an instance of a generality that is already established internally. The epistemological issue is ethical – how to do justice to what is beyond the inner domain, how to treat the others as less than full-blown indifferent presences beyond my scope whose demands are not my concern, but as more than particular cases of pre-existing generalities. It is clear that the fear that invites the myth is that we fail to do justice to what comes through the senses.

Inspired to some extent by Sellars's quest, McDowell has also been looking for a satisfactory empiricism that exorcises the Given. At least since his *Mind and World*, he has been recommending a minimal empiricism that, while avoiding the myth, takes seriously the idea that there should be a genuine tribunal of experience. The image of perceptual knowledge he advocates is one in which experience plays a role that is greater than that of observational beliefs immersed in a network of inferences.[13] Experience can alter the internal determinations of a belief system from outside, even if the deliveries of the senses have to play a role in a game of asking for and *giving* reasons that is taken to be central to thought.[14] McDowell claims that the deliveries of the senses can both exert a pressure over thought and not be contaminated by thought activity if they are passively accepted in the space where this game is played. The receiver of an (explicit) gift has an action to perform – that of acknowledging the gift being offered – but that action does not make a difference to the content of the gift;

the content is received passively. Likewise, experience provides an offer that thought is to accept without interfering in the message: thought can change or challenge the deliveries of the senses at a later stage when they are to become the content of a belief. What McDowell tries to show is that sensorial intuitions can be accepted in a passive way. Receptivity, according to him, is apt to provide reasons coming from outside thought in the form of passively acquired conceptual content. Provided along with content, the deliveries of the senses are not blind or silent, but present themselves as ready to be thought.

McDowell inherits from Sellars a characterisation of empirical thought (and empirical knowledge) in terms of the placement of a claim in a logical space of reasons. A logical space is an ensemble of logical possibilities associated with a feature such that each point in the space is a state of this feature.[15] Within a logical space of reasons, a reason is given, and if it commands endorsement, it is accepted: it is a space of recognition. It is in this space that the game of asking and giving reasons takes place. In this game, reasons are pieces, and nothing is a reason if it is not recognised as such by the reason-mongering players. From the point of view of receptivity as hospitality, it is interesting if reasons coming from outside through the senses ensure that the space of reasons is not an enclosed totality. If the space of reasons is supplemented by what comes from experience, the connection between reason and experience is not one of inclusion or incorporation, but rather one in which reason is slowly supplemented by experience.

It is important for McDowell to distinguish the non-mythical empiricism he seeks from positions where beliefs are the only bearers of reason.[16] For Davidson, there are no reasons coming from experience itself; sensibility can play a role in the formation of beliefs, but no rational force is present until a belief is fully constituted. McDowell acknowledges that it is hard to avoid this way of seeing the contribution of sensibility once you reject the mythical idea that deliveries by the senses are external to the space of reasons, yet fully ready to affect the interior of this space. In *Mind and World*, he posits that these deliveries are presented with propositional content, and therefore are distinct from ordinary beliefs only in the sense that they are acquired passively. In his earlier position, experience was something fully presented with its ready content. Later, McDowell is convinced that intuitions with propositional content are hardly distinguishable from something internal to thinking. He recognises that his earlier position, according to which sensorial intuitions have propositional content, makes it 'hard to deny that experiencing is taking things to be so, rather than what I want: a different kind of thing that entitles us to take things to be so'.[17] A minimal empiricism has to conceive of intuitions as distinct from beliefs yet capable of being received, with an appropriate measure of passivity, in the interior of the space of reasons. In any form of minimal empiricism faithful to the Kantian rebuttal of the Given (which encourages what Meillassoux diagnoses as weak correlationism) conceptual capacities shape the form of sense intuition. In his earlier position McDowell understood those conceptual capacities to be present – albeit passive – in the deliveries of the senses themselves, which have a propositional form just like any belief. In his later position, made clear in 'Avoiding the Myth of the Given', he limits the role of concepts to the workings of the senses and allows intuitions (which he prefers to call by the Kantian German term *Anschauungen* to avoid confusion) to be neither themselves embedded in concepts nor propositional like beliefs.[18]

In both his earlier and his later positions, McDowell holds that a non-mythical empiricism can be achieved if we understand the deliveries of the senses as already bearing concepts. He urges an understanding of sensibility in which a cooperation of intuitions and concepts is at play. Conceptual capacities are passively present in the workings of the senses, and an appropriate reception of what is on the other side of the gate depends on the response we are ready to provide. Our capacity to respond makes it possible for us to have sensorial intuitions that show us how things are out there and convey a message about them: carrying concepts, they are no longer mute.[19] The senses can only work as receivers of verdicts when aided by concepts – without them, there is little to be delivered. McDowell's later position, however, posits *Anschauungen* as having less than full-blown propositional content – they appear and carry information about the surroundings that is not ready to be accommodated by thought. This is an interesting move: the senses deliver something that is not ready to be thought; they detect something that is not fully present to thinking. McDowell explains this by writing that *Anschauungen* have content which is conceptual but stops short of being propositional.

The idea that *Anschauungen* are not fully present to thinking points towards something in them that escapes propositional content. From the point of view of the metaphysics of the others, there is an infinity in what is delivered by the senses; exteriority is never fully encompassed.

## The Complexities of Receptivity

McDowell's minimal empiricism was crafted as a way to avoid both the image he dreads in Davidson – that of being confined to our own ruminations, unable to be impacted by anything outside our own correlation – and the myth of the Given – which makes experience imposing but scarcely able to provide more than exculpations.[20] He intends to escape from both poles while preserving the idea that experience provides verdicts, that there is an absolute we can access through the passive elements that appear in receptivity. As much as the correlation blocks us from contact with the absolute according to Meillassoux, our spontaneity seems to McDowell to block us from hearing the voice of experience. Initially, he thought passivity would be enough to make us touch the absolute that spontaneity blocks and make sure that experience provides verdicts. In his more recent position, he stresses that *Anschauungen* are distinguished from beliefs and have a different structure – although they are conceptual, they also have a voice that is different from that of thinking.[21] This distinction makes him prone to pay greater attention to the process of receptivity. Much along the lines of a traditional empiricist architecture in which sensibility precedes rational judgement, he divides receptivity into two stages: the one in which conceptual intuitions are met, and the one in which they are integrated. Although in McDowell's assessment there is no receptivity without concepts, detection can be separated from full-blown assimilation to the inside. Content is not ready for thinking in its delivery by the senses. The assimilation of what the senses provide – like an act of hospitality – falls short of full integration.

Much of McDowell's change of position has been prompted by his exchanges with other philosophers, especially Charles Travis. In a series of articles, Travis challenged McDowell's conception of receptivity, and in particular the idea that experience has content. He argues that perception 'makes the environment present to us' and as such it doesn't represent anything, but simply brings things in. Therefore, it doesn't have content but only *relata*. When things look one way or another to me, they can at most indicate their presence through a propositional attitude. What perception should be able to do is make the outer world accessible. Travis's image is that perception directly detects objects and features of the environment. The idea that perception provides contents through conceptual capacities is suspicious for him because we must be able to separate seeing objects, or particulars of any sort, and see that something is the case. When McDowell acknowledged that there are two stages to receptivity, he certainly moved in the right direction, but both stages cannot be conceptual. Perception should be able to provide awareness of a particular case independently of concepts.

Travis makes clear that fine-tuning is required to achieve an image of the complexities of receptivity that avoids both the Given and an account of the senses that renders thinking frictionless spinning in the void. The metaphysics of the others indicates that the adequate alternative is to hold firmly that in receptivity, hospitality is in play. The positions of McDowell and Travis shed light on the way perception is to be conceived of in order to see the senses as performing acts of hospitality. McDowell, not surprisingly, sees Travis as lapsing into the myth of the Given as he postulates that detection of outer items through the senses comes in a ready-made format, as if perception required no contribution from inner capacities. McDowell believes the way to remedy this lapse is to postulate that the detection of objects and their features cannot take place unless conceptual capacities have been acquired. Detection of objects is mediated by concepts – objects cannot make themselves available without conceptual exercises. At the same time, he realises that *Mind and World* was still too close to Davidson's claim that only belief-like contents can affect thinking. His gambit there was that passivity in reception was enough to ensure there is no frictionless spinning in the void.

Travis wants to be able to detect what is perceived without concepts, while McDowell insists that detection without mediation is not available. Both approaches are interesting for an account of perception guided by the metaphysics of the others. An important lesson from the debate is that receptivity is not just passive acceptance of something that is ready for thinking – hospitality is not directed to what is already native. If the deliveries by the senses are the others, these deliveries are not made of anything fully present, but rather of incitements. Nothing is presented to thought in terms of content, but rather in terms of traces that point to infinity. This is how the Levinasian Other appears in perception: the senses bring in traces that interrupt by asking for something, triggering a call for attention – the attention required for hospitality. If we take content to entail full presence, Travis is right in arguing that there is no content to the deliveries from the senses. On the other hand, McDowell is right in making sure that mediation is part of receptivity – perception requires being hospitable, which is not just allowing an invasion to happen. The idea that perception provides traces entails that there are no full presences added to thought by the senses, while making sure that nothing is assimilated without mediation.

We can picture the situation as follows. Travis made McDowell move away from a position that was too close to the Davidsonian pole, but he is still not far enough from it to embrace the idea that perception provides no content. Travis, on the other hand, steers too close to the opposite pole by assuming no (conceptual) mediation in sense detection. The idea that the senses deliver traces and incitements finds a middle position between the two poles of this oscillation, which is perhaps smaller than the one between Davidson's abandonment of any epistemology of experience on the one hand, and the Given on the other. This centrist position holds that perception requires actively receiving traces that come in premediated form but resist being fully thought. Hospitality is not turning the outsider into a native, but simply welcomes it in – that is, to respond to the appeal provided by the senses. Receptivity involves both sensing the incitement and responding to it, for there is no incitement unless a response can be provided. This is the nature of supplementation: only something less than full presence can be incited into being supplemented. The centre position takes into consideration both the idea that passivity is not enough to distinguish the outer from the inner (Travis) and the requirement of mediation (McDowell).

However, McDowell takes mediation to be conducted exclusively through concepts. In his later position, *Anschauungen* themselves bear concepts even if they have no propositional content. A general metaphysics of the others suggests instead that there is more to mediation – and to a capacity to exercise receptivity – than conceptual abilities. Mediation is the interference of any agency – which could be but need not be the exercise of concepts – in receiving a message. In fact, there is more to the others than instantiations of concepts – even if the concept is unique to them, as in McDowell's *de re* senses where concepts are used to determine a singular thought with the help of demonstratives.[22] Levinas describes the violence of ontological knowledge in terms of making the Other 'become concept', which is already to take away alterity.[23] By contrast, consider McDowell's claim that everything is thinkable (and can be turned into concepts and propositions). He argues that while reality is not itself thought, it is made of thinkables – and in his later position, it is not that *Anschauungen* provide propositions, but that they provide items that can be turned into propositions.[24] I call his move a modal recoil: while the outside reality and our sense intuitions about it are not made of thoughts, concepts or propositions, they can safely be turned into thoughts, concepts and propositions. But it is interesting that the modal recoil is a recoil, a reducing of one's assumptions: it is possible not to conceptualise the conceptualisable (not to think the thinkable or turn into a proposition what can be turned into a proposition). If for McDowell conceptualisation appears as an imperative – without it, experience would not take place – the metaphysics of the others would rather take it as looming possibility. Based on Levinas's portrayal of the face that says, *you can kill me but please don't*, we can formulate the interruption brought about by perception as if the perceived speaks like this: *you can conceptualise me (in such and such a manner) but please don't*. When we see the perceived in terms of this asking, it becomes clear that in experience there is an exposure to the vulnerability of the others. It is as if the other, infinite and transcendent, can be turned into a fully present content for thought but asks to be received as something that escapes the grip of the concept.

Receptivity can therefore accept the demand not to conceptualise. What is perceived is perceived by asking for something. Still, this will not make perception an exercise in immediacy. I will elaborate below on how there is more to mediation than the employment of concepts. Right now, it is enough to say that mediation can be performed by deictic operators – there is something indexical to receptivity. Indeed, perception is hostage to circumstance; it is only with respect to a position that what is perceived can be articulated. Receptivity concerns the outer border – to perceive is to relate to the other outside, guided by a call, by an interruption, a plea for attention, a tenderness or a curiosity. In any case, it is guided by something that appears on the doorstep. Indeed, indexicalism entails that there is nothing to be perceived but deixis. No interiority can perceive without the deployment of deictic operators. What is perceived is already indexically placed. Mediation is done by deixis, and concepts are useful in as much as they provide implicit indexicality. We could perhaps rephrase Kant's motto: intuitions without indexicals are blind (or mute). Receptivity, like hospitality, is made of reorientations. But the others, infinite in their traces, always remain exterior. Supplementation is not integration, and never reaches completion.

Detecting the others, like welcoming someone at the doorstep, is this exercise in deixis. The capacities to respond, in contrast, depend on what is available indoors, which according to indexicalism is itself deictic. This deictic mediation, however, could seem dangerously close to the mythical Given: it could seem that being nearby is enough for something to be perceived. Indeed, Sellars has identified in Russell's notion of *knowledge by acquaintance* the typical footprints of a mythical empiricism.[25] Russell contrasts knowledge by acquaintance with knowledge by description; the latter is a kind of knowledge that deploys conceptual (and propositional) capacities, while the former requires no more than acquaintance – acknowledging something or someone by shaking hands or visiting a place. To know someone by acquaintance, it is not enough to shake hands with her. One needs to be aware that acquaintance has been made – awareness meaning accessing the handshake, in memory or otherwise, and discriminating between the person acquainted and all (relevant) others.[26] This knowledge, knowledge *of an* acquaintance, is what according to Sellars is not mediated by concepts. Russell seems to require acquaintance to entail cognitive contact.

It is difficult to completely dispel the impression that deictic receptivity is mythical – especially because it doesn't require conceptual mediators. But we can argue that deictic mediators make no foray into the Given. First, it is worth remarking that perceptual contact does not suppose cognitive contact. Perceptual contact without cognitive contact is possible, to paraphrase Wettstein's motto quoted earlier.[27] So, there is no need for knowledge of an acquaintance. Second, there is no perception by merely standing beside something; deictic operators cannot be reduced to cartographical positions, mostly because cartography is itself situated. The outer with which perception is engaged is built by an act of indexical attention, and not from a geographical position supposedly calculated from nowhere. Deictic operators are mediators

150    Indexicalism

because they require engagement of some sort. To be sure, they do not require conceptual engagement, but they involve a call from outdoors.

## Importance and Supplement

Whitehead's notion of importance is central to his analysis of perception.[28] His account of perception revolves around a standing location that determines a percipient event from which perception takes place. Perception is thoroughly situated with respect to other perceived events, hence to other actual entities – defined as final facts, which are 'drops of experience, complex and interdependent'.[29] Just as with Leibniz's monads, each of them has a defined connection with each element of the universe through perception.[30] In Leibniz, other monads are perceived according to their salience in the viewpoint of the perceiving monad. Likewise, for Whitehead, importance guides perception: what affects something in the exercise of perception is what matters in the surrounding environment. The concern for the environment is guided by a *locus standi* from which there are interests, aims, purposes and a sense of situation – it is from somewhere that an actual entity reaches towards others. Whitehead claims that perception requires 'concentrated attention [meaning] disregard of irrelevancies: and such disregard can only be sustained by some sense of importance'.[31] Perception cannot be unfocused. One can think here of the tick studied by von Uexküll: there are a few things that matter in the environment, such as whether the branch is ending, whether there is a mammal passing, whether there is a hairless region on the body of the prey.[32] The tick is equipped to detect these things, for they matter. Anything else goes unperceived; any other event is unnoticed, cannot be taken into consideration, has no importance. Importance provides orientation, a sense of direction that makes both pursuing a goal and evading danger possible. The frog navigates its surroundings in order to detect and catch flies, and not just any flying object that seems like an insect.[33] Like von Uexküll's tick, the frog is to a great extent oblivious to what is sufficiently different from flies. There would be no perception if nothing in the environment mattered; nothing happens to a tick if no salient feature is detected in the surroundings, nothing happens to a frog if not enough of a fly looms about.

Importance is a general notion. Tied to a matrix of differences and indifferences – like an indexicalist interiority – it modulates by providing orientation. And modulation is mediation: an untuned radio is deaf to what is being broadcast by different stations. If the station is not tuned, the signal is silent in the sense in which McDowell once envisaged that intuitions could be mute. If no difference makes a difference – if I am indifferent to all differences – I am in a white blindness where everything is noise and nothing is signal. Importance is the tuning that enables signal to be distinguished from noise. Signal is important. It is through matrices of importance that senses are tuned to what they can receive. The very idea that a perceiver is affected requires a distinction between signal and noise, between what matters and what can be left unperceived.

As a broad mediator, matrices of importance have a special case in concepts. Concepts encapsulate importance – they focus attention as if they are asking questions of what is being sensed. Importance is what makes intuition speak. The concept of *cardinal* is central for one to be both aware of cardinals and capable of distinguishing them from other birds. Without the concept, the passing cardinal goes undetected. To acquire the concept of cardinal is to become sensitive to some features in birds; the concept gives those features importance. Because importance makes intuitions speak, it makes us able to respond to incitements. What concepts do in terms of mediation, however, is in fact the job of determining what is of importance. Whitehead remarks that '[b]abies and animals', which do not deal in concepts, 'are concerned with their wants as projected against the general environment'.[34] Further, non-conceptual animals find different ways to operate receptivity because they find other ways to attend to importance. It is importance in general and not its conceptual instance that ultimately provides content to sense experience.

Whitehead takes perception to be everywhere. Each actual entity both perceives *and* is perceived by several others. He postulated the connection between each entity and the rest in terms of what he called *prehension*. Prehensions can be negative or positive; while a negative one is 'the definite exclusion of [. . . an] item from positive contribution to the subject's own real internal contribution',[35] a positive one is a feeling acquired through perception. Hence, what ties actual entities to each other are feelings and exclusions. A prehension is always marked by a change in the prehending actual entity. Every event is prehended, and furthermore, there can be no event that is not prehended somewhere. The very notion of event is tied to perception – ultimately, events are perceived events.

Whitehead distinguished conceptual prehension as one kind of prehension among others.[36] Concepts provide one kind of mediation – one kind of measure of importance and one kind of prehension – among several others. As this type of prehension is in an interplay with others, perception is not shaped solely by concepts. It is rather that when conceptual feelings are available, they play a role in the overall ecology of receptivity. Due to his extended notion of experience that includes bodily perception as much as what is channelled by sensorial organs, Whitehead believes that even among concept-mongers, receptivity is shaped by other articulation operators – we do not respond only with our concepts, but with all the modulators at the gates of all of our bodily sensors. The interplay between different kinds of prehension and different modulators and senses of importance provides a richer picture of the endeavour of hospitality in perception. In particular, Whitehead describes the operations of *aversion* and *adversion*. These take place when physical and conceptual feelings are present. In aversion, the concept attenuates or eliminates what is physically felt, while in adversion the concept enhances the intensity of a physical feeling.[37] Both operations act to produce new states of affairs. So, for example, when I recognise a leaf as coming from an oak tree, I avert to attenuate the straight lines and sharp angles I physically feel and advert to emphasise the curves that are otherwise only barely distinguishable. It is through operations of this sort that receptivity engages mediation – and concepts are just one case among others. Perception takes place through an assembling of various, sometimes conflicting capacities. The outcome is, in general, unpredictable.

In Whitehead's picture, awareness is not a necessary condition for perception. Although concentrated attention is required in the form of recognising what is important, this is not necessarily done through awareness – neither a tick nor a frog is aware of what it perceives and what it does not. Furthermore, Whitehead was adamant in expanding experience beyond the acquisition of sensorial input.[38] The body as a whole is experiencing when it ages, sickens, falls in love or gets tired. Partly as a consequence of bodily changes, no agent of receptivity holds to a fixed sense of importance: an ageing animal preys on different stock, a well-trained driver is better at spotting dangerous road situations. Apart from changes in the body, there are other ways to affect what is important. Whitehead finds *lures for feeling* in propositions, theories, concepts, narratives. A lure for feeling affects what is important and makes what was previously unfelt available for perception.[39] After an accusation, the accused is perceived with different eyes; an ornithological theory enables distinctions that were previously unperceived; a concept such as 'mansplaining' ensures that masculine self-assurance is audible; a narrative of the details of how white people captured slaves in Africa brings racism to the fore. All these things are capable of changing what is important – much like aversion and adversion, they call attention to what was previously unnoticed and attenuate what was previously salient. If importance is changeable, a transcendental condition for sensibility, it is not fixed once and for all but rewired according to what takes place in the history of a perceiving actual entity and its surroundings.[40]

Whitehead postulates perception both as response and as creation. It responds, according to what matters, to the surroundings while it creates both a specific way to register what is perceived and an event associated with the perception. There is a spontaneity not only triggered by receptivity but also required by it – like the law of hospitality urging the host to go beyond the established practices of welcoming. The idea of a lure for feelings shows that incitement by experience can change what is deemed important. Importance is also shaped by curiosity and tenderness – an openness to what is outside, an attention to calls. From an indexicalist point of view, importance draws the borders of an interiority by shaping deictic operators. It determines what is the same and what is other, what is close and what is far, what is different and what is indifferent. From the point of view of receptivity as hospitality, the power of importance to draw these borders makes clear that the perceiver is not a full presence, for it is vulnerable to what matters outside. The others speak to the perceiver's sense of importance but can also interrupt it. This is what the notion of lure for feelings enables – a modification of the sense of importance.

The metaphysics of the others extends these capacities to modify what is important to anything outer that attracts perceptual attention. To have sensoria open to the world is to be vulnerable to incitements and to lures. Perception is where I am hostage to the others. Perception involves pleas for responses. Any other, because it is an other, can attract my attention and be a lure for feelings

– can promote, for example, curiosity or tenderness. This is what Lawrence's snake, Coetzee's pregnant stray cat and Lispector's cockroach mentioned in Chapter 2 all do, with differing degrees of intensity. Sensibility is an open door for interruption – and if interruption paves the way for hospitality, it triggers the need to respond finitely to an infinite demand. Receptivity enforces the law of hospitality, the one that both respects the procedures of hospitality and transgresses them.[41] Interruption through sensibility can change everything inside the perceiver – spontaneity is at the service of infinite receptivity in the same way that Levinas emphasised that freedom follows from infinite responsibility.

Just as responding to what is asked is an exercise in freedom, perception involves acts of spontaneity driven by sensorial attention.[42] Furthermore, the plea for conceptual capacities not to be deployed and for the perceived other not to be turned into a concept – *you can conceptualise me but please don't* – is what makes perception supplementary: the act of perception is never complete, never captures the full presence of the other. Sensibility deals in incitements and responses – the deliveries from the senses are no more than traces of the others. To receive these incitements is to provide a finite response to an infinite demand. (Whitehead's account of the ubiquitous nature of perception accommodates the elusiveness of what is perceived by claiming that the same actual entity could be prehended in different ways by different subjects – there are indefinitely many prehensions because perception entails creation.)

## Perceiving is Responding

Whitehead takes importance to be key to the way receptivity relates to coordination. To apprehend anything – as much as to prehend anything – one needs to connect it with something else. The idea that a fact can be apprehended on its own, in isolation and without being articulated in a network of facts, is, for Whitehead, mistaken. The idea that isolated facts can make sense, let alone be perceived, is a myth. 'A single fact in isolation is the primary myth', he writes. 'This mythological character arises because there is no such fact. Connectedness is of the essence of all things of all types.'[43] A single fact is no fact; if we consider events, it is even clearer: events take place only with respect to points of reference grounded in other events. The metaphysical connectedness of things – which can be thought of in terms of the standing location of whatever exists – entails that nothing is accessible in isolation. To perceive is to coordinate; it is to integrate what is apprehended with what is already assimilated. Perception is assimilation, and because it depends on what has already been perceived, it is always a unique and creative action. In perception, a standing location matters precisely because it is instrumental in articulation. 'Abstraction from connectedness involves the omission of an essential factor in the fact considered', Whitehead writes. 'No fact is merely itself [. . .] It follows that in every consideration of a single fact there is the suppressed presupposition of the environmental co-ordination requisite for its existence.'[44] All perceivers must make this suppressed presupposition. To a great extent, receptivity requires previous receptivity; the conditions of possibility for perception are that something has already been perceived.

The myth of the isolated fact is close to the myth of the Given. In fact, the former is perhaps a generalisation of the latter. Whitehead's myth teaches that no item that is not coordinated can be delivered by the senses; no ready-made, isolated fact independent of any effort of articulation can be delivered by the senses. The message is that intuitions without coordination are blind (or mute). Or rather that it is only through articulation that senses can deliver – there is no separation between the deliveries by the senses and the environmental coordination. Sensibility requires a sense of importance and modulators therein, without which there is no coordination of what can be perceived with what has already been experienced. Receptivity requires coordination, and this is one of the things concepts do – they coordinate the newly seen with what is already known or assumed. They bring with them a matrix of differences and indifferences that determine which features one should pay attention to when spotting a cardinal, and which features are irrelevant. Concepts coordinate by modulating importance. The drive to assimilate engages concepts to turn sensible intuitions into conceptually formulated propositions for thinking. The myth of the Given is the assumption that intuitions can provide thought content without the help of concepts because predications of the form '$x$ is red' are already present in having sensations. In other words, there is no need for concepts to articulate the content of what is delivered by the senses – receptivity dispenses with concepts. Rejecting the Given amounts to claiming that concepts are the primary way to coordinate what is perceived with what provides content to sensibility. The need for coordination in perception then becomes the need for concepts.

The rejection of the myth of the Given acquires a different purchase when it is combined with the rejection of the broader myth of the isolated fact. Conceptual articulation – the idea that only through the deployment of conceptual capacities can experience constitute a tribunal – is not the only way to provide coordination and therefore to make perception possible. As we will see, concepts are not the only coordinators, and receptivity can take place among entities that are not concept-mongers. Moreover, conceptual assimilation could violate the alterity of the other perceived – the alterity that asks not to be turned into a concept. Concepts can instead be mobilised in the context of responding to an incitement – they are tools that can be used to respond to perceived appeals like those of the snake, the stray pregnant cat or the cockroach.

Responding in itself is a way to articulate. The myth of the isolated fact shows that receptivity is not the capture of a (self-sufficient, fully present) content. There is no non-articulated content – an isolated fact cannot be perceived because it cannot be assimilated. Perception articulates by giving specific responses to specific demands; responses make use of everything available to the perceiver, including concepts. Sensibility, from the point of view of the metaphysics of the others, is a way to receive demands in the form of incitements and to respond to them – to a large extent, the complexities of receptivity mimic the intricacies of responsibility. The gist of the metaphysics of the others in which perception is the very place where the others are met is that the senses bring us others, and therefore infinite responsibility. Perception doesn't stop short of the encounter with a transcending Other.

An episode of perception is never a one-off; it is always enmeshed in previous, concomitant perceptions and associated with the experiences that produce expectations. Habituation is an operation in sensibility and, as Whitehead points out, an important ingredient in experience.[45] Sensibility is also always charged with affective tones that prepare for each exercise of receptivity: surprise, anxiety, tiredness and perplexity are some of these affective tones, shaped by importance and guiding coordination. Receptivity, like hospitality, is about responding to what is asked, which is often conflicting and often requires ways to resettle what has already been accommodated. Coordination is also an operation of hospitality. It is where experience in the sense in which

Levinas describes responding to the Other meets experience in the way Whitehead describes prehensions. Indeed, coordination in perception is where sensibility resembles the free acts we ought to perform when infinite responsibility is at stake.

The call of the Other takes place in sensibility because this is where ordinary dealings with the others take place. The others appear to my senses, and it is through them that they can interrupt the course of my action and the flow of my thought. This openness to interruption is what makes receptivity what it is: like a doorstep on which guests appear, receptivity is what makes thought hinge on the others. Perception makes my thinking hostage to what comes from outside. To be sure, a great amount of my activity in sensibility is ordinary application of usual concepts – an effort to vindicate my expectations. The singular call of an other in perception more often than not goes unnoticed. But then again, at least for most people and in most circumstances, encountering the human other is not much more than an effort to vindicate expectations. Levinas's remarks concerning the sanctity of the Other – a transcendence that places the Other as prior – can nevertheless be equally applied to every exercise of receptivity. This is how the metaphysics of the others extends the transcendence of infinite responsibility beyond the realm of human faces. Receptivity – the moment of hospitality in thinking – is what transcends spontaneity and makes it transcendentally possible as a free activity. As soon as spontaneity is in action, it meets its responsibility towards the others whom sensibility continuously makes apparent. Spontaneity is tied to receptivity because it is shaped by responsibility.

Levinas, in his *Totality and Infinity*, draws a distinction between the fruition of what is outer through sensibility and the metaphysical desire for the Other that comes from sensing a face. The distinction there grounds his dichotomy between refuting and contesting. From the point of view of the metaphysics of the others, there could be a phenomenological distinction between, say, fruition through the senses and interruption through them. But fruition and interruption do not belong to separate spheres of sensibility – they do not command two different faculties of receptivity or two separate realms concerning responsibility. There are others that refuse me and others that contest me; there is nevertheless no principled way to distinguish between them – I have to manage with my freedom and my spontaneity the infinite responsibilities that arrive at the shores of my senses. From this point of view, the distinction between fruition and interruption is not established in any form before the experience; that is, it is not shaped before the others demand or incite a response. The others all appear to my senses as invoking an infinite responsibility. As we saw earlier, the metaphysics of the others constitutes a form of process philosophy moved by others – nothing in the others that interrupt a nexus provides an excuse to treat them as providing no more than fruition. No other comes with a mark displaying whether they can contest me or refuse me. The others require responses that can take the form of any reshuffling once in perception. I am hostage to whatever my senses bring to me – which perhaps amounts to saying that no guest comes with fixed, separate quarters and a key of her own.

The metaphysics of the others pictures perception as an effort to do justice to the others. Receptivity is to attend to an external interruption within one's internal space and resources. As such, it is an exercise in responsibility – an exercise in responding. It has no constraints other than the ones provided by the situation at hand; responsibility requires freedom to act. Perceiving the other is perceiving in infinity; so the apprehension of an other through a concept, for instance, is a decision that follows an interruption which brings about an infinite responsibility. Each intuition comes with an interruption, an infinite demand that is never fully responded to nor met. Yet the deliveries of the senses prompt responses – the incitements are not captured in isolation but only within exercises of receptivity. The responses are themselves not fully present but are traces to be supplemented by further perceptions, further demands, further appeals. As a result, the emerging image is one in which, rather than an exercise in extracting the intelligibility behind what is experienced, perception is the ground for justice towards the others.

Receptivity is about working out verdicts. As a consequence, perceptual experience is itself a tribunal: not one conducted by getting ready-made verdicts through the senses, but one in which a plea for justice comes from the deliveries by the senses, which themselves respond by mobilising whatever is there to be coordinated. However, an episode of receptivity is a personal tribunal more like the efforts to do justice to what we hear in a conversation than like the endeavours of institutionalised juridical bodies. To a great extent, the decisions made in perception prompted by the others that are prompting interruptions can be scrutinised in a public language – but the decisions concerning receptivity are personal. If we stick to the idea that sensorial apparatuses have a functioning of their own, they cannot be put in place without a drive. The drive is our personal choice that results from the spontaneity that is entangled in our faculty of receptivity.

The metaphysics of the others therefore inverts a standard metaphysical order that places perception at the service of intelligibility. In this usual order, the senses are employed to grasp intelligence. In the inverted order, the senses drive thinking. In a strange way, this inverted order perhaps moves in the direction of Heidegger's remark that reason, glorified for centuries, is in fact an obstinate adversary of thinking.[46] If by *reason* we understand the effort to extract intelligibility from what our senses make available, and we associate thinking with the effort to do justice to what appeals to me, the autonomy of perception could be a way to emancipate thinking from the imperatives of reason. The imperative to extract the intelligibility of things has been a burden on the way we attempt to make plain what is at work in perception. Receptivity has to come to terms with how rationales are to be found in what we inspect. Instead of bringing us near to the Great Outdoors, perception has been considered in terms that explain its role in the project of elaborating a total view of what is available to the senses. In contrast, freed from the burden of making things intelligible in a total view, perception can be considered in the broader light of how to do justice to incitements.

## Metaphysical Empiricism

The metaphysics of the others takes experience as the meeting point with the others. In this sense, it places experience ahead of any general epistemological project concerning the extraction of the intelligibility of events, things and processes, and ahead of (theologico-)political projects concerning how to deal with any other. It draws therefore on the idea of a general, broad empiricism that is fully open to pre-predicative episodes of perception. Levinas attributes to Wahl a new empiricism that gives full priority to feelings and the intricacies of sentiment.[47] Levinas welcomes this empiricism because it is not tied to the production of empirical judgements. Wahlian empiricism is a missing link between Levinas and Whitehead – it is a commitment to a general framework of experience that gives priority to an open drawing board integrating both theories and pure sensations that Wahl draws both from his understanding of phenomenology and his contact with Whitehead.[48]

This metaphysical empiricism is also a missing link between Levinas and Deleuze, both students of Wahl. Deleuze describes his empiricism in terms of Whitehead's notion of experience – empiricism for Deleuze entails pluralism, the twin claims that 1) the abstract needs explanation (it is never the ultimate *explanans*) and 2) novelty is a major constituent to be accommodated in a sound conception of reality.[49] These claims help invert the metaphysical order in which the purpose of extracting intelligence precedes the perception and guides it. Rather, it is the repetition of singularities that gives the impression that there are unities towards which experience converges, and that recalcitrant differences would ultimately disappear. Deleuze sees expectations from Hume's point of view, according to which they change not what repeats, but what contemplates repetition. Because repetition is always the redoing of something in (at least slightly) different circumstances, it is made of differences and acts as a platform that makes further difference possible.[50] A message conveyed repeatedly through different media ends up modified – as illustrated in the game of 'Chinese Whispers' (or 'Telephone', as it is commonly known in the United States). The extraction of intelligence from processes, events and things can then be described simply as further repetition (in a different medium) and not as a privileged instance that condenses any other in the abstract once and for all. Hume despairs of induction because he finds this insurmountable gap between particular and repeated observations and universal conclusions. Hume's problem of induction is read by Deleuze as an awareness that no amount of repetition pre-empts difference. Difference is precisely what makes experience indispensable – the insufficiency of induction is only a problem within a metaphysical framework in which experience is subsidiary to an abstract state of affairs. If experience is not a tool to extract intelligence but rather an irreducible ingredient of what is concrete, repetitions are no more revealing than difference.

Despite his distance from Hume's account of experience – and of matters of fact – Whitehead also takes perception to precede any abstraction. Indeed, for him, because experience is an ingredient of reality, epistemic states are not only found among conceptmongers but elsewhere as well. Epistemology is therefore to be conceived of as a chapter of general metaphysics, the one that deals with the ubiquitous connections between actualities where affects and effects play a central role. Epistemology is chiefly concerned with experience, which is what brings things together; since every connection is through prehensions, it carries a considerable metaphysical import. Metaphysical empiricism is a claim about experience in reality – it is not a thesis about (our) access to it. Our access is an example of how experience is in play. It is not only our ignorance that can be remedied with an appeal to experience but also any insufficiency, any absence of ready-mades, any incompleteness. Wherever there is room for supplement, there is room for experience.

It then becomes inviting to couple metaphysical empiricism with the idea that there is always room for supplement and nothing is complete or fully present. This incompleteness – which is not a lack, but rather that room for supplementation – drives a relation with the others, a capacity to be affected which I understood above as the *Sophist*'s *dynamis koinonias*. It is a drive towards the Outdoors, towards the others. This drive is what makes perception matter: it is through perception that the others can affect me and supplementation can take place. This drive is where Levinas finds the metaphysical desire for the Other – which he contrasts with fruition – and the guiding obsession with the Other – which orients proximity.[51] In both cases, there is an attraction to the Other that guides my subjectivity. The possibility of supplement does not result in indifference; there is an attraction towards the outer that eventually prevails over the efforts of self-protection. In his letters from Muzot, Rilke writes about how nature fails to protect its creatures but instead exposes them to risk, just like our nature does.[52] According to the metaphysics of the others, perception is what makes one vulnerable to the others – it is through the interruptions provided by the senses that supplement is brought in.

## Pan-perceptualism

Whitehead's metaphysical pan-perceptualism, according to which existents are connected through perception, envisages perceptual experience as beyond both what has conceptual capacities and what can explicitly formulate empirical judgements. There is more to what is accessed through perception than what commands awareness, and as we saw above, there are also non-conceptual prehensions. The metaphysics of the others endorses the idea that traces of the others do not depend on a conceptual capacity to interrupt. Coordination is enough for the senses to respond to what draws them. Further, the metaphysics of the others welcomes the pan-perceptualist idea that perception is everywhere – that it is through perception, a *dynamis koinonias*, that what exists interacts. Certainly, if pan-perceptualism is a total theory, indexicalism and the metaphysics of the others can only accept it with a paradoxical grain of salt. Still, it is in this direction that a metaphysics of the others would tend.

The limitation of perception to existents endowed with concepts is difficult to defend. McDowell himself attempts to rescue Sellars (and most Kantian approaches) from the charge that non-rational animals cannot have perceptual knowledge by saying that the myth of the Given has to do with knowledge of a certain sort.[53] In this light, it could be inferred from this concentration on a special sort of knowledge (and perception) that non-rational beings can enjoy the Given – because there is no involvement of conceptual capacities in the deliveries by their senses – without falling into the myth. It seems that they have a special dispensation from the problems of appealing to a myth because, after all, they are not rational. According to this picture, for example, animals perform no act of receptivity, but are merely saddled (or inculcated, or infused) with complete messages from outside. Then they are able to receive something (or be given something) that rational beings cannot receive – rational beings are obliged to perform some action in order to make contact with what comes from outside, while creatures that cannot deal in concepts make this contact free of charge. Perhaps because they are beasts, they enjoy a natural excuse. But we cannot appeal to such an excuse, not even occasionally, once we are endowed with the capacity for conceptual receptivity.

The problem with this way of understanding the special character of rational (and conceptual) receptivity is that it entails that any other receptivity is no more than a seeming receptivity, and that we talk about the perceptual experience of non-rational beings as an exercise of courtesy. The internal elements – purportedly constituted by conceptual capacities in play in the space of reasons – are crucial in explaining rational dealings with the other things (through perception), but are non-starters as far as other, non-rational beings are concerned. It is precisely this restriction of receptivity to concept-mongering animals that the metaphysics of (any) others intends to exorcise (or overcome).

McDowell, however, does not want to go quite this far. He wants to insist that there is perception beyond the bounds of conceptual abilities. He closes his *Perception as a Capacity for Knowledge* by saying that '[p]erception as an operation of rationality is our distinctive species of something that is generically animal'.[54] He wants to defend the *sui generis* character of perception as an operation of concepts precisely because it allows reasons for one's perceptual judgement. Conceptual capacities enable one to state that things are thus and so because one perceives things as being thus and so. McDowell seems to believe that this approach cannot generalise to all sorts of perception, as he wants to make room for genuine perception in non-conceptual beings. He concentrates on something more restricted than perception in general, seeing perception as a genus, and perception specifically as an operation of rationality as a species within that genus. He writes that if 'our concern is with a species, we do not have to restrict ourselves to things that are true of all instances of the genus of which it is a species'.[55] He reckons his overall characterisation of rational perception has no purchase concerning perception in general – there are no lessons about perception in general to be drawn from examining how concept-endowed entities go about it.[56] McDowell says little about the possible conclusions one can draw from the species of perception he focuses on as to the genus of perception in general.[57]

The metaphysics of perception would rather take receptivity to range beyond concepts. In any case, receptivity is an action prompted by an offer within the scope of one's sensibility. The idea of an offer presupposes a reception in the sense that it cannot be an offer if there is nothing to receive it.[58] The senses, engaged in receptivity, are somehow addressed by an incitement that comes with a demand for an answer. Conceptual receptivity modelled in terms of capacities at play in the senses is an example of the broader hospitality that the senses are urged to perform. As an attempt to do justice to the others, receptivity has no fixed articulation; it is a genuine action filled with spontaneity. If deliveries by the senses are connected by a natural law to a state of affairs either in the outer world or in the inner physiology of the perceiver, there cannot be anything but an excuse from responsibility. To use the image from Derrida discussed in the last chapter, in this case there would be no law of hospitality beyond the appropriate laws of hospitality.[59] There would be no free response to what is outside. This is equally true if a perceptual state is generated by chance. The only way out of excuses is if there is agency in receptivity. This is why we can think of the perceptual senses as doors, the agency of receptivity as hospitality and the others that incite or appeal as knocking at the door.

The hospitality of perception is an affair of traces and supplements. Davidson was adamant in rejecting what he labelled the third dogma of empiricism – which is equivalent to Sellars's myth of the Given in the sense that much of traditional empiricism seems to hinge on it – according to which there is a dualism between conceptual scheme and empirical content. The broader lesson to be learned from this rejection is that there is no way to separate the content of empirical incitements and modulated responses. Or rather, the spontaneity–empirical message of dualism is to be exorcised. Spontaneity is to be thought of in terms of any resource available to the perceiver for the action of receptivity. It cannot be separated from the incitements that prompt responses; each purported empirical message is itself presented in terms of a content only because receptivity has already been at play. It is through spontaneity that different coordinations provide an empirical message to the impact of the outside on the senses. There is no way to specify the empirical content contacted by the senses without the resources of receptivity – which is entangled with spontaneity. This can be understood as a consequence of the impossibility of eliminating the saying by focusing on the said: that is, as a consequence of Levinas's claims about the saying as indispensable and irreducible to the said. Through the saying, the trace of the Other offers an engagement. The others appear to the senses as traces that command an infinite responsibility while always being short of full presences. The senses perceive the others, but the content of this perception cannot be expressed without considering the whole process of receptivity. In receptivity, passivity stands only in being exposed to the traces of the others. The only possible way to make explicit what is provided by such intuition is in terms of something towards which perception is called to do justice. The incitement is then received by the responses perception provides in its effort to do justice to what carried out the interruption.

Receptivity in the metaphysics of the others is close to the (Lockean) idea of indirect perception – also in contrast to what is recommended by McDowell (and Travis).[60] The object of perception is never perceived directly but only through the efforts of responding to incitements. The object of perception guides the receptivity process by making spontaneity be deployed in the effort to respond to incitements. But in perception, the object is never fully present; the others are perceived only indirectly and only in traces, retaining their infinite character while provoking the movement of receptivity. Receptivity is the place of transcendence. The interiority is open to what transcends it through perception, which is what makes receptivity possible; however, without the capacity to respond, nothing can be received. Both the others indirectly perceived and the mediators in spontaneity capable of responding, which are imbricated, are required in receptivity.

Whitehead also adopts an indirect-perception view modelled on Locke. His *res vera*, indirectly perceived, guides prehensions without being present in experience. He models the interior of actual entities on a Cartesian conception of subjectivity, where an image of what is perceived is created and it is only through that image – which he calls the *subjective form* – that the perceived object comes into view. Just as in Locke, perception works through proxies. Whitehead conceives of subjectivity as shaped by prehensions; in a sense, he clearly advocates that the outdoors is responsible for everything in an actual entity. Prehensions are described by Whitehead as incomplete actual entities, since there is nothing to the subjectivity of an actual entity other than prehensions.[61] The efforts of receptivity constitute each actual entity. While receptivity itself is not conceived in the way favoured by the metaphysics of the others – for there is no supplementation, no interruption and no responses to incitements – the role of receptivity in the economy of subjectivity is similar in both positions. Receptivity is how a subjectivity is built from outdoors.

Whitehead's pan-perceptualism thus assigns a remarkable metaphysical role to experience which is, for Whitehead, broader than the activity of the sensorial organs. His conception of experience involves every bodily element; he claims that 'the derivation of emotion from the body is among our fundamental experiences'.[62] Further, he admits no distinction between the interior of an actual entity and its receptivity apparatus. Everything is engaged in receptivity; interiority is readiness for experience.[63] The senses offer a fragment of a much more complex, nuanced and continuous stream of experience that involves every element of an entity's life; he suggests that the analysis of experience based on the senses 'is analogous to the endeavor to elucidate the sociology of modern civilization as wholly derivative from the traffic signals on the main roads'.[64] In fact, it is on the basis of his broad notion of experience, where everything that happens to an entity is an experience, that he grounds his metaphysics of perceivers. For Whitehead, the body is where experience takes place and is a 'society of functionings within the universal society of the world'.[65] He suggests that bodily experiences offer a basis from which to conceive the world as some sort of society of experiences.

Whitehead holds that perception involves experience in the present time and is the basic ingredient of any actual event. Since prehensions are taken to be what affects the prehending entity, he conceives efficient causation in terms of perceptual experience. Causal effects are thought of in terms of affects. Whitehead distinguishes two basic modes of perception. One is that of *presentational immediacy*, where a portion of what is present comes into view.[66] The other is *efficient causation* itself – the effect of a causation that is itself receptivity. It is an indistinct form of perception, as even 'the detailed geometrical relationships are, for the most part, incurably vague'.[67] Efficient causation cannot present something to view; it is just as much about receiving something from outside as the other modes of perception are. In fact, Whitehead's account of causation as perception shows a relevant feature of his metaphysics of perception: there is no need for anything but experience. For Whitehead, it is a mistake to postulate an underlying metaphysical structure to the exercise of receptivity – no substances, no states of affairs, no causal connections, just entities and their perceptual experiences. To suffer the effect of anything is already receptivity. He holds that to be affected is to perceive, and therefore finds no good reason to separate the effect of a cause and the perception of it.

Pan-perceptualism is, accordingly, a claim about the coincidence between the concrete and the sensible. The concrete is made out of an assemblage of sensibilities – it is at a crossroads of different sensibilia. The difference between perceivers of different types – between the birdwatcher who entertains the concept of cardinal, the tick capable of spotting mammals and indifferent to whether the mammal is a pig or a human, and the red billiard ball – is that they operate receptivity differently. The billiard ball arguably operates with less diverse modulators than the tick and the birdwatcher, who exhibit a greater degree of flexibility in receptivity. These are differences in the capacity to feel – differences in sensibilia – no less than differences in capacity to intensify and attenuate experience by being susceptible to lures.

The metaphysics of the others is at odds with pan-perceptualism. On the one hand, the metaphysics of the others is grounded in the indexicalist priority of the exterior. Exteriority is then conceived in terms of receptivity: the others interrupt through sensibility. If it is the case that in my vulnerability to the others, obsession and metaphysical desire for them can be found in perception, it seems a sound speculative move to postulate that sensibility is what brings the others to any interiority. Such a move will make receptivity ubiquitous, and as a consequence will make exteriority a constitutive furniture of the universe.

On the other hand, the speculative move projects my known receptivity to the rest of the others – it assumes they have receptivity. This is the point where perhaps we can best contemplate the result of a paradoxico-metaphysics. It is also where we contemplate a sophisticated ontologist landscape. Indexicalism brings deixis to the fore as constitutive of reality. A total theory of exteriority, even one committed to deixis, is still a total theory. As such, it should not be interruption-proof – speculation, and the totality it achieves by projecting the same on to the other, is itself open to interruption. The metaphysics of the others holds that interruption precedes speculation in the same way as, in Levinas's terms, metaphysics precedes ontology. The speculative move is itself hostage to the others. The paradoxical totality that ensues is again a landscape of horizons: it includes transcendent elements and itself does not preclude transcendence. The paradoxico-metaphysics of the others illustrates interrupted speculation because it is built on a thorough orientation towards exteriority. It is guided by the priority of the others and by the challenge of Tsing's injunction. Yet it is paradoxical; and it is so also in the sense that it is not complete and envisages no completion. The metaphysics of the others is itself to be placed within an exterior border – a horizon – that determines its vulnerability.

### Proximity, Conversation and Experience

Receptivity is connected to proximity. Proximity alone does not provoke receptivity – perception deploys a sense of importance, modulators, operations without which nothing is felt. An interiority is endowed with a capacity for receptivity because it is in relations of proximity. It is situated, not in the sense of lying in a place on the map viewed from nowhere, but rather in the sense that it has acquired a proximity in its history of attending to incitements. In Levinas's analysis, proximity is what enables recurrence and substitution: I act for the Other who is close. Proximity comes from my sense of orientation. The nearby outer is what makes me positioned and situated where I am. It is the Other that affects my sensibility, the call that interrupts me and makes me respond. Proximity does not come from any substantive description of my position; it is defined by what can knock at my door. This is why proximity engenders further proximity. In addition, as Levinas insists, proximity is anarchic. It is not ruled by anything that has not been sanctioned by receptivity. It is indifferent to family relations, to convergence of interests, to orders and to geographies. This is another unruly element affecting receptivity – together with the spontaneity that endows the perceiver with agency. There are others that go unnoticed. As with the spontaneity entangled in receptivity, proximity affects receptivity because of infinite responsibility. Infinity precedes any attempted totality, and this is why proximity is crucial. Proximity, anarchic and therefore never reducible to anything else, is what determines the pressure of what is asked and the urgency of a response. Proximity also changes with time – just as a lure for feeling can affect perception, several different features in experience can alter proximity, from sharing addresses and seasons to knowledge of biographies and histories. Proximity is a condition of possibility for receptivity; it is also what brings infinity to the border of an interiority. The exteriority of the Great Outdoors is mediated by proximity, which itself never stops short of infinity. Anything can be in the proximity and anything can be asked. That proximity is affected by receptivity shows that, as with Whitehead's lure for feelings, the transcendental is not indifferent to the empirical.[68]

It is only with respect to what is in my proximity that I determine my actions and my engagements – as Levinas claims, proximity is what orients substitution and recurrence. Proximity is what situates me. It contrasts with universality: while commitments to the universal are blind with respect to what is of importance for me, commitments to the proximal are precisely oriented towards what I care about. Universal talk is committed to a totality, to

The Hospitality of Perception    169

substantive descriptions, to the impersonal. Proximal talk, in contrast, brings in exteriority, indexicality and personal engagement. There is no universal love, no universal trust, no universal taste – a history of proximity in its anarchic character can never be fully exorcised. The metaphysics of the others adds that similarly there is no universal thinking, no universal experience, and crucially, no universal reality. Proximity once more makes clear the paradoxical character of the metaphysics of the others: it posits situated reality and its task is to give a maximally general account of a proximal reality never fully amenable to universalisation. Proximity brings in the Great Outdoors, not by attempting to encompass it, but rather by being vulnerable to it. This is exactly why proximity has to be anarchic; it has to be open to exteriority.[69] Proximity and receptivity are tied together in that together they promote interruption. The metaphysics of the others conceives of experience not as resulting in a report or judgement, but rather in a response that is indistinguishable from the appeal that triggered the senses. The response is both a consequence and a shifter of proximity. The anarchic character of proximity, as much as freedom or spontaneity, follows from infinite responsibility.[70]

As a consequence, proximity is no mere habituation. This is why perception is central here – I perceive what calls my attention either by its effects on me or by the appeal I notice. Perception makes interruption possible. More than habituation, engagement is its mark. An interruption takes place when an engagement is called for – a knock on the door. Proximity is hardly determined by fixed borders; it is drawn by deixis. In this sense as well, proximity contrasts with universality just as substantives contrast with indexicals. Like the focusing of our eyes, it is prompted by what the eyes themselves deliver, and shifts between landscapes of expected images and interrupting salient features. Accordingly, previous observations are revised, reconsidered, placed in different contexts.

Proximity, interruption and the embedded urge to respond brought about by reception itself make perception something close to a conversation. Perception is an exchange of interruptions and responses – heteronomous when the Great Outdoors interrupts, autonomous when a response is given. Infinite responsibility guides not only autonomy and proximity but also the ongoing nature of the perceptual conversation. There is no final report that ends the inquiry, precisely because exteriority precedes totality –

and the Great Outdoors is not a big loft attached to the house. The metaphysics of the others makes perception an ongoing, plural, unruly conversation that can be interrupted but never brought to a close. Its metaphysical character is indeed that of conversation and not of report – of treaty more than treatise.

Rather than a single act of being presented with something, perception is a sequence of responses to the different others that appear on the horizon. Like a conversation, it cannot be understood without reference to its history. This is another mis-giving of the mythical Given: it portrays the deliveries by the senses as atomic, non-inferential pieces of data. A content is received in a flash. This problem does not fully disappear when McDowell pictures receptivity in terms of a passive exercise of conceptual capacities or in terms of sensible *Anschauungen* brought to the fore as snapshots. Here again, we see how the myth of the Given is an instance of the broader myth of the isolated fact, and that exorcising the former may not amount to dispelling the latter. There are no isolated facts, not even as contents of perceptual episodes: perception involves proximity, interruption, responses and the history of what has already been perceived. Concepts are part of the ongoing conversation as much as demands and responses are. The image of perception as a conversation models receptivity on the complexities of hospitality where, say, intuitions and concepts exist in a multilayered interplay in which senses are like an *agora* where multiple voices can be heard speaking. Senses are more like a negotiating chamber than a *camera obscura*, more like a gathering than a border control. If the senses speak, then they speak in a conversation – not like the words of a report, but like the talk of guests and hosts.

Perception is a conversation following appeals from the others. It is oriented by the tension between accommodating concepts and the Great Outdoors, in the sense of what is requested by the perceived – *you can conceptualise me but please don't*. The demand expresses the unbound nature of perception; it is an openness to exteriority. The demand of the perceived is perhaps a law of receptivity that, like Derrida's law of hospitality, enables and transgresses the laws of hospitality; such a law of receptivity orients the practices of coordination that constitute perception. The law of receptivity sets in place a conversation. In this sense, perception is a friction and hostility can be as much a response as sanctity, as Levinas terms the giving of wholehearted welcome. The demand haunts the deliveries by the senses – it is the very mark of the obsession or the metaphysical desire for the Great Outdoors. Exteriority is not only a condition, but an orientation in the subjective life of an interiority, a life that takes place within horizons and is animated by a will to transcend. This orientation towards transcendence – of which the desire to know is a pale corollary – makes perception (in a broad sense) indispensable to whatever is placed among others. It is not, however, a single-track orientation towards the other that captures attention, curiosity or tenderness – it is rather an environment of responses to multiple others that, guided by the law of receptivity, faces infinite responsibilities. A finite perceiver cannot but continuously update a portfolio of welcoming and hostile responses. Each response is an intervention in the ongoing perceptual conversation.

### Deictic Absolutes

Writing about the weird and the eerie – in contrast with similar notions such as the *Unheimlich* – Mark Fisher notices that the allure they possess

> is not captured by the idea that we 'enjoy what scares us.' It has, rather, to do with a fascination for the outside, for that which lies beyond standard perception, cognition and experience. This fascination usually involves a certain apprehension, perhaps even dread – but it would be wrong to say that the weird and the eerie are necessarily terrifying. I am not here claiming that the outside is always beneficent. There are more than enough terrors to be found there, but such terrors are not all there is to the outside.[71]

A fascination gives us the impulse towards the outdoors: the weird and the eerie are not just the frightening unusual, but what brings a lure for curiosity, a moment of suspension, an opening to what is unknown that eludes speculation. The irruption of the Other also illustrates the priority of perception – the priority of what is said by current perception over the establishment composed by cognitive and affective habits. This is how interruptions shape perceptual conversations. They form no closed, cybernegative circuits – that would resemble a barren totality – but spell an open-ended journey of transcending subjective landscapes. The metaphysics of the others fleshes out the claim that exteriority can never reach an end. Just as hospitality is not always a harmonious scenario, conversations are seldom strategies to build consensus, and what attracts perceptual attention rarely commands full-blown surrender. The extremes of giving up all of one's concepts, agendas and habits when faced with a recalcitrant experience, and of shutting out what is perceived or shelving it in a distant drawer, are not usually adopted. Still, the conversation that informs receptivity involves conflicts that can be insurmountable. These conflicts reveal the political nature of receptivity: the senses form an arena in which demands are accommodated or ignored and claims for justice are either met or dismissed.

Nick Land exposes the political relations of concepts and intuitions, in a picture in which Kant's philosophy appears as that of a colonial enterprise. Land talks about the conceptual apparatus having too strong a purchase on the object. He portrays Kant's project as that of a general colonial scheme for reason where there is no certainty of success, for

> [w]hen confronting the heterogeneity of intuition, reason must engage in a kind of Pascal wager; assuming an intelligible system of nature because it has nothing to lose by not doing so. The submission of the outside in general to the inside in general, or of nature to the idea, i.e. conquest, is not guaranteed by any principle [. . .] the conqueror feels exultation in the attainment of victory, precisely because there was no reason to expect it.[72]

The strategy of colonisation is to decide that the intuitions will submit to concepts come what may – that the upper hand is to be taken as certain. Such a strategy intends to submit exteriority to universality; it is a drive towards totality based on systematically dismissing any force of the law of receptivity. As such, it proceeds to think the thinkable, to conceptualise what is amenable to conceptualisation. Land takes this project to be one that aims to 'expand indefinitely whilst reproducing itself as the same' and to 'touch the other without vulnerability'.[73] The metaphysics of the others is an alternative to this colonial strategy. It rejects the taming of exteriority into totality as much as the exorcism of deixis in substantives. The infinite responsibility brought about by the Great Outdoors makes explicit that unabashed exteriority is in proximity, and perception itself is where it makes demands. In a thoroughly non-correlationist vein, the metaphysics of the others pictures the Great Outdoors as revolting against the strategy of colonisation. Although the metaphysics of the others reaches the absolute only in a deictic, conversational manner, it exposes the Great Outdoors in its explicit exteriority. This exteriority is in fact what is taken to be absolute – not the substantives found outside but the deixis itself.

Beyond countering correlationism and the ontological commitment to an enclosed totality, the metaphysics of the others contrasts with what can be described as a broader project within the history of Western metaphysics. This project is akin to what Land finds in the colonial strategy that responds to a drive for security and control. It is the endeavour to extract the intelligence of objects, processes and events. Heidegger diagnoses this effort to separate the intelligence and the intelligible from the sensible things where they are found as a stage in the unveiling history of nihilism.[74] The history of nihilism is described as the very saga of metaphysics. Heidegger takes metaphysics to have been pursuing the concealed intelligible structure that enables what exists to be what it is – metaphysics intends to capture the causal mechanisms, the substantial connections and the underlying forms that make things what they are. The metaphysical project has been to expose the principles through which things function. It seeks reasons to guide a thought towards uncovering what animates the sensible. The extraction of intelligence turns the sensible into no more than a carcass with instantiated principles that themselves made it what it was. On the other hand, the extracted intelligence is now available, just as the energy of a river is available in the dam or the nutrients of an animal are available in cattle management. The procedure is to capture the intelligence of what appears in perception, to surprise the other in order to seize its secrets. The separation of the sensible from the intelligible gradually generates dispensable sensible things on the one hand and intelligence that can be made artificial on the other. A world where God is dead is described as a world made into resources, with no genuine exteriority. The thrust of Nietzsche's claim that God is dead is that the intelligence of the world has been inherited by different hands that are not necessarily human – the intelligence is artificial, detached and itself a resource. Nihilism is the road towards making things flimsier, paler and less substantial. Once intelligence is rendered artificial, nothing concrete affects the senses as genuinely exterior. Perception is then at the service of completing exteriority to make it a totality.

In his *Einblick in das was ist*, Heidegger depicts the gradual conversion of the world into a *Ge-Stell* – and of things into objects.[75] Instead of letting things unfold and make themselves present of their own accord, *Ge-Stell* makes their availability exposed. Gradually, what was allowed to reveal itself from its concealment becomes something permanently shown and therefore available. The being of things is persecuted in order to force them into displaying themselves. The persecution is the extraction of intelligence; it commands the standing reserve – things made available into objects. Heidegger claims that *Ge-Stell* is what makes *Nähe* impossible; there is no nearness to a reservoir, just a capacity to make use of what it reserves. What is at stake is the development of technology whose essence is *Ge-Stell*. Technology requires intelligence to be extracted, and by doing this it puts in place an era of being that makes metaphysics and science as we know them possible. This endangers being, persecuting it with joint efforts to hunt its intelligence. The hunting leads to a mastery of things that places them in standing reserve. The procedure ousts being from its truth, since *Ge-Stell* replaces the world and guards none of its truths. The epoch Heidegger is portraying is that of a pursuit, one that puts being itself in danger. The pursuit is what triggers most current cognitive efforts – those of attempting to understand the mechanisms of things by conjoining perception and concept handling. It is also what places receptivity at the service of the goal – the others perceived are the others pursued. Recalcitrant experience is therefore either dismissed, or used to fuel a refinement of the intelligence being extracted. Once *Ge-Stell* begins replacing things with objects at its disposal, the road is open to placing things in an accessible standing reserve arranged according to an artificial intelligence. There is no nearness – and in a sense no deixis – but only a cartography indicating where the resources are available. This epoch of being started with the early efforts to understand the *physis* of things and heads towards the transformation of the world into a storage space.

Heidegger provides a broadly accurate picture of what is at stake in the age of extraction of intelligence. His picture is insightful – he points to the relative need of the human to carry the technological movement towards its completion, but in the process the very essence of the human will have to develop an essential relationship with *Ge-Stell*, and therefore make explicit the blind spots and the pitfalls of a blind Prometheanist faith. It is also fertile, as it can be coupled with an analysis of how capitalism is tied both to the history of nihilism and the endeavour to extract intelligence that is guided by the essence of technology. His way to respond to the picture is less clear, and not as insightful or fertile. In the last of his Bremen Lectures, entitled '*Die Kehre*' ('The Turn'), he sets out to hint at a way to move away from the state of affairs he depicts to end the current epoch of being in pursuit. Maybe the shadows of another dispensation of being are here, but we can never know when and how it will come. The danger itself carries its own antidote. His recipe involves forgetting – '[i]n the essence of danger there essences and dwells a grace, namely the grace of the turn of forgetting'[76] – and glancing – 'when the world as guardian of the essence of being makes its entrance, there takes place the flashing entry of world into the unguarding of the thing'.[77] The alternative is to allow things to come in a flash and then return to forgetfulness. (It is interesting to compare the idea of an insight with that of a baroque realism elaborated in Chapter 1 above based on Deleuze's remarks on dissonance.)[78] Instead of cherishing the thesis, Heidegger recommends valuing the insight – not the permanent light but the flash. The insight, he claims, is itself situated in the world. Heidegger seems to suggest a different epistemological regime – one in which instead of extracting the intelligence of things, we have insights about them and among them, insights that are not kept, stored or put at the service of a worldview, but rather forgotten. This is an epistemological regime where thinking is not tied to an archive.

The metaphysics of the others can provide an alternative to the current regime of intelligence extraction. It is perhaps to some degree in line with Heidegger's proposal when he recommends a turn towards situated insights. It is not only more explicit, but also different in motivation. It is driven not by the danger that being is in, but rather by the appeal of the others and the effort to do justice to what is perceived. When we move towards indexicalism, we commit to a situated metaphysics faithful to exteriority. The metaphysics of the others places the Other ahead of any extracted intelligence and therefore perception before reason. Such ongoing paradoxico-metaphysics can never fully extract the intelligence of any process – processes are situated and therefore singular, intelligence relies on silencing some others, and extracting is itself at odds with the law of receptivity that ensures the open-ended character of the Great Outdoors. Perception as a locus of infinite responsibility is less about inspecting than about crafting alliances. The orientation towards the exterior triggers the disruption of agendas and not their consolidation. Only when the law of receptivity is dismissed, and the drive towards exteriority immunised against, can perception issue reports instead of making moves in an unending conversation. An indexical turn that could end the age of pursuit entails a reconstruction of metaphysics that makes it situated, conversational, paradoxical, supplementary and oriented towards the others. Paradox ushers a critique of metaphysics (which is otherwise innocuous to the general metaphysical project) into metaphysics and brings what is exterior to the project to its kernel.

The supplementary nature of perception makes the very project of intelligence extraction ultimately impossible – it can be undertaken, however, as a finite enterprise. The choice between unattainable totality and persisting exteriority is cosmic, but the appeal of the latter comes both from its advantages – concerning the effort to attend to the law of receptivity that seems to make perception crucial for the process of being among others – and from the consequences of the age of pursuit. As an alternative to the epistemological regime of intelligence extraction, the metaphysics of the others favours an epistemology where the others are not instantiations of abstractions, not screens on which an ever-growing Same is projected. Such a regime is perhaps one oriented by concern, by responding to the others and their perceptual demands. Perception becomes central, not as the lobby of a structure of intelligence-processing but as an *agora*, a negotiating table where the diverse others – including the ones that have been perceived before and have shaped memories – find a way to coexist. The multiplicity of others is an ingredient of such a *xenophilic* turn in epistemology. The turn moves away from the efforts at making each perceived other a piece in a totality and towards a genuine mosaic of appeals connected by infinite responsibilities. This is how the others in perception act as supplements – they supplement because they interrupt agendas. Others in perception act by bringing about experience, which puts at risk what was settled. Experience is the very name of alterity, and the Other is precisely the unit of content of a perceptual experience.

Tsing's injunction is met by making explicit why encompassing totalities cannot be interruption-free. This is ultimately the role of perception. Others come and tell a different story, or simply do not fit into what is being told. An epistemological regime in line with the metaphysics of the others is one in which intelligence is reshuffled in an ever-ongoing conversation involving all sorts of interrupters. Instead of extraction of intelligence and extermination of exteriority, the focus is on the management of supplementation through no pre-existing intelligence. When supplementation is what is managed, a reference to what can be or has been complete can only lead astray. In contrast, the injunction points towards the abandonment of totality as a regulative ideal. The metaphysics of the others, an enterprise saddled with perception, takes external borders to be both nearby and in engagement. The exorcism of universality starts in the reversal of a metaphysical order that places deixis at the service of the uncovering of substantives – a metaphysical order that places the saying at the service of the said and perception at the service of intelligence. This reversal guides the metaphysics of the others – a commitment to no absolute substantives; that is, a claim that totality and not the absolute is to be exorcised, since deixis is what is, paradoxically, absolute.

## Notes

1. Kirby, *The Optician of Lampedusa*, pp. 26–8. Kirby's text deals with the experience of an optician sailing in a boat called the *Galata* in the Mediterranean and finding the drowning bodies of refugees all around the boat.
2. Kant, *Critique of Pure Reason*, pp. 65, 93.
3. Kant, *Critique of Pure Reason*, p. 71.
4. This is how Quine formulated the independence of the tribunal of experience; see, for example, Quine, 'Epistemology Naturalized'. Stimuli in nerve endings are part of the integrated presence formed by an organism and its environment. There is little a person can do about her nerve-ending stimuli – she is coerced into accepting the feeling in her body just as when she is overwhelmed by natural forces.
5. When discussing the issue (*Mind and World*, p. 8, footnote), McDowell credits Zvi Cohen with the suggestion that when we transfer agency to what was delivered to our senses, we should speak of 'exculpations' rather than 'excuses'. An exculpation defence in a trial refers to a case in which the deed is admitted but culpability is rejected. In an excuse defence, one is said to have merely done what one was supposed to do. In the latter case, but arguably not in the

former, there is an element of a norm in place – if the deliveries of the senses offer me an excuse, I have received them as I should have, and it is considered that it was *in my power not to do so*. In the former case, the deliveries of the senses act on my thinking and *I cannot help myself*. The choice of excuses or exculpations therefore provides different accounts of the empiricist claim that the content of perceptual experience is to be accepted as it comes: an appeal to exculpations exempts the empirical thinker from any responsibility, since the impingements of the senses are matters of fact, while an appeal to excuses says that the thinker provided the expected or the usual response and therefore cannot be held responsible.

6. McDowell explores this resilience of receptivity evoking the Müller-Lyer illusion (*Mind and World*, p. 11, footnote). It is clear from cases like this that sensibility is independent of thoughts. If one rejects the claim that responses involve no agency, one could argue that even in such cases, what the senses provide is different when we know we are faced with, say, an optical illusion. See Bensusan and Pinedo, 'Minimal Empiricism without Dogmas'.
7. See McDowell, 'The Disjunctive Conception of Experience as Material for a Transcendental Argument', and Pritchard, *Epistemological Disjunctivism*.
8. McDowell, *Mind and World*, p. 11.
9. It clear at this stage that according to this book (and indexicalism), the problem with an (epistemologically) naturalist approach is its underlying metaphysical assumption of a nature devoid of deixis – and therefore bifurcated from perception. Notice that adopting the naturalist stance in the epistemology of perception doesn't necessarily entail a generally naturalistic epistemological outlook. Davidson famously held that perception is to be described in terms of nervous systems, and experience has no epistemological role, while holding an epistemology of how thought responds to the world to be thoroughly non-naturalistic (Davidson, 'A Coherence Theory of Truth and Knowledge', and Davidson, 'Epistemology Externalized').
10. Sellars, *Empiricism and the Philosophy of Mind*.
11. Sellars, *Empiricism and the Philosophy of Mind*, p. 21.
12. Sellars phrases the second and the third theses in terms of acquired and non-acquired abilities. The topic of acquisition is important for him because it ties up the capacity to predicate with an *a priori* knowledge. For my argument, it matters only that abilities alien to sensorial organs are in place so that there is action indoors during receptivity.

13. McDowell's position has been contrasted on many occasions with that of Robert Brandom (*Making It Explicit* and *Rorty and His Critics*), according to which beliefs are to be evaluated by their inferential role, and observational beliefs are no exception. Brandom shares with McDowell the Sellarsian legacy of conceiving empirical knowledge in terms of a game of asking and giving reasons, a space of reasons, but draws from Sellars the lesson that experience as such can play no special role in this game when it is properly understood. McDowell wants to insist that experience has an (external) impact on thought that is different from that of observational beliefs. In *Mind and World*, he insists that this can be demonstrated by considering intuitions as candidates for judgement, and emphasising that they are *passive* exercises of the same capacities deployed in beliefs. For a criticism of his position, see Bensusan and Pinedo, 'Minimal Empiricism without Dogmas', and Travis, 'The Silence of the Senses'. McDowell has since changed his position considerably, but throughout these changes he has remained faithful to the idea that experience has to place an audible external constraint on (empirical) thought.

14. Brandom, *Making It Explicit*, ch. 3, describes the process of inferring and seeking justification as a game in which a central element is that of giving reasons – to repeat, *giving* them. Yet this giving is different from the Given, if for no other reason than because a reason needs to be accepted as such in order to play its role as a reason (for something).

15. Wittgenstein, in the *Tractatus*, writes about a logical space of facts in which things don't belong; likewise, he considers a logical space of colours in which 'red' is a point but 'square' is not; a logical space is composed of points that are possible values of an attribute or a type. See, for example, Wittgenstein, *Tractatus*, 1.13, 3.4 and 6.3751. Later, Wittgenstein abandons the idea of a logical space (for instance, of colours) in favour of that of a grammar that allows a finer analysis of the relations between the multiple states of something. Interestingly, Sellars chooses to talk about a logical space of reasons instead of a grammar of reasons.

16. Cf. Davidson, 'On the Very Idea of a Conceptual Scheme', 'A Coherence Theory of Truth and Knowledge' and 'Three Varieties of Knowledge'.

17. McDowell, *Having the World in View*, p. 269. Here he accepts that his position in *Mind and World* was dangerously close to Davidson's idea that beliefs are only altered through other (observational) beliefs.

He then proceeds to change his view on intuitions by making them have a (non-propositional) form different from the (propositional) form of beliefs.
18. McDowell, *Having the World in View*, pp. 256–72.
19. McDowell, 'Scheme-Content Dualism and Empiricism', pp. 89–90.
20. A comparison between the geography of positions considered by McDowell at the beginning of *Mind and World* and the one offered by Meillassoux in *After Finitude* is insightful. McDowell spots an oscillation between a Davidsonian incapacity to draw lessons from outside through experience, and a position which assumes that experience mythically provides us with information. In other words, an oscillation between a Davidsonian correlationism and an empiricism of objectivity that believes the senses alone can provide objectivity to thought (a pre-critical position). McDowell then endeavours to find a way out of this oscillation. Notice that correlationism is perhaps the best way to characterise the problem with Davidson – who is clearly as much on the realist side as anyone within the Kantian heritage. Davidson's access to the outer world is only possible through our concepts and their intelligibility. My suspicion, however, is that as much as McDowell attempts to break out from frictionless spinning in the void through an appeal to minimal empiricism, he still ends up on correlationist shores. This is because he embraces theses such as the unbounded character of the conceptual – that everything is thinkable. He intends to remain faithful, nevertheless, to the claim that singular thought can grasp something exterior.
21. Cf. McDowell, *Having the World in View*, ch. 3.
22. McDowell, '*De Re* Senses'.
23. Levinas, *Totality and Infinity*, pp. 43–4.
24. See, for example, McDowell, *Mind and World*, pp. 24ff (lecture 2). For his later position on intuitions and propositions, see *Having the World in View*.
25. See Russell, 'On Denoting', and Sellars, *Empiricism and the Philosophy of Mind*, pp. 63–4.
26. For a distinction between access and discrimination, see Pritchard, 'Epistemological Disjunctivism and the Basis Problem' and *Epistemological Disjunctivism*.
27. See Chapter 1 above.
28. See, for example, Whitehead, *Modes of Thought*, pp. 1–19.
29. Whitehead, *Process and Reality*, p. 18.
30. Cf. Whitehead, *Process and Reality*, p. 41.
31. Whitehead, *Modes of Thought*, p. 9.

32. von Uexküll, *Milieu animal et milieu humain*.
33. Lettvin et al., 'What the Frog's Eye Tells the Frog's Brain'.
34. Whitehead, *Modes of Thought*, p. 9.
35. Whitehead, *Process and Reality*, p. 41.
36. Whitehead, *Process and Reality*, pp. 239–55.
37. Whitehead, *Process and Reality*, p. 254.
38. Whitehead, *Modes of Thought*, pp. 20–31.
39. Whitehead, *Process and Reality*, pp. 184–6.
40. That importance can change according to experience itself is a form of transcendental empiricism that can be traced back from Deleuze to Whitehead.
41. See Chapter 2 above.
42. One can think of the tension between theories and recalcitrant experience or the impact of an *experimentum crucis* on worldviews. The new external perceived element may ask for a complete reshuffle indoors. Accepting the force of the law of hospitality entails a readiness for unlimited revision of anything that has been previously held – including cherished principles (say, of logic), much in the sense Quine indicates is possible as a consequence of his rejection of the two dogmas of empiricism (Quine, 'Two Dogmas of Empiricism').
43. Whitehead, *Modes of Thought*, p. 9.
44. Whitehead, *Modes of Thought*, p. 9.
45. Whitehead writes that Hume was unable to elucidate in his system the phenomenon of experience, which is the derivation of expectation that he soundly described. Whitehead, *Modes of Thought*, pp. 82–3.
46. The idea is in the last sentence of Heidegger's *Holzwege* essay, 'The Word of Nietzsche: "God Is Dead"'.
47. Levinas, *Proper Names*, pp. 110–11.
48. Wahl, *Vers le concret*.
49. Deleuze, *Dialogues*, p. vii (preface).
50. Deleuze, *Difference and Repetition*.
51. The two notions, metaphysical desire and obsession, are parts of the slightly different architectures of concepts in *Totality and Infinity* and *Otherwise than Being*, respectively. In both cases these notions indicate a direction towards the Other. In the latter work, obsession is tied to proximity and these two notions are central in the book, while they are almost absent in *Totality and Infinity*. For present purposes, metaphysical desire and obsession can be taken to be fairly similar notions.
52. Rilke, *Letters of Rainer Maria Rilke*.

182    Indexicalism

53. McDowell, *Having the World in View*, pp. 3–4.
54. McDowell, *Perception as a Capacity for Knowledge*, p. 57.
55. McDowell, *Perception as a Capacity for Knowledge*, p. 21.
56. In 'Knowledge and the Internal', McDowell specifies the kind of *internalism* he wants to defend concerning human perception. It is crucial for him to have an account of epistemic states in terms of points in the space of reasons. He rejects the alternatives that leave no space for the internal in accounting for knowledge, such as reliabilism and its variants. He leaves it up in the air whether non-rational perception has to be accounted for in the internalism he recommends in the human case.
57. To be fair, McDowell elsewhere seems to envisage a broader lesson to be drawn from his account of perception among concept-mongers. In his response to Travis's 'Unlocking the Outer World', he writes that 'if one wanted to say something about the perceptual capacities of non-rational animals, it would be this: for non-rational animals too, perceiving things, for instance seeing them, requires more than just sense impressions, though the extra that is required cannot be, as with us, that conceptual capacities must be in act in their perceptual awareness' (McDowell, 'Travis on Frege, Kant and the Given', p. 32).
58. Derrida analyses the gift as often requiring at least a measure of gratitude in return, and therefore inserts it in the circle of economic exchange (Derrida, *Given Time*). A gift that is not named, on the other hand, can escape this predicament of (loose) economic exchange.
59. Derrida and Dufourmantelle, *Of Hospitality*, pp. 75ff.
60. McDowell recommends disjunctivism as a form of direct perception where access to what is perceived is granted in the good cases. Pritchard recommends an analogous disjunctivism in 'Epistemological Disjunctivism and the Basis Problem' (see also McDowell, 'Travis on Frege, Kant and the Given'). In Pritchard's terms, disjunctivism combines acceptance of the requirement of access with rejection of that of discrimination, as defined as following: (ACCESS) If S and S* do not differ in the facts that they are able to know by reflection alone, then they will not differ in the degree of epistemic justification they have for their beliefs. (DISCRIMINATION) If the experiences had by S and S* are indiscriminable, then S and S* will not differ in the degree of epistemic justification they have for their beliefs.
61. Whitehead, *Process and Reality*, p. 19.
62. Whitehead, *Modes of Thought*, p. 160.

63. Whitehead, *Modes of Thought*, pp. 105ff (lecture VI).
64. Whitehead, *Modes of Thought*, p. 31.
65. Whitehead, *Modes of Thought*, p. 164.
66. Whitehead, *Process and Reality*, p. 168.
67. Whitehead, *Process and Reality*, pp. 169–70.
68. Just as a lure for feelings both enables and results from an experience, proximity makes receptivity possible and is informed by it. Here again one can see shades of a transcendental empiricism that can be traced back to Husserl and Wahl.
69. Levinas, *Otherwise than Being*, p. 101.
70. Proximity is not tied to families, neighbourhoods, nationalities, ethnic groups or even species. A politico-demographic project that is easily construed in terms of the anarchic character of proximity is Donna Haraway's *make kin not babies* or *make kin not populations* (Haraway, *Staying with the Trouble*, pp. 99ff, and Haraway and Clarke, *Making Kin not Population*). Haraway recommends less demographic expansion – and hopefully less associated demographic reduction – of humans and other animals favoured by humans, and more attention to what is already there and requiring of kinship to thrive.
71. Fisher, *The Weird and the Eerie*, pp. 8–9.
72. Land, 'Kant, Capital and the Prohibition of Incest', p. 75.
73. Land, 'Kant, Capital and the Prohibition of Incest', pp. 63–4.
74. Heidegger, 'The Word of Nietzsche: "God Is Dead"'.
75. Heidegger, *Bremen and Freiburg Lectures*.
76. Heidegger, *Bremen and Freiburg Lectures*, p. 69.
77. Heidegger, *Bremen and Freiburg Lectures*, p. 70.
78. Deleuze, *The Fold*.

# Coda: The Circumscription of Potosí

## Epistemic Abundance

Peter Linebaugh, writing in the foreword of Silvia Federici's book *Re-enchanting the World*, claims that the 'universalization of knowledge and technology is a colonial legacy'.[1] The colonial project has in its epistemic regime a special licence for indignity – in the name of knowledge, the rights of the others are systematically ignored and trespassed upon.

The epistemic regime which places knowledge ahead of anything else, the endeavour to extract intelligence from what is perceived, postulates that facts command more attention than any other concern.[2] As a consequence of the isolation and priority of epistemic matters, spontaneity of thought is conceived as constrained only by what brings about correction. It matters that convictions are right, and not much more. To the epistemic is given a unique dispensation not shared with any other normative system: the licence to deal solely with one's own competence. What matters is to gain and maintain knowledge which is universal – indifferent to political choices, to community ties, to circumstances or situations. That knowledge is placed ahead of justice – facts are alien to considerations concerning the Other. The others are primarily placed in an ontologist project: that of retaining what is common, repeatable and intelligible, geared towards taming peculiarities and oblivious to any appeal for justice that is not also an appeal for correctness.

Levinas describes this epistemic regime oriented by ontologism in terms of seizing what we meet in order to betray it, so that it becomes a concept.[3] This is because relations with the others are subordinated to relations of knowledge, and the spontaneity of thought precedes justice. Under this regime of extraction of intelligence, the epistemic enterprise is such that it never becomes fully hostage to receptivity. In contrast, a metaphysics of the others enables receptivity to provide a friction beyond any effort of accommodation. Its corresponding epistemology points towards exercises of response. Response is part of a conversation that springs from an appeal, from a detection of otherness in the perceptual field. It is not about immunising against the alien; rather, it ushers in a *xenophilic* turn in epistemology – a model based not in intelligence extraction but rather in interruptions and ongoing conversations. The epistemological landscape is not a desert containing rare and invaluable gems to be extracted in order to render everything intelligible; it is not a landscape where intelligibility is condensed in precious, sizeable pieces. The universalisation of knowledge and technology that Linebaugh describes is attached to this desert image: the indifference to anything brought into proximity by the senses except what reveals an overall intelligibility that can be detached from everything else. It is as if each sensible experience carries no more than a relevant (or marginally redundant) universal message that is to be extracted and incorporated into a mosaic of intelligibilities – an image of the world to be (eventually) completed. Experience is a component of the epistemic project of maximising the extraction of intelligibility in order to secure the sameness of future experience – to render the future secure. In contrast, the metaphysics of the others is situated and posits no portability of intelligence; intelligence is tied to (conversational) responses, and responding itself is not portable. Rather, the xenophilic turn in epistemology assumes a rainforest abundance of intelligibility in which the senses continuously bring supplements – and it makes no sense to secure gems of intelligence for a future of scarcity to come. This epistemic abundance posits no end to curiosity, no irrelevance for receptivity. On the one hand, even if solutions are established, the questions are constantly modified; on the other hand, responses are themselves always situated.

Epistemic abundance also means an inextinguishable provision of supplement. Previous responses, as well as knowledge already acquired, are placed in different conversational circumstances by being further interrupted. In the image of an ongoing conversation with ever-appearing interlocutors, asking for responses has no end. There are situated questions in every epistemic scenario, and each of them impacts not only the construction of knowledge but equally the balance of justice. Conversations are never mere inquiries and interchanges are never only investigations. In this xenophilic environment, knowledge is not a found (portable) treasure but rather a deictic position that is hostage to several interlocutors. That knowledge ought to be situated is a consequence both of indexicalism, which assumes no substantive reality, and of its corollary metaphysics of the others, which posits responses and not solutions as its staple. Portability – and ultimately universality – is exactly what substantives provide. The absence of substantives to be grasped throws knowledge into permanent commerce with exteriority. Because receptivity is never made redundant, exteriority ties knowledge to a horizon.[4] Abundance is then precisely the predicament of exteriority: there is no scarcity of circumstances when horizons furnish (what is assumed to be) substantives with addresses.

### The Potosí Principle

This book engages with proximity and deictic absolutes to argue against the usual interference of totality in metaphysics. For reasons that I am only partly aware of, the book took its definitive shape in Potosí, in the Andes, at about 5,000 metres above sea level. The place was arguably the centre of the world when modernity was taking shape, in the 1600s. While I was there, the mountain I could see from my doorstep was the Sumaq Urqo (or Cerro Rico). This mountain filled with silver and tin had a role in the high reputation universality was to enjoy in the coming modern times. It is the underlying geology behind many of the adventures of modernity – an economic ground that underpins capital and its conquering diaspora. The minerals that compose the mountain are now spread across the world through many unknown paths: 16 million kilos of silver were sent between 1503 and 1660 to Sanlúcar de Barrameda in Seville. They shaped fortunes, companies, cities and architectures, but also gave shape to manufacturing and therefore to capital itself. The endeavour to spread the regional around the globe is called colonisation – Columbus's voyage began to globalise crops, plants, animals, habits, diets, customs and practices. Sumaq Urqo was itself globalised. Its matter is the matter of universal and permanent capital. Its forces were extracted, and what remains in Potosí is its carcass. (There are now worries that the mountain might collapse altogether, as it is becoming even hollower.)

The details of how the mountain made possible the increasing universality of capital – images, documents, traces of various kinds – disappeared from town. Some of this material is in Seville, and some in a colonial museum in Madrid: the Cristóbal Colón Museum. There are other numbers too, less widespread, and other minerals. At the beginning of the twentieth century, a select number of tin magnates became millionaires around Potosí; right now, the lithium fever and other open-air multi-mining projects are still lingering. The plundering of the place, which has enriched the Western world and made modernity possible, features extensively in a book I have been browsing: the catalogue of an exhibition held in Madrid, Berlin and La Paz called *Principio Potosí*.[5] The book starts out by asking what would happen if we replaced Descartes' *ego cogito* with Cortés' contemporary *ego conquiro* in the narrative of modernity in art. The paintings of colonial Bolivia follow the rules of the canon both in form and content, but depict indigenous celebrations. The colonial enterprise takes that which does not fit and turns it into a particular instance of something known. Substantive metaphysics, and its attempt to attain a view from nowhere, is intriguingly similar to an immaterial colonial museum. Colonial unification, as Nick Land has suspected, is a way of weakening underlying forces of resistance.

Substantive metaphysics renders innocuous the deictic operations behind any thematisation of what is around. If philosophy is to have any impact, it has to be fed with wild and perhaps brutal suspicions. The project of substantial metaphysics is one in which a total view is set as the ultimate goal, a goal towards taming dissent. The idea of a unified, substantive universe is an attempt to exorcise biases by making them invisible. To be sure, colonial museums are alive and kicking, and this is because their message still resonates – not only do they have their fans but they have their role. Perhaps just like metaphysics. As Levinas notes:

> The security of the peoples of Europe behind their borders and the walls of their houses, assured of their property (*Eigenheit* that becomes *Eigentum*), is not the sociological condition of metaphysical thought, but the very project of such thought. A project impossible of accomplishment, ever deferred, a messianic future as that missing present [. . .] All materialism is marked by this, as is all idealism.[6]

The metaphysical project he has in mind is one that bets on an appropriate thematisation of the universe as a totality that, once accomplished, is eventually immune from any interruption. In other words, it is the project of trading exteriority for totality – which assumes that curiosity is more akin to desire as lack than to an unquenchable craving for more. It is a project that assumes that totality is innocuous, or even ultimately redeeming. Susan Benso writes that what 'has made Western philosophy unethical is not the committing of the metaphysical murder, but the denial of the murdered and of the murderous act'.[7]

Potosí, whose name comes from the sound of explosions inside the mountain, has been at most an odd centre of the world, in the sense that it financed the world. Potosí was not an inspiration about how to live; it was a massive sacrifice of the local to the universal. The universal is the mineral trade, itself often synonymous with the flow of capital: Potosí is the world's prime example of capital deterritorialisation. Its population was composed of silver treasure hunters, the administration the Spanish crown had moved in and the *mitayos* – the indigenous enslaved people captured to work the mines. The local, on the other hand, was above all the mountains, the earth full of minerals. Those stones and dust were made global; they spoke directly to capital because they were particular instances of it – no matter the indigenous celebrations taking place in town. Potosí was always a European town, no doubt about it.

Potosí was the closest the conquerors ever got to the American El Dorado. Humboldt, narrating his travels in South America, diagnoses a curse of abundance: El Dorado would soon become a pretty unpleasant place to live.[8] Abundant places are places of poverty. Alberto Acosta wonders how much would it cost to reverse the curse – does a curse have a price? What is the value of a hidden treasure?[9] Potosí was a dream place: treasures and the cheap labour to extract them. Sumaq Urqo is a symbol of a global landscape juxtaposed with a local neighbourhood. An expression for anything of great value spread quickly: *it's worth a Potosí*. To undo the colonial mining order, one needs to undo the extraction and the dissemination of the value held inside the Cerro. But how do you put value back in? Do you need to stop taking it as value? Think of reparations. How would they take place? The silver removed from the mountain is still circulating somewhere on the planet – gold and silver are the ultimate vessels of value. It was not thrown in the seas in great quantities, so it is still located in invaluable pieces of silver. The silver could be collected and sent back to the mountain. Maybe then it could be buried in Sumaq Urqo, or sold in the local market. Now Sumaq Urqo doesn't need money – its current inhabitants do. But is paying undoing, or is it overdoing? The Cerro cannot take buried pieces of silver as part of its body; once minerals are taken from the ground, they cannot be placed back in. This is the fate of the Anthropocene: the soil of the Earth is like passion, according to Martin Dysart, the psychiatrist in Peter Shaffer's *Equus*. It can be destroyed by a specialist, but it cannot be (re-)created.

Potosí is also an icon of what Heidegger described as the dispensation of being where what there is is in danger: every place can be found to be on top of a Sumaq Urqo. Abundance is a curse in which everything is in danger of falling. Treasure can be found anywhere – and a treasure is a piece of global value in a local environment. The image of value illustrates perhaps much of the point of exorcising the global that can usher in a genuinely postcolonial epoch: the market is an aggregate of the needs and greeds of everyone. It is global at least in its seed. The market value of something is its importance viewed from nowhere. In sharp contrast is the positioned importance of Sumaq Urqo for the mountains, minerals, animals, vegetation and humans around it. Potosí spells the translation of the local into the global. The silver, tin and copper inside the mountain could have no other destination but the market. The global operation – the colonial operation – turns what exists into existence-for-the-market. That is the curse, the mode of existence of abundance. The local, as local, becomes invisible.

The Yasuní National Park in the Ecuadorian Amazon is an area of rainforest that is home to twenty threatened mammal species and several groups of indigenous peoples who live in isolation: the Tagaeri and Taromenane clans of the Waorani. The park, together with the Waorani reserve, covers an area of more than 10,000 square kilometres. There are more species of trees there than in all of the US and Canada combined. Beneath it lies 846 million barrels of oil. As a local initiative, Yasuní ITT (a trust founded in 2010) aimed to collect $US3.6 million from pledges to keep the oil where it is. By 2012 the pledged sum of money added up to a tiny fraction of the target amount. Not enough money to spare the park – not enough money to keep it local. Bataille writes that only when growth is limited does a real surplus emerge.[10] It is a test of force: the unknown surplus of the spared mineral on one side and the Potosí principle on the other. Acosta is suspicious of the compensations requested for leaving the mineral buried: is capital the only alternative medium? It is, insofar as it is the only game in town.

One of the Bolivian participants of the *Princípio Potosí* exhibition was the *Mujeres Creando* collective and María Galindo, one of the founders of the movement. Galindo contrasts the scripted patriarchal global identities that make women what they are supposed to be with the creativity of each unexpected situated alliance between concrete women. She likens decolonialisation to depatriarchalisation. She finds in patriarchal structures the same drive towards substantive discourse on bodies and performances that grounds a convenient continuity between pre-colonial and Hispanic patriarchy. Galindo brings up the issue of colonial wombs: they are the site of the demographic conflict between the coloniser and the native. Indigenous women gave birth to the new coloniser population, carrying European names and the surnames of the fathers. There is no *arché* to the womb; it is placed as the arena of the biopolitical dispute. Yet Galindo wants to distance herself from a general agenda of women, or of indigenous people, that is grounded in identities – there are no identities that shortcut the creativity of infinite responsibility to one's proximity. A neighbourhood is the stuff of all sorts of alliances that are not crafted in substantive, pre-existing identities but rather thrive in ethical responses. These alliances are fragile, precarious and dependent on gestures of hospitality, but there are no ethnic shortcuts to ethics. She insists on the creativity of engagement, on opposition to political programmes that could be formulated anywhere. It is not enough to act locally – if thinking is global, colonialism prevails. The alternative is to be excruciatingly local, to reach each description from an indexical environment, instead of understanding substantives as lying somewhere prior. Thinking locally, one might act globally: the indexical environments are themselves connected, but only through indexicals.

Situated metaphysics is a remedy neither for the colonial predicament nor for the substantive metaphysics that comes with it; it is, nevertheless, a departure from the colonial attachment to increasingly integrated wholes. It is about interruption and response, and posits no intelligence that can be extracted once and for all. The intelligible is not what renders what was found irrelevant – experience is not a ladder to be laid aside once used

– but what is never immune to supplement. A metaphysics of the others contrasts with the ongoing metaphysical project of finding the substantives that provide a complete picture of reality because it builds on absolutes that are deictic. It builds on deixes that are never just a *façon de parler*.

### Ch'ixi

In this book I have been proposing a self-destructive metaphysics – destructive if we take the quest for totality as an inextricable guide to all things metaphysical. Indexicalism is a metaphysics without totality, and is in this sense a departure from metaphysics; its relation with totalities cannot be anything but paradoxical. Paradox, and paradoxico-metaphysics, is perhaps the very way out of substantive metaphysics – a substantive totality is an impossibility. Deixis is always recalcitrant. It follows that a general feature of reality is that there is no general feature of reality. Indexicalism entails that exteriority is a general feature of reality that dismantles any other. It is the claim that substantives are derivative and cannot be deprived of their indexical addresses. Its metaphysics of the others points towards a receptivity taken as hospitality: there is a drive towards the exterior in the form of a metaphysical desire, a constitutive obsession or a persistent curiosity. This is a consequence of the insufficiency of intelligibility – reality is always on the verge of supplement.

Insufficiency prevents completion: metaphysical insufficiency entails that no completion is possible, either in the form of an original totality that has degenerated into a lack, or as a goal to attain. Metaphysical insufficiency is what ushers in the paradoxical character of the metaphysical endeavour. Completion can be conceived in terms of purity – or in terms of what engenders no paradox. Silvia Rivera Cusicanqui tells the history of the colonial Andes as a failure of the colonial purity project of establishing a subservient array of republics portraying themselves as countries just like those in Europe.[11] The failure lies in the fact that there is an indigenous underground always tainting the European-like institutions. The failure is impurity, or rather what she calls *ch'ixi*, an Aymara word for stained or mottled. *Ch'ixi* is the native Aymara who is irrevocably supplemented in her way of living through contact with Europe as much as *ch'ixi* is the Spanish language, institutions and art forms in the colonised Andes. Rivera opposes the idea of *ch'ixi* to that of the hybrid; the former is an active friction between poles that gives rise to permanent recombination.[12] Accepting the impure enables a new form of expressing what is one's own in a stained, contaminated way. She writes:

> the idea of ch'ixi, which literally refers to the mottled gray, formed from an infinity of black and white points that are unified in perception but remain pure, separate. It is a way of thinking, talking and perceiving that is based on the multiple and the contradictory, not as a transitory state that must be overcome [...] but as an explosive and contentious force that enhances our capacity for thought and action. It is thus opposed to the ideas of syncretism, hybridity and to the dialectics of synthesis, which are always in search of the one, the overcoming of contradictions through a third element, harmonious and complete in itself.[13]

The creative power lies in a persistent friction that is not to be resolved by integration or the prevalence of a pole. There is no convergence. To be tainted or stained is to have been supplemented – traces of something external amounting to incompletion. Rivera's *ch'ixi* is a response to violent miscegenation and forced integration: something that is *ch'ixi* is tainted by the others, but is neither becoming one with the others nor becoming the others. It is not becoming. It is perhaps better described as something that comes back to itself in a recurrence after being interrupted by the outside. Rivera holds that there is a permanent struggle between the Indian – she prefers this word for political reasons[14] – and the European in the Andean subjectivity. This struggle is an internal tension contrasting with a single total view and enabling non-ending, ongoing conversations.

A *ch'ixi* metaphysics embraces an irredeemable pluralism. As such, it makes room for a *diaphonía* that cannot but add indexical addresses to any substantive description. Just like the Andean tainted submission to colonial standards, the local, the indexical and the situated underlie efforts towards substantivism while being rendered invisible by them. Satisfying Tsing's injunction requires room for something left out of one's narrative – friction from outside. The metaphysics of the others pictures perception as this permanent source of stain in existing intelligibility. It is therefore in line with a task for xenology described by Viveiros de Castro as the new mission for anthropology: the permanent decolonisation of thought.[15]

In his effort to contrast his dialogical *analetics* with Hegelian dialectics, Enrique Dussel distinguishes between a drive towards averting exteriority and a drive to be permanently converted to it.[16] A permanent conversion would be akin to permanent decolonisation; Dussel understands analetics as a friction with unforeseen others that provides no negation, no bifurcation and no synthesis. Both dialectic and analectic are movements where the interplay between two poles makes them change, but the dialectic change is convergent. The analectic change, on the other hand, is such that the point of departure is itself divergent. The Same and the Other are different in both cases – in dialectic movement, the Same is ultimately the Only, whereas in analectic movement the Other does not head to a completion. Dussel conceives of analetics as a thorough departure from a drive towards totality; it is guided by a conversation with the exterior.[17] He is a Levinasian who describes colonisation as the covering up of the Other. He conceives of the (analectic) interplay between Same and Other as a way to make explicit what is at stake in the political struggles around this covering up. Colonialism is the endeavour of unification in which a single intelligibility is forced into whatever is found – unless the Other acts as a dialectical mediation placed at the service of the increased intelligibility. The drive towards exteriority is concealed by the totality-oriented colonisation project; in Dussel's terms, it is as if an underlying analetics provides some of the movement towards a unified intelligibility. Analogously, it is as if underlying conversations set the engine that makes the substantive narrative take shape. These situated conversations hold the key to the endemic insufficiency that a metaphysics of substantives covers up. Substantives are insufficient to do justice to the insufficiency of what exists. This insufficiency is what fuels indexicalism, and the metaphysics of the others.

### *Being Up for Grabs*

This insufficiency was also a central concern in my book *Being Up for Grabs*. There, a route through necessity led to the idea that, while the hyper-chaos is not all-encompassing as it is for Meillassoux, what is up for grabs is the cornerstone of reality. Accident is not everywhere, but it is a *sine qua non* for the understanding of anything concrete. Due to this primacy of contingency over anything else, that book presented not a complete metaphysics but rather three narratives, called ontoscopies, each of them failing to be sufficient. The three narratives made clear that contingency comes out of pluralism, so that not only was what Peirce labelled necessitarianism rejected in each of the three ontoscopies, but also none of them was deemed sufficient to fully address an up-for-grabs reality.[18] Metaphysical insufficiency also informed the friction between each of the three ontoscopies. In the book, this insufficiency that grounded contingency and plurality – and both the accounts of contingency and the plurality of them – enabled a multinarrative metaphysics that is arguably a step towards meeting Tsing's injunction. The upshot was that contingency is a metaphysical cog behind everything, including the story told in the book.

Indeed, to be contingent is to be dependent on something else – to be in the hands of something else, so to speak. Being up for grabs is being hostage to something other. There is a family resemblance between a metaphysics of contingency and a situated metaphysics: not only do both press in the direction of shaking off the burden of necessity that metaphysical endeavours usually carry, but the latter can only make sense if situations are themselves to a large extent accidental. Indexicalism makes the accident of being in an indexical environment the ultimately relevant piece in the furniture of the universe; the contingency of a situation is all that there is. As such, it certainly constitutes no totality – there is no complete account of all situations. A situated metaphysics is not a metaphysics of situations; that would take situations to be substantives. It is not about extracting the intelligible features of a situation in general – or of kinds of situations – from an experience with distinct situations. A situated metaphysics is in fact hostage to situations, and does not present a complete view of them. It is therefore not clear from a situation – from an indexical environment, say from being in front of the Sumaq Urqo – how anything is contingent on it. This is what ushers in paradox: it is a general account of reality according to which reality affords no general accounts. The metaphysical situation contemplated by the metaphysics of the others – and by indexicalism – is to be before the Great Outdoors; that is, metaphysics lies in facing exteriority. This is where reality can be grasped – a reality that depends on deixis and cannot be viewed from nowhere. A situated metaphysics cannot but be paradoxical, yet still its attraction stems from two conflicting and yet intertwined, generally accepted ideas: that a general account always transcends a situation and that transcendence itself is situated.

The path from indexicalism to a worked-out situated metaphysics shows how crucial it is to steer clear of substantives. Possibly, the attachment to the idea that substantives are central to reality is what makes most of what lapses into paradoxico-metaphysics seem intolerable. From an indexicalist, situated perspective, several paradoxes are the consequence of a lack of attention to the plurality of situations. Implicit appeals to standing locations against a substantivist background could be the key to the puzzlement brought up by paradoxical scenarios. In any case, several paradoxes depend on the mix of indexical and substantive language: typical examples include the liar paradox (with indexicals like 'I'm Cretan' or 'This sentence'), Russell's paradox (with 'a member of itself') and the Richard-Berry paradox (with 'less than a number of words').[19] I won't explore the paradoxes further here from the point of view of the friction between substantives and indexicals, but I think a closer look into these formulations would provide intuitions about the tight links between paradoxico-metaphysics and the pervasiveness of deixis that is indexicalism's starting point.

In *Being Up for Grabs*, there are several moments in which the focus on insufficiency paves the way for a situated metaphysics (and its paradoxical condition). The chapter that discusses doubts proposes a contrast between the neo-Pyrrhonism of Sextus Empiricus, according to which belief is prey to endemically insufficient reason – uncovered through *diaphonía* – and an ontology of doubt (perhaps close to the original Pyrrhonic idea) according to which reality is not always determined to be one way or another. The contrast between unknown determinations and the lack of determinations to be known brings home the idea that one can suspend judgement about whether there are determinations in reality. Suspension of judgement, in both cases, is an activity of thought guided by a quest for insufficient reasons – it produces a *diaphonía*. It is therefore an exercise in hearing another equally grounded voice. The starting point of this exercise is what appears, the phenomenon, which is a common ground to show that each voice has insufficient reason. It is interesting to remark that the neo-Pyrrhonist phenomenon is not defined in terms of sensorial input or of a fixed set of accepted appearances. It is hardly definable; the starting point of the suspension of judgement is situated, dependent on circumstances. A situated phenomenon orients suspension of judgement; *epokhé* takes place in the *agora*, it is shaped by circumstances. If we embrace this situated notion of phenomenon, there are no universal doubts, because insufficiency is grounded in circumstance. If the starting point for suspending judgement is situated, it seems that something like a situated metaphysics is in the vicinity. Still more so if an ontology of doubt – in contrast with standard neo-Pyrrhonism – is adopted, for the indeterminacies in reality are then dependent on the circumstances that shape the phenomenon on the basis of which we find out that something is not determinate. The indeterminacies of reality are themselves relative to the phenomenon taken as the starting point of the enterprise of doubting – and doubting is, according to the ontology of doubt, a way to uncover real indeterminacies. Understood along these lines, the ontology of doubt is very close to a situated metaphysics.

Further, the book presents two other ontoscopies, one based on fragments and another on rhythms. In the former, contingency is conceived in terms of a process monadology where the basic units enjoy a triple mode of existence as fragments, composers and compositions. In the latter, rhythms are the vehicles of contingency, as they interact with each other in indeterminate ways. A metaphysics of fragments thought of in terms of a monadology entails that a totality is always being composed. Since fragments are composers and compositions, they can be units of spontaneity that can be interrupted – and in this respect, this ontoscopy is close to the idea of interrupted nexûs. It falls short of the metaphysics of the others because, as a monadology, it is not situated; it makes fragments still part of a landscape viewed as a totality. Clearly, a metaphysics of fragments could instead embrace the idea that fragments supplement each other from outside, replacing monadological assumptions with indexicalist ones – making no room for a sideways-on view of what the fragments are composing. Similarly, a rhythm-based account of contingency approaches the metaphysics of the others by postulating a plurality of interrupted timings. In the book, the rhythm-oriented ontology has no room for interiorities – rhythms just infect each other, in a way that can equally be described from the point of view of a totality constantly being modified. Certainly, one could conceive of interiorities that are rhythmical and exteriority as what interrupts the inner pace. The metaphysics of the others prefers to understand interruption in terms of demands that are received and trigger responses.

Interruptions do not impose anything; they simply break the pace of spontaneity and open alternative courses of action.

However, the main friction between indexicalism and the metaphysics of the others found in this book and in *Being Up for Grabs* lies in the substantive character of contingency. Both endeavours provide departures from the idea of a necessary totality composing reality. Indexicalism, however, posits no account of what replaces that necessary totality – it only attempts to be faithful to the idea of exteriority. In contrast, a metaphysics of contingency attempts to find a substantive underlying structure behind deixis and what makes exteriority disruptive: a structure that means that things are dependent on their circumstances. This dependence ushers in a metaphysics of situations rather than a situated metaphysics. While to postulate contingency as central is not a non-interrupted speculative gesture – like the one Meillassoux makes to attempt to establish his principle of facticity – it appeals to a neutral term common both to interiorities and to the Great Outdoors. Further, as substantives make no (explicit) reference to deixis, to say there is contingency connecting what exists is to picture a substantivist world bound to deictic operations. In other words, the indexicalist complaint about the metaphysics of *Being Up for Grabs* is that it deals with the insufficiency in reality in a substantivist manner. Instead, I now posit that yes, things are up for grabs, but because there is genuine exteriority, genuine interruption and an underlying deictic structure to reality. To be sure, for several purposes both theories converge in their primacy of insufficiency and in their rejection of necessitarianism. In both cases, metaphysics is stripped of its attachment to substantial structures and necessary connections in favour of an attention to insufficiency, accidents and circumstances.

## Absolutely Situated

The metaphysics of the others finds the absolute in exteriority. As a consequence, the absolute is less in totality than in transcendence, and therefore cannot be reached or grasped without resorting to a situation. This means the absolute is not a substantive situation but rather a deixis that reveals the Great Outdoors as permanently unveiled – and concealed – in perception. Receptivity in a broad sense – going beyond sensorial perception towards whatever is capable of being affected – is a consequence of the absolute deixis that distinguishes the inner from the outer, the interior from the exterior, the same from the other. Because indexicals are situated, they are not symmetrical, and in the conversational approach to receptivity, what is said by the others has the priority of the impact that creates responsibility. The infinite conversation, a consequence of the central attention given to exteriority, is infinite in time and in responsibility, but also in the number of intervening characters. There are no limits to the demands that come from the exterior, and to do justice to them all is a ceaseless and impossible endeavour. Yet this endless conversation is brought about by the metaphysics of the others. It results in no thesis about everything except that thinking about reality is situated, but concludes that absolutes cannot but be deictic.

This book itself was written within the borders of Potosí. It was not fully conceived in the surroundings of Sumaq Urqo, but was chiefly engendered in colonised Latin America. Situated metaphysics is a way to counter the urge for universality that associates the metaphysical effort with the colonial enterprise. The metaphysics of the others opposes the extraction of intelligence with an ongoing conversation where what is said never makes the saying of it redundant. It postulates a metaphysical hospitality that differs from the colonial project as much as exteriority bounds totality. When the quest for exteriority met the rush for totality, totality responded with conquest. Conquest, nevertheless, requires the security of the peoples of Europe that Levinas talks about. Its price is a discomfort with disagreement that has to make truth silence justice – and epistemic dominance conceal epistemic injustice.

Metaphysical hospitality counters the drive towards totality with different tools. It favours an impact of the others triggered not by impingements, either in the form of appeals to inclinations or to the force of imperatives, but rather by asking. In the Dardenne brothers' film *Two Days, One Night*, Sandra is constrained into asking sixteen of her workmates to give up their wage bonuses in order to let her keep her job. The film portrays how she interrupts plans and projects by asking each of them to let go of an advantage to respond to her. People respond differently, but they have to respond somehow. Asking is difficult: it can only take place in an environment where freedom exists, because responsibility is infinite. The metaphysics of the others is a metaphysics of asking. Asking also requires proximity. The rush for totality abolishes proximity: abolishes the local, conceals the minerals of Sumaq

Urqo, while unveiling a reservoir of silver. The rush for totality is not going to be simply imposed on the prevailing metaphysical project. If any attempt at totality is bound by the Great Outdoors, which has an impact on thinking through receptivity, there are demands underlying commands. In other words, the seduction of the exterior is a force within the very rush for totality. Seduction, as Levinas often points out, is not foreign to asking. Exteriority is not a greater force capable of stopping the prevailing rush: rather, it deconstructs totality.

The impact of indexicalism in the colonial course of things is that of reinstating locality, intending to interrupt the project of turning the world into the leftovers of an extracted artificial intelligence. It entails a metaphysics of the others which is also a thorough criticism of the metaphysics that has prevailed in recent centuries. The outcome of the criticism, paradoxically, is to show that metaphysics is situated and there is no substantivist road towards the absolute. From within Potosí, the rush for totality looks like an effort to tame the weird and the eerie. From here, the entrails of the history of metaphysics become visible – and they have addresses.

## Notes

1. Federici, *Re-enchanting the World*, foreword by Peter Linebaugh, p. xv.
2. The contrast between facts and concerns – or matters of fact and matters of concern, as Latour presents it (Latour, 'What Is the Style of Matters of Concern?') – is perhaps itself a contrast between totality, of which facts are like jigsaw pieces, and exteriority as concern for the others.
3. Levinas, *Totality and Infinity*, pp. 43–4.
4. The idea of a situated epistemology has been considered in social constructivist projects. The metaphysics of the others is a different scenario, for though it also assumes the relevance of one's interlocutors, it does not restrict them to (power-oriented) human groups. For more on situated knowledges, see Haraway, 'Situated Knowledges'.
5. Creischer et al., *Principio Potosí*.
6. Levinas, *Proper Names*, p. 57.
7. Benso, *The Face of Things*, p. 131.
8. Humboldt, *Cosmos*.
9. Acosta, *La maldición de la abundancia*.

10. Bataille, *La part maudite*.
11. Rivera reconsidered the Principio Potosí exhibition (Rivera, *Principio Potosí Reverso*) to make clear that the exhibition was still committed to a single narrative concerning the Europeans in their purity and the colonised natives. Instead, she offers narratives in which the local population is inevitably tainted, and therein lies their resistance. Interestingly, both the exhibition and her reconsidered version emphasise the relevance of the Andean baroque. The baroque view does not intend a complete exhibition of everything; rather, it cherishes the contrast between what lies illuminated and what is concealed as a consequence. See Deleuze, *The Fold*, and also Chapter 1 above, 'Tense Realism and Baroque Realism'.
12. Rivera, *Principio Potosí Reverso*, p. 5.
13. Rivera, *Sociología de la imagen*, pp. 310–11, my translation.
14. The choice of the word 'Indian' as opposed to 'natives' or 'peasants' or 'original peoples' is tied to the struggle of what Fausto Reinaga called 'the Indian Revolution', which raised an effort of awareness of the Indians as bearers of a thoroughly non-European way of living. See, for instance, Reinaga, *La revolución india*.
15. Viveiros de Castro, *Cannibal Metaphysics*, p. 40.
16. Dussel, *Para una ética de la liberación latinoamericana I*, pp. 102–3.
17. Dussell, *Para una ética de la liberación latinoamericana I*, chs 13–16.
18. Peirce, 'The Doctrine of Necessity Examined'. See above, Chapter 2, 'Process Metaphysics of the Others'.
19. Formulations of the liar paradox include 'All Cretans are liars, and I'm Cretan', 'I'm lying now' and 'This sentence is false.' Russell's paradox can be formulated thus: 'The set of all sets which are not members of themselves is both a member of itself and not a member of itself.' Richard-Berry's paradox is that any natural number that cannot be described in less than, say, twenty words can be described in less than twenty words by 'the smallest number which cannot be described in less than twenty words', that is, in twelve words. For a relevant discussion of paradoxes, see Priest, *Beyond the Limits of Thought*, and Cogburn, *Garcian Meditations*.

# Bibliography

Acosta, Alberto, *La maldición de la abundancia*, Quito: CEP, 2009.
Aira, César, *The Conversations*, trans. Katherine Silver, New York: New Directions, 2014.
Århem, Kaj, 'Ecosofia Masuna', in F. Correa, *La selva humanizada: ecología alternativa en el tropico húmedo colombiano*, Bogotá: Instituto Colombiano de Antropología CEREC, 1993, pp. 109–26.
Aristotle, *Categories and De Interpretatione*, Oxford: Clarendon Press, 1963.
Artaud, Antonin, *To Have Done With the Judgement of God*, Los Angeles: Black Sparrow Press, 1975.
Badleh, Jalal, *De Derrida à Lévinas, la dette et l'envoi*, Paris: L'Harmattan, 2015.
Bataille, Georges, *La part maudite*, Paris: Minuit, 2014.
Barad, Karen, *Meeting the Universe Halfway: Quantum Physics and the Entanglement of Matter and Meaning*, Durham, NC: Duke University Press, 2007.
Benso, Silvia, *The Face of Things: A Different Side of Ethics*, Albany: SUNY Press, 2000.
Bensusan, Hilan, *Being Up for Grabs: On Speculative Anarcheology*, London: Open Humanities Press, 2016.
— 'The Cubist Object: Black Boxes, Über-realism and the Metaphysics of Perspectives', *Speculations*, 2, 2012, pp. 169–86.
— *Pacífico Sul – ou Teoria Geral da Referência*, Rio de Janeiro: Confraria do Vento, 2012.
— 'O realismo especulativo e a metafísica dos outros', *Eco-pos*, 21.2, 2018, pp. 94–110.
— 'Towards an Indexical Paradoxico-Metaphysics', *Open Philosophy*, 1, 2018, pp. 155–72.
Bensusan, Hilan, and Jadson Alves de Freitas, *A diáspora da agência: ensaio sobre o horizonte das monadologias*, Salvador: EdUFBA, 2018.

Bensusan, Hilan, and Manuel de Pinedo, 'Minimal Empiricism without Dogmas', *Philosophia*, 35.2, 2007, pp. 197–206.
Bernardo, Fernanda, and Gérard Bensussan, *Os Equívocos da Ética/Les Équivoques de l'Éthique. A propósito dos/A propos des Carnets de Captivité de Levinas*, Porto: FEAA, 2013.
Blanchfield, Brian, *Proxies: A Memoir in Twenty-Four Attempts*, London: Picador, 2017.
Blood, Benjamin, *Pluriverse: An Essay on the Philosophy of Pluralism*, London: Routledge, 2014.
Bluck, Richard, *Plato's Sophist*, ed. Gordon Neal, Manchester: Manchester University Press, 1975.
Brandom, Robert, *Making It Explicit: Reasoning, Representing, and Discursive Commitment*, Cambridge, MA: Harvard University Press, 1994.
— (ed.), *Rorty and His Critics*, Oxford: Blackwell, 2000.
Coetzee, J. M., 'The Old Woman and the Cats', in *Cripplewood-Kreupelhout*, New Haven: Mercatorfonds/Yale University Press, 2013, pp. 7–28.
Cogburn, Jon, *Garcian Meditations: The Dialectics of Persistence in Form and Object*, Edinburgh: Edinburgh University Press, 2017.
Coole, Diana, and Samantha Frost (eds), *New Materialisms: Ontology, Agency, and Politics*, Durham, NC: Duke University Press, 2010.
Creischer, Alice, Max Jorge Hinderer and Andreas Siekmann, *Principio Potosí*, Cologne: Walther König, 2010.
Critchley, Simon, *The Ethics of Deconstruction: Derrida and Levinas*, Edinburgh: Edinburgh University Press, 1999.
Davidson, Donald, 'A Coherence Theory of Truth and Knowledge', in D. Henrich (ed.), *Kant oder Hegel?*, Stuttgart: Klett-Cotta, 1983, pp. 307–19.
— 'Epistemology Externalized', *Dialectica*, 45.2–3, 1991, pp. 191–202.
— 'On the Very Idea of a Conceptual Scheme', *Proceedings and Addresses of the American Philosophical Association*, 47, 1974, pp. 5–20.
— 'Three Varieties of Knowledge', in A. Phillips Griffiths (ed.), *A.J. Ayer Memorial Essays: Royal Institute of Philosophy Supplement*, Cambridge: Cambridge University Press, 1991, pp. 1358–2461.
de Sousa, Eudoro, *Horizonte e Complementaridade*, Lisbon: Imprensa Nacional, 2002.
Deleuze, Gilles, *Dialogues*, trans. Hugh Tomlinson and Barbara Habberjam, New York: Columbia University Press, 1977.
— *Difference and Repetition*, trans. Paul Patton, New York: Columbia University Press, 1994.

— *The Fold: Leibniz and the Baroque*, trans. Tom Conley, Minneapolis: University of Minnesota Press, 1993.
— *The Logic of Sense*, trans. Mark Lester, London: Athlone Press, 1990.
Deleuze, Gilles, and Félix Guattari, *Anti-Oedipus, Capitalism and Schizophrenia*, vol. 1, trans. R. Hurley, M. Seen and H. Lane, Minneapolis: University of Minnesota Press, 1972.
— *A Thousand Plateaus – Capitalism and Schizophrenia*, vol. 2, trans. Brian Massumi, London: Bloomsbury, 2013.
Derrida, Jacques, *The Beast and the Sovereign*, trans. Geoffrey Bennington, Chicago: University of Chicago Press, 2009.
— *Given Time*, trans. Peggy Kamuf, Chicago: University of Chicago Press, 1992.
— *Of Grammatology*, trans. G. C. Spivak, Baltimore: Johns Hopkins University Press, 1976.
__ *Writing and Difference*, trans. Alan Bass, London: Routledge, 1978.
Derrida, Jacques, and Anne Dufourmantelle, *Of Hospitality: Anne Dufourmantelle Invites Jacques Derrida to Respond*, trans. Rachel Bowlby, Stanford: Stanford University Press, 2000.
Descola, Philippe, *Beyond Nature and Culture*, trans. Janet Lloyd, Chicago: University of Chicago Press, 2013.
Dewey, John, *Experience and Nature*, Chicago: Open Court, 1925.
Dolphijn, Rick, and Iris van der Tuin, *New Materialism: Interviews and Cartographies*, London: Open University Press, 2012.
Donnellan, Keith, 'Reference and Definite Descriptions', *Philosophical Review*, 75.3, 1966, pp. 281–304.
Dussel, Enrique, *Para una ética de la liberación latinoamericana I*, Buenos Aires: Siglo Vinteuno, 1973.
Escobar, Arturo, 'Sentipensar con la Tierra: las luchas territoriales y la dimensión ontológica de las epistemologías del sur', *Revista de Antropologia Iberoamericana*, 11.1, 2016, pp. 11–32.
Federici, Silvia, *Re-enchanting the World: Feminism and the Politics of the Commons*, Oakland: PM Press, 2019.
Fine, Kit, 'Tense and Reality', in *Modality and Tense: Philosophical Papers*, Oxford: Oxford University Press, 2005, pp. 261–320.
Fisher, Mark, *Capitalist Realism: Is There No Alternative?*, Winchester: Zero Books, 2009.
— *The Weird and the Eerie*, London: Repeater Books, 2016.
Garcia, Tristan, *Form and Object: A Treatise on Things*, trans. Mark Allan Ohm and Jon Cogburn, Edinburgh: Edinburgh University Press, 2014.

Gratton, Peter, *Speculative Realism: Problems and Prospects*, London: Bloomsbury, 2014.
Grice, Herbert Paul, *Studies in the Way of Words*, Cambridge, MA: Harvard University Press, 1989.
Haraway, Donna, 'Situated Knowledges: The Science Question in Feminism and the Privilege of Partial Perspective', in *Simians, Cyborgs, and Women – The Reinvention of Nature*, New York: Routledge, 1991, pp. 183–201.
— *Staying with the Trouble: Making Kin in the Chthulucene*, Durham, NC: Duke University Press, 2016.
Haraway, Donna, and Adele Clarke (eds), *Making Kin Not Population*, Chicago: Prickly Paradigm Press, 2018.
Harman, Graham, *Immaterialism: Objects and Social Theory*, Cambridge: Polity, 2016.
— *Quentin Meillassoux: Philosophy in the Making*, Edinburgh: Edinburgh University Press, 2011.
— *Speculative Realism: An Introduction*, Cambridge: Polity, 2018.
— *Towards Speculative Realism: Essays and Lectures*, Winchester: Zero Books, 2010.
Hartigan Jr, John, *Aesop's Anthropology: A Multispecies Approach*, Minneapolis: University of Minnesota Press, 2014.
Heidegger, Martin, *The Beginning of Western Philosophy: Interpretation of Anaximander and Parmenides*, trans. Richard Rojcewicz, Bloomington: Indiana University Press, 2015.
— *Being and Time*, trans. Joan Stambaugh, Albany: SUNY Press, 1996.
— *Bremen and Freiburg Lectures: Insight into That Which Is and Basic Principles of Thinking*, trans. Andrew J. Mitchell, Bloomington: Indiana University Press, 2012.
— 'Insight Into That Which Is', in *Bremen and Freiburg Lectures, Insight Into That Which Is and Basic Principles of Thinking*, trans. Andrew J. Mitchell, Bloomington: Indiana University Press, 2012.
— 'The Word of Nietzsche: "God Is Dead"', in *The Question Concerning Technology and Other Essays*, trans. William Lovitt, New York: Harper Perennial, 1977, pp. 53–114.
Heraclitus, *Fragments*, trans. Brooks Haxton, New York: Penguin, 2003.
Humboldt, Alexander von, *Cosmos: A Sketch of the Physical Description of the Universe*, trans. Elise C. Otté, Baltimore: Johns Hopkins University Press, 1997.
Husserl, Edmund, *Cartesian Meditations: An Introduction to Phenomenology*, trans. Dorion Cairns, Dordrecht: Kluwer, 1977.
Irigaray, Luce, 'Questions to Emmanuel Levinas: On the Divinity of

Love', in *Re-reading Levinas*, trans. Margaret Whitford, London: Athlone Press, 1991, pp. 109–18.

Jabès, Edmond, *Le livre de l'hospitalité*, Paris: Gallimard, 1991.

Kant, Immanuel, *Critique of Pure Reason*, trans. Norman Kemp Smith, New York: Palgrave Macmillan, 2007.

Kaplan, David, 'Demonstratives', in *Themes from Kaplan*, ed. Joseph Almog et al., Oxford: Oxford University Press, 1989, pp. 481–563.

Kirby, Emma Jane, *The Optician of Lampedusa*, London: Allen Lane, 2016.

Klossowski, Pierre, *Les lois de l'hospitalité*, Paris: Gallimard, 1965.

Kohn, Eduardo, *How Forests Think: Toward an Anthropology Beyond the Human*, Berkeley: University of California Press, 2013.

Kripke, Saul, *Naming and Necessity*, Cambridge, MA: Harvard University Press, 1972.

— 'Speaker's Reference and Semantic Reference', *Midwest Studies in Philosophy*, 2, 1977, pp. 255–76.

Kunst, Bojana, 'Nearness', in *The Swedish Dance History*, Stockholm: INPEX, 2010, pp. 21–30.

Lacan, Jacques, and Jacques-Alain Miller, *The Seminar of Jacques Lacan: The Psychoses*, Book 3, trans. R. Grigg, New York: W. W. Norton, 1997.

Land, Nick, 'Kant, Capital and the Prohibition of Incest', in *Fanged Noumena: Collected Writings – 1987–2007*, ed. Robin Mackay and Ray Brassier, London: Urbanomic, Sequence Press, 2011, pp. 55–80.

Latour, Bruno, 'Irreductions', in *The Pasteurization of France*, trans. Alan Sheridan and John Law, Cambridge, MA: Harvard University Press, 1993, pp. 151–236.

— 'What Is the Style of Matters of Concern?', in N. Gaskin and A. J. Nocek (eds), *The Lure of Whitehead*, Minneapolis: University of Minnesota Press, 2014, pp. 92–126.

LeGuin, Ursula, *Finding My Elegy – New and Selected Poems*, Boston, MA: Houghton Mifflin Harcourt, 2012.

Leibniz, Gottfried, *Leibniz-Arnault Correspondence*, trans. S. Voss, New Haven, CT: Yale University Press, 2016.

— *The Philosophical Works of Leibnitz: Comprising the Monadology, New System of Nature, Principles of Nature and of Grace, Letters to Clarke, Refutation of Spinoza, and his Other Important Philosophical Opuscules, Together with the Abridgment of the Theodicy and Extracts from the New Essays on Human Understanding*, trans. George Martin Duncan and Ralph M. B. Easley, New York: Andesite Press, 2017.

— *Theodicy: Essays on the Goodness of God, the Freedom of Man*

*and the Origin of Evil*, trans. E. M. Huggard, La Salle: Open Court, 1985.
Lettvin, Jerome Yisroel, Humberto Maturana, Warren Sturgis McCulloch and Walter Pitts, 'What the Frog's Eye Tells the Frog's Brain', *Proceedings of the IRE* 47, 11, 1959, pp. 1940–51.
Levinas, Emmanuel, *Difficult Freedom: Essays on Judaism*, trans. Seán Hand, Baltimore: Johns Hopkins University Press, 1990.
— *Existence and Existents*, trans. Alphonso Lingis, The Hague: Martinus Nijhoff, 1978.
— *On Escape*, trans. Bettina Bergo, Stanford: Stanford University Press, 2003.
— *Otherwise than Being or Beyond Essence*, trans. Alphonso Lingis, Pittsburgh: Duquesne University Press, 2006.
— *Proper Names*, trans. Michael B. Smith, Stanford: Stanford University Press, 1996.
— *Time and the Other, and Additional Essays*, trans. Richard A. Cohen, Pittsburgh: Duquesne University Press, 1987.
— *Totality and Infinity: An Essay on Exteriority*, trans. Alphonso Lingis, Pittsburgh: Duquesne University Press, 1969.
Lewis, David, *On the Plurality of Worlds*, Oxford: Blackwell, 1986.
Lima, Tania Stolze, 'O dois e seu múltiplo: reflexões sobre o perspectivismo em uma cosmologia tupi', *Mana* [online], 2.2, 1996, pp. 21–47.
Lispector, Clarice, *The Passion According to G.H.*, trans. Idra Novey, New York: New Directions, 2012.
McDowell, John, '*De Re* Senses', *Philosophical Quarterly*, 34.136, 1984, pp. 283–94.
— 'The Disjunctive Conception of Experience as Material for a Transcendental Argument', in A. Haddock and F. Macpherson (eds), *Disjunctivism: Perception, Action, and Knowledge*, Oxford: Oxford University Press, 2008, pp. 376–89.
— *Having the World in View: Essays on Kant, Hegel, and Sellars*, Cambridge, MA: Harvard University Press, 2009.
— 'Knowledge and the Internal', *Philosophy and Phenomenological Research*, 55.4, 1995, pp. 877–93.
— *Mind and World*, Cambridge, MA: Harvard University Press, 1994.
— *Perception as a Capacity for Knowledge*, Milwaukee: Marquette University Press, 2011.
— 'Scheme-Content Dualism and Empiricism', in Lewis E. Hahn (ed.), *The Philosophy of Donald Davidson*, La Salle: Open Court, 1999, pp. 87–104.
— 'Travis on Frege, Kant and the Given', in Johan Gersel et al. (eds), *In*

*the Light of Experience – Essays on Reasons and Perception*, Oxford: Oxford University Press, 2018, pp. 23–35.

McTaggart, John Ellis, 'The Unreality of Time', *Mind*, New Series, 17.68, 1908, pp. 457–74.

Meillassoux, Quentin, *After Finitude: An Essay on the Necessity of Contingency*, trans. Ray Bressier, London: Bloomsbury, 2009.

— 'L'Inexistence divine', in Graham Harman, *Quentin Meillassoux: Philosophy in the Making*, Edinburgh: Edinburgh University Press, 2011, pp. 175–238.

Menassé, Adriana, and Hilan Bensusan, '¿Es tiempo de abandonar el barco humano?', *Stoa*, 6.12, 2015, pp. 85–112.

Mooney, Timothy, 'Deconstruction, Process and Openness: Philosophy in Derrida, Husserl and Whitehead', unpublished manuscript, <https://philpapers.org/rec/MOODPA> and <https://https://philpapers.org/rec/MOODAW>.

— 'Derrida and Whitehead: Pathways of Process and Critique of Essentialism', unpublished manuscript, <https://philpapers.org/rec/MOODPA> and <https://https://philpapers.org/rec/MOODAW>.

Nagel, Thomas, *The View From Nowhere*, Oxford: Oxford University Press, 1986.

Noys, Benjamin, 'Drone Metaphysics', *Culture Machine*, 16, 2015, pp. 1–22.

— *The Persistence of the Negative: A Critique of Contemporary Continental Theory*, Edinburgh: Edinburgh University Press, 2010.

Peirce, Charles Sanders, 'The Doctrine of Necessity Examined', *Monist*, 2.3, 1892, pp. 321–37.

Perry, John, 'The Problem of the Essential Indexical', *Noûs*, 13.1, 1979, pp. 3–21.

Plant, Sadie, and Nick Land, 'Cyberpositive', in R. Mackay and A. Avanessian (eds), *#Accelerate: The Accelerationist Reader*, Falmouth: Urbanomic, 2014, pp. 303–14.

Plato, *Sophist*, trans. William Cobb, Savage, MD: Rowman and Littlefield, 1990.

Povinelli, Elizabeth, *Geontologies: A Requiem to Late Liberalism*, Durham, NC: Duke University Press, 2016.

Priest, Graham, *Beyond the Limits of Thought*, Oxford: Oxford University Press, 2002.

Pritchard, Duncan, 'Epistemological Disjunctivism and the Basis Problem', *Philosophical Issues*, 21, 2011, pp. 434–55.

— *Epistemological Disjunctivism*, Oxford: Oxford University Press, 2012.

Putnam, Hilary, 'The Meaning of "Meaning"', *Minnesota Studies in the Philosophy of Science*, 7, 1975, pp. 131–93.
— 'Models and Reality', *Journal of Symbolic Logic*, 45.3, 1980, pp. 464–82.
Quine, Willard van Orman, 'Carnap and Logical Truth', *Synthese*, 12.4, 1960, pp. 350–74.
— 'Epistemology Naturalized', in *Ontological Relativity and Other Essays*, New York: Columbia University Press, 1969, pp. 69–90.
— 'Quantifiers and Propositional Attitudes', *Journal of Philosophy*, 53.5, 1956, pp. 177–87.
— 'Two Dogmas of Empiricism', *Philosophical Review*, 60, 1951, pp. 20–43.
Reinaga, Fausto, *La revolución india*, La Paz: La Mirada Salvaje, 2010.
Rilke, Maria Rainer, *Letters of Rainer Maria Rilke*, vol. 2, trans. Jane Bannard Greene and M. D. Herter Norton, New York: W. W. Norton, 1947.
Rivera, Silvia, *Principio Potosí Reverso*, Madrid: Museo Nacional Centro de Arte Reina Sofía, 2010.
— *Sociología de la imagen: Miradas ch'ixi desde la historia andina*, Buenos Aires: Tinta Limón, 2015.
Rössler, Otto, *Endophysics: The World as an Interface*, Singapore: World Scientific, 1998.
Russell, Bertrand, 'On Denoting', *Mind*, New Series, 14.56, 1905, pp. 479–93.
Sellars, Wilfrid, *Empiricism and the Philosophy of Mind*, Cambridge, MA: Harvard University Press, 1997.
Severino, Emanuele, *The Essence of Nihilism*, London: Verso, 2016.
Sextus Empiricus, *Outlines of Scepticism*, ed. J. Annas and J. Barnes, Cambridge: Cambridge University Press, 2000.
Shaviro, Stephen, *The Universe of Things: On Speculative Realism*, Minneapolis: University of Minnesota Press, 2014.
Sousa Santos, Boaventura, *Epistemologies of the South: Justice against Epistemicide*, Boulder: Paradigm, 2014.
Stengers, Isabelle, *Cosmopolitics I*, Minneapolis: University of Minnesota Press, 2003.
Tarde, Gabriel, *Monadology and Sociology*, trans. Theo Lorenc, Melbourne: RePress, 2012.
Travis, Charles, 'The Silence of the Senses', in *Perception: Essays after Frege*, Oxford: Oxford University Press, 2013, pp. 23–58.
— 'Unlocking the Outer World', in *Perception: Essays after Frege*, Oxford: Oxford University Press, 2013, pp. 223–58.

Tsing, Anna, *The Mushroom at the End of the World: On the Possibility of Life in Capitalist Ruins*, Princeton: Princeton University Press, 2015.
Viveiros de Castro, Eduardo, *Cannibal Metaphysics*, trans. P. Skafish, Minneapolis: University of Minnesota Press, 2014.
— 'Cosmological Deixis and Amerindian Perspectivism', *Journal of the Royal Anthropological Institute*, 4.3, 1998, pp. 469–88.
— 'O nativo relativo', *Mana* [online], 8.1, 2002, pp. 113–48.
— 'Perspectivismo e multinaturalismo na América Indígena', in *A inconstância da Alma Selvagem*, São Paulo: Cosacnaify, 2002, pp. 345–400.
— 'Perspectival Anthropology and the Method of Controlled Equivocations', *Tipití: Journal of the Society for the Anthropology of Lowland South America*, 2.1, 2004, pp. 3–20.
von Uexküll, Jacob, *Milieu animal et milieu humain*, trans. Charles Martin-Freville, Paris: Payot-Rivages, 2010.
Wahl, Jean, *Traité de Métaphysique*, Paris: Payot, 1968.
— *Vers le concret – Études d'histoire de la philosophie contemporaine: William James, Whitehead, Gabriel Marcel*, Paris: Vrin, 2004.
Wettstein, Howard, *The Magic Prism: An Essay in the Philosophy of Language*, Oxford: Oxford University Press, 2007.
Whitehead, Alfred North, *Adventures of Ideas*, New York: The Free Press, 1967.
— *The Concept of Nature*, Cambridge: Cambridge University Press, 2015.
— *Modes of Thought*, New York: The Free Press, 1968.
— *Process and Reality: An Essay in Cosmology*, Gifford Lectures, University of Edinburgh, 1927–28, ed. David Ray Griffin and Donald W. Sherburne, New York: The Free Press, 1978.
— *Science and the Modern World*, New York: The Free Press, 1997.
Wittgenstein, Ludwig, *Philosophical Investigations*, trans. G. E. M. Anscombe et al., Chichester: Wiley-Blackwell, 2009.
— *Remarks on the Foundations of Mathematics*, trans. G. E. M. Anscombe, Oxford: Blackwell, 1956.
— Tractatus Logico-Philosophicus, London: Anthem Press, 2021.

# Index

Note: 'n' indicates chapter notes.

absolute(s), 7, 8, 12, 20, 27, 40, 47, 61, 74, 80, 89, 90–4, 95–6, 104, 116, 118, 145, 171, 173, 177, 186, 191, 197, 198, 199
abundance, abundant, 184, 185, 186, 188, 189
Acosta, Alberto, 188, 190, 199, 201
actual entity, actual entities, 2, 16, 25, 27, 28, 80, 103, 105, 109, 110, 112, 113, 123, 150, 151, 153, 165
address(es), 6, 7, 8, 17, 20, 55, 57, 104, 105, 163, 168, 186, 191, 192, 194, 199
agency, agent, 25, 50, 61, 79, 80, 103, 110, 112, 113, 136, 147, 152, 164, 168, 177n, 178n
Amerindian, 85, 86, 87, 128, 129
analetic(s), 193
anarchic, 55, 56, 104, 168, 169, 183
animism, 85, 87
*Anschauung(en)*, 144, 145, 147, 148, 170
anthropocene, 189
anthropology, 10, 84, 85, 87, 88, 89, 128, 129, 192
*arché*, 112, 113, 190
Aristotle, 13, 23, 24, 42, 64, 72n, 81
Artaud, Antonin, 66, 67, 70, 77n
artificial intelligence, 11
ask, asked, asking, 29, 50, 75n, 82, 83, 101, 103, 106, 108, 109, 110, 113, 118, 119, 125, 142, 143, 147, 148, 156, 168, 179n, 185, 198, 199
asymmetry, 29, 95, 96

Barad, Karen, 44, 45, 47, 75
baroque, 39, 41, 42, 175, 200n
Bataille, Georges, 189, 200n
being up for grabs, 72n, 74n, 128n, 193, 195, 197
Benso, Silvia, 119, 120, 121, 122, 130n, 132n, 133n, 188, 199n
beyond, 2, 4, 7, 8, 14, 15, 19, 20, 28, 32, 33, 39, 42, 43, 51, 52, 60, 66, 70, 78, 79, 82, 87, 88, 92, 93, 95, 96, 97, 100, 102, 103, 104, 107, 108, 118, 124, 125, 128
bifurcation, 2, 4, 9, 46, 60, 92, 193
big Other, 67, 68, 69, 70
Blanchfield, Brian, 12
border(s), 79, 92–3, 95, 96, 97, 99, 100, 101, 102, 109, 115, 124, 148, 153, 167, 168, 177
Brandom, Robert, 179

capital, capitalism, capitalist, 67, 68, 175, 186, 187, 188, 190
*ch'ixi*, 191, 192
Coetzee, J. M., 117, 118, 132n, 154
coexistence, 10, 24, 27, 80, 103, 110, 112
Cogburn, Jon, 13n, 18, 32, 64, 71n, 73n, 129n, 200n
cognition, cognitive, 1, 3, 4, 5, 35, 48, 49, 50, 51, 52, 70, 149, 171, 174
conceptual, conceptualize, 30, 86, 91, 139, 143, 144, 145–6, 147–50, 151–3, 154, 155, 156, 161, 162, 163, 164, 170, 172, 180n, 182n
concrescence, 103, 105, 112
concrete, concreteness, 17, 21, 23, 25,

Index   211

48, 80, 103, 112, 126, 135–6, 160, 166, 173, 193
contingent, contingency, 3–4, 26, 91, 93–6, 97, 103, 194, 196–7
conversation, 49, 78, 83–4, 102, 113–14, 167–72, 173, 176, 177, 185, 192, 193, 198
correlation, correlations, correlationism, 3–4, 5, 17, 20, 71, 89–97, 104, 107, 108, 129, 132, 144, 145, 172–3, 180n
cosmopolitics, cosmopolitical, 113
*cosmorealpolitik*, 103
cubist, 32, 41, 74n

Dardenne brothers, 198
Davidson, Donald, 79, 128n, 143, 146, 147, 164, 178n, 179n, 180n
de re/de dicto, 14–17, 22, 34–5, 37, 40, 45, 48, 57, 66, 70n, 71n, 74n, 79, 86, 133n, 148, 180n
de-determination, 63–5
definite descriptions, 37, 74
deictic, deictics, deixis, 4, 7, 9, 11–12, 16–19, 20, 22–3, 24–5, 26, 27–9, 30, 31, 32, 36–9, 41, 42, 43, 45, 48, 51–2, 55, 59, 61–2, 65, 66, 73, 78, 79, 85, 86, 87–8, 92, 93, 98, 99, 101, 103–4, 128n, 129n, 135, 148–9, 153, 167, 169, 171, 172–3, 174, 177, 178n, 186, 187, 191, 194, 195, 197–8
  deictic absolutes, 7, 12, 171, 176
  deictic operations, operator(s), 22–3, 24, 26–32, 36, 37, 38, 39, 41, 42, 43, 48, 51, 55, 61, 65, 87–8, 92–3, 98, 148–9, 153, 197
Deleuze, Gilles, 13n, 41–2, 67, 70n, 72n, 75n, 76n, 77n, 91, 114–17, 131n, 132n, 160, 175, 181n, 183n, 200n
demand, demanding, 50–1, 52, 75n, 101, 106, 108, 109, 111, 113, 122, 138, 142, 148, 154, 156, 158, 163, 170, 172, 176, 196, 198
Demonstrative(s), 15, 16, 17, 20, 22, 23, 34, 37–9, 79, 148
Derrida, Jacques, 33, 58, 71n, 76n, 117, 118, 122–3, 124–5, 132n, 133n, 139, 163, 170, 182n
Descola, Philippe, 85, 86, 118, 128n, 132n

*diaphonía*, 9, 37, 44, 47, 48, 57–8, 81–2, 100, 102, 138, 192, 195
Donnellan, Keith, 35, 37, 74n
drone, 66, 77n, 104
Dussel, Enrique, 93, 200n
*dynamis koinonias*, 101, 105, 113, 123, 161

empirical, 33, 107, 135, 137, 138, 140, 141, 142, 143, 161, 164, 168, 178n, 179n
empiricism, 2, 136–7, 138–44, 145, 149, 159–61, 164, 178n, 179n, 180n, 181n, 183n
epistemic, 52, 160, 182, 184–5, 198
epistemologies of the South, 10, 13n
Escobar, Arturo, 10, 13n
experience, 2–3, 5–6, 7, 11, 17, 21, 46–7, 54, 58, 59, 60, 80, 90, 91, 92, 102, 105, 107, 109, 112, 116, 121, 126, 131n, 135–7, 140, 141, 142–3, 145, 147, 148, 150, 151, 152, 153, 155, 156–7, 158, 159–61, 162, 165–7, 168–9, 171, 172, 174, 176, 177n, 178n, 179n, 180n, 181n, 182n, 185, 190
exterior, exteriority, 4–6, 7–9, 10, 11, 12, 14, 19–21, 22–3, 25–6, 28–9, 31, 32, 37, 41, 48, 50, 51–2, 53, 55–6, 58, 59, 60–2, 65, 68–9, 70, 71n, 78–80, 81, 82, 83, 92–3, 95, 96, 97, 98, 99, 100, 101, 102, 103, 104, 106, 108, 109–10, 113, 115, 117, 118, 119, 121, 122–3, 124, 125–6, 129n, 137–8, 140, 141, 142, 145, 149, 167, 168–9, 170–1, 172–3, 175–7, 180n, 186, 188, 191, 193, 194, 196, 197–9, 199n
externalism, 48, 51

face, 52, 103, 116, 117, 118–21, 126, 148, 157
Federici, Silvia, 184, 199n
Fine, Kit, 40–1, 74n
Fisher, Mark, 67–8, 77n
furniture of the universe, 15–16, 19, 61, 91, 123–4, 167, 194

Galindo, Maria, 190
Garcia, Tristan, 13, 62–5, 72n, 76n, 77n
Ge-Stell, 56–7, 59, 69, 119, 121, 174

Given, myth of, 138–47, 149, 155–6, 162, 164, 170, 179n, 182n
Great Outdoors, 1, 2, 3, 4–6, 8, 11, 12, 14, 15, 17, 20, 28, 32, 49, 51, 70 71n, 78–80, 81–2, 83, 84, 95–6, 97, 99, 114, 115, 116–18, 119, 124, 126, 127, 159, 168–70, 172–3, 175, 194, 197, 199

Haraway, Donna, 11, 66, 77n, 84, 128n, 183n, 199n
Harman, Graham, 1, 3, 5, 13n, 59–65, 72n, 76n, 96, 98, 110
Hartigan, John, 85, 128n
Hegel, Georg W. F., 13n, 22, 72n, 91, 93, 193
Heidegger, Martin, 3, 42–3, 56–8, 59, 61, 69, 75n, 76n, 77n, 96, 99, 109, 119–21, 131n, 133n, 159, 173, 174–5, 181n, 183n
horizon, 9, 16, 42–4, 53, 56, 61, 75n, 83, 93, 97, 98, 99, 122, 125, 133n, 167, 171, 186
hospitality, 5, 106, 124–6, 127, 133n, 135, 137, 138, 139, 140–3, 145, 146–7, 149, 152–4, 156–7, 163–4, 170, 171, 181n, 190, 191, 198
Husserl, Edmund, 30, 73n, 107–9, 120, 131n, 133n, 183n
hypostasis, 23, 62, 101

impingement(s), impinged, 138, 140, 178n, 198
importance, 4, 115, 150–3, 154, 155, 156, 167, 168, 181n, 189
incitement(s), 137, 138, 140, 146–7, 151, 153, 154, 156, 158, 159, 163–5, 168
indexicals, indexical, indexically, indexicalism, 5, 6, 7, 8, 9–10, 11–12, 14, 16–17, 18–23, 24–5, 26–33, 34–44, 48, 50, 51, 53–6, 57–9, 60, 63, 65, 66, 71n, 73n, 75n, 78–9, 83, 86, 87, 92–3, 97, 98, 99, 101, 103–5, 109, 110, 113, 117, 119, 124, 127, 130, 136, 148–9, 151, 153, 162, 167, 169, 175–6, 168, 186, 190, 191, 192, 193, 194–5, 196, 197, 198, 199
infinite, infinity, 49, 148, 149, 154, 156–8, 164–5, 168, 169, 171, 172, 175, 176, 180n, 181n, 190, 192, 198, 199n
interiority, interiorities, 5, 22–3, 24, 25, 26–32, 36, 41, 42, 48, 50, 51–2, 53, 54, 55, 56, 61, 78, 85–6, 87–8, 89, 92, 93, 95, 96, 99, 101, 102, 103–6, 113, 115, 118, 124, 126, 151, 153, 165, 167, 168, 171, 196, 197
interrupted nexus, 103, 110, 111, 112, 114, 123, 196
interrupted speculation, 8, 103, 167
interruption(s), 12, 53, 83, 100, 102–3, 106, 108–11, 112–14, 115–16, 117–18, 119, 120, 121, 125, 126–7, 135, 137, 141, 148, 154, 157–8, 161, 164–5, 167, 169–71, 176, 185, 188, 190, 197
isolated fact, myth of, 154–6, 170

Jabès, Edmond, 125, 127
justice, 9, 56, 81, 82, 83, 98, 108, 142, 158–9, 163–4, 172, 175, 184, 185, 193, 198

Kant, Immanuel, 33, 60, 89–90, 91, 107, 135, 136, 137, 139, 144, 149, 162, 172, 177n, 180n, 182n, 183n
Kaplan, David, 35, 38–9, 74n
Klossowski, Pierre, 125, 133n
Kohn, Eduardo, 88, 129n
Kripke, Saul, 35–8, 52, 64, 74n
Kunst, Bojana, 53, 75n

Lacan, Jacques, 67, 68, 77n
Land, Nick, 172–3, 187
Latour, Bruno, 9, 25, 63, 73n, 80, 91, 103, 110, 128n, 199n
Lawrence, D. H., 117–18, 125
LeGuin, Ursula, 114, 132n, 140
Leibniz, Gottfried, 24–6, 29, 35, 72n, 73n, 74n, 103, 112, 123, 130n, 131n, 150
Levinas, Emmanuel, 5–6, 9, 17, 19–21, 22, 23, 28, 29, 30–2, 41, 48, 49–52, 59, 70n, 71n, 72n, 73n, 74n, 75n, 76n, 78, 79, 80, 81, 83, 92–3, 95, 98–102, 103, 104, 106–10, 113, 115, 117, 118–26, 128n, 129n, 130n, 131n, 132n, 133n, 140, 142, 147, 148, 154, 157, 159–60, 161, 164, 167,

168, 170, 180n, 181n, 183n, 184, 187, 193, 198, 199, 199n
Lima, Tania Stolze, 85, 128n
Linebaugh, Peter, 184, 185, 199n
Lispector, Clarice, 118, 132n, 154
local, locality, 46, 60, 103, 188–90, 192, 198, 199, 200n
*locus standi*, 27, 47, 105, 150

McDowell, John, 29–30, 73, 140, 142–8, 151, 162, 163, 165, 170, 177n, 178n, 179n, 180n, 182n
McTaggart, John, 39–40, 41, 74n
Marx, Karl, 13n
measurement, 11, 38, 41, 44–8, 79
*megista gene* (greater kinds), 17, 130
Meillassoux, Quentin, 3–4, 71n, 76n, 89–98, 129n, 131n, 132n, 144, 145, 180n, 193, 197
metaphysics, metaphysical, 4–6, 7, 8, 9, 11, 14, 15, 16, 18, 19, 20, 21, 24, 28, 32, 33, 34, 35, 36, 40, 44, 50, 60, 63, 65, 66, 69, 71n, 72n, 75n, 77n, 78–81, 83, 87, 89, 90, 91–3, 97, 98, 99–100, 101, 103, 105, 106, 109, 110, 114, 115, 121, 122, 135, 139, 154, 159, 160, 161, 163, 166, 167, 170, 171, 173, 174, 175, 176, 178, 181, 186, 187, 188, 190, 191, 192, 193, 194, 196, 197, 198, 199, 200n
   metaphysics of paradox, 7
   metaphysics of subjectivity, 91–3, 96, 104–5, 110, 132n, 193
   metaphysics of the others, 4–6, 8, 9, 10, 11, 12, 79–80, 82–4, 89, 92–3, 96, 99, 102, 103, 104–5, 110, 111, 113, 115, 116, 117, 118, 119, 122, 135, 141, 142, 145, 146, 147–8, 153, 156, 157–8, 159, 161, 162, 164–5, 167, 169–70, 172–3, 175, 177, 185–6, 192, 193, 194, 196, 197–8, 199
   paradoxico-metaphysics, 14, 18, 32, 41, 71, 79, 102, 167, 175, 191, 195
   situated metaphysics, 9, 10, 11, 21, 175, 190, 194, 196, 197
monadological, monadology, 24, 25, 26, 27, 28, 30, 60, 61, 63, 72n, 73n, 79, 80, 106, 107, 109, 110, 112, 130n, 196
Mooney, Timothy, 133n

nexus, nexûs, 103, 110, 111, 112, 114, 123, 126–7, 158, 196
non-human, 1, 21, 52, 56, 60, 79, 84–8, 94, 117, 118–19
nothingness, 17, 20, 43, 100
Noys, Benjamin, 13n, 66, 77n

object-oriented, 3, 5, 13n, 21, 59–63, 65, 96, 110
objects, 3, 11, 13n, 16, 34, 48, 56, 59–65, 74, 96–7, 110, 116–17, 119, 121, 136, 138, 146, 173, 174
obsession, 99, 120, 124, 126, 140, 161, 167, 171, 181n, 191
ontological argument, 20, 48, 55
ontologism, 100, 121, 184
other, Other, 4–12, 13n, 16–17, 19–21, 22–3, 25–32, 48, 49–52, 53–5, 57–65, 70, 70n, 71n, 72n, 73n, 74n, 75n, 78–84, 89, 92–3, 95, 96, 98–111, 113–28, 135, 140, 148, 153–4, 156–9, 161, 162–7, 168–9, 171–7, 181n, 184, 191, 192, 193, 197–9
*ousia prote* (first substance), 23, 64
outside, 9–10, 14, 15, 17, 22, 25, 26, 28, 33, 50, 51, 52, 58, 70, 75n, 78, 81, 83, 90, 91, 95, 96, 98, 100, 101, 106, 113, 114, 123, 124, 126–7, 136, 137, 138, 140, 142–3, 145, 147, 148, 153, 157, 162, 164, 166, 171, 172, 173, 180n, 192, 196

pan-perceptualism, 135, 161–2, 165–7
paradox, paradoxical, paradoxically, 6–7, 10, 11–12, 16, 18–19, 33–4, 53, 78–9, 83, 84, 93, 97, 99, 105, 122, 124, 162, 167, 169, 176, 177, 191, 194, 195, 199, 200n
Parmenides, 17, 20, 43, 100, 130
Peirce, Charles Sanders, 111–12, 131n, 194, 200n
perception, 5, 6, 15, 25, 27, 28, 47, 48, 52, 58, 59, 60, 61, 80, 84, 103, 114, 115–16, 120, 126–8, 135–42, 145–77, 178n, 182n, 192, 197

Perry, John, 34–5, 37, 73n, 74n
perspectivism, perspectivist, 72n, 84–9, 128n, 129n
*physis*, 42, 57, 59, 76n, 81, 83, 109, 121, 174
Plato, 13, 17, 19, 20, 76n, 100–1, 130n
pluriverse, 10, 13
Poincaré, Henri, 45–7
position, 9, 11, 15, 16, 17, 21–3, 29, 30, 34, 35, 37–9, 40, 44, 46–7, 53, 54, 55–7, 61, 62, 65, 71n, 78, 87, 88, 96, 115, 129n, 143–9, 179n, 180n, 186
Potosí, 35, 186–90, 199, 200n
Povinelli, Elizabeth, 88, 129n
Predication, 23, 24, 62, 140, 141, 155
prehension(s), prehending, 151–2, 154, 157, 161, 165, 166
Priest, Graham, 69, 200n
Princípio Potosí, 187, 189n, 200n
Pritchard, Duncan, 178n, 180n, 182n
process, process philosophy, 5, 8, 17, 20–1, 22, 28, 52, 72n, 73n, 75n, 79, 80, 103–6, 110–13, 123, 129n, 130n, 131n, 133n, 145, 158, 159, 160, 164, 165, 173, 174, 175, 176, 179n, 180n. 181n, 182n, 183n, 196, 200n
proper names, 34, 35, 52
proximity, 5, 12, 20, 53–61, 76n, 79, 83, 84, 92, 104, 113, 116, 118, 124, 126, 135, 161, 167–9, 172, 181n, 183n, 185, 186, 190, 198
public language, 48–9, 83, 132n, 159
Putnam, Hilary, 35, 36, 49, 50, 64, 71n, 74n, 75n

Quine, Willard V. O., 46, 70n, 75n, 177n, 181n

realism, 9, 14, 29, 42, 71n, 74n, 98, 120
 baroque realism, 39, 42, 175, 200n
 capitalism realism, 67–8, 77n
 deictic realism, 12
 indexicalist realism, 41
 speculative realism, 1–2, 5–6, 8–9, 13n, 72n, 76n, 90, 97, 98, 128n
 tense realism, 39, 200n
receptivity, 5, 47, 126, 135–49, 151–9, 162–72, 174–6, 178n, 183n, 185, 186, 191, 197–8, 199

recognise, recognition, 118, 139, 143, 144, 152
recurrence, 53–4, 73n, 104, 108, 109, 168, 192
reference, reference fixing, 22, 35–40, 47, 52, 64, 65, 74n, 154
response, responding, 50, 51, 52, 83, 100, 101, 102, 106, 108, 109, 113, 118, 119, 125, 127, 131n, 135, 137, 144, 147, 153, 154, 156, 158, 164, 165, 168, 169, 170, 171, 178n, 182n, 185, 186, 190, 196
responsibility, infinite responsibility, 29, 50, 51, 55, 56, 76, 104, 108, 120, 121, 122, 125, 126, 127, 128, 131n, 138, 141, 154, 156, 157–8, 163, 164, 168, 169, 172, 176, 178n, 190, 198
Rilke, Rainer Maria, 161, 181n
Rivera Cusicanqui, Silvia, 191–2, 200n
Robinson, robinsonology, 114–17, 119, 127, 132n
Rössler, Otto, 11, 13n
Russell, Bertrand, 46–7, 74n, 149, 180n, 195, 200n

Sellars, Wilfrid, 141–3, 149, 162, 164, 178n, 179n, 180n
sensibility, 58–9, 76, 80, 135–7, 139–41, 143–5, 154–7, 163, 167, 168, 178
sensitivity, 140
Severino, Emanuele, 43, 75n,
Shaviro, Steven, 128n
singularity, singularities, 10, 110, 122, 160
situated, situation, 8, 10,
solipsism, 30–1, 107–9
speculation, speculative, 1, 2, 3, 7–10, 11–12, 21, 94–5, 96–9, 102–3, 105, 108, 121, 167, 171, 197
spontaneity, 50, 81, 108, 111–12, 120, 126, 135, 136, 142, 145, 154, 157, 163–5, 168, 184, 196–7
Stengers, Isabelle, 9, 131n
Stranger (Plato's), 17, 20, 100–1
substantives, substantivism, substantivist, 4, 11, 12, 15–20, 22, 23, 24, 26, 27, 36, 38–42, 43, 44, 45, 54, 55, 61, 62, 65, 70, 71n, 72n, 76n, 87, 93, 98,

101, 103–4, 109, 111, 117, 119,
    128, 168, 172–3, 177, 186, 187,
    190–1, 192, 193, 194, 195, 197,
    199
substitution, 31, 53–6, 73n, 104, 110,
    118, 120, 121, 124, 126, 127,
    168
Sumaq Urqo, 186, 188–9, 194, 198
supplement(s), supplementation,
    122–6, 127, 139, 140, 141, 143,
    147, 149, 150, 154, 158, 161,
    165, 166–7, 185, 191, 192, 196
sympoiesis, sympoietic, 84, 127

tense, 39, 41, 47, 74n, 78
tentacular, 11, 66
thematisation, thematized, 52, 55,
    57–8, 121, 187
tick, 150, 152, 166
*tode ti* (substratum), 23
totality, 6, 7, 8, 9, 19, 20–1, 22–3,
    24–6, 28–33, 37, 40, 41, 42, 47,
    49, 55, 57, 61–2, 65, 67, 68–70,
    72n, 73n, 75n, 76n, 78, 79, 80,
    83, 87, 89, 95–6, 97–9, 100, 104,
    106, 107, 109, 115, 122–4, 125,
    128n, 129n, 130n, 131n, 132n,
    133n, 141, 143, 157, 167, 168,
    171–3, 176, 177, 180, 181n, 186,
    187–8, 191, 193, 194, 196–7,
    198–9
Tournier, Michel, 114–17, 119, 132n
trace(s), 8, 51, 63, 81, 83, 104, 121,
    123, 137, 146–7, 149, 154, 158,
    164, 187
transcendence, transcendent,
    transcending, 2, 3, 4, 6, 8, 9, 19,
    21, 25, 28, 31, 33, 42, 50, 51, 52,
    75n, 78, 79, 80, 90, 93, 95, 96,
    97, 98, 99, 101, 102, 106, 108,
    110, 120, 123, 124, 148, 156,
    157, 165, 167, 171, 195, 197
transcendental, (ultra)transcendental,
    2, 33, 60, 90, 107–9, 114–15,
    117, 120, 153, 157, 168, 178n,
    181n, 183n
transparency, 2–4, 6, 7–8, 92, 94, 95,
    96, 97, 104, 105, 110
Travis, Charles, 145–7, 165, 179n,
    182n
Tsing, Anna, 81–3, 88, 102, 128n,
    129n, 167, 176, 192, 194

Valentim, Marco Antonio, 84
Viveiros de Castro, Eduardo, 72n,
    85–9, 128n, 129n, 192, 200
von Uexküll, Jakob, 150, 181n

Wahl, Jean, 22–3, 58, 72n, 76n, 112,
    131n, 159–60, 181n, 183n
Wettstein, Howard, 35, 51, 74n, 149
Whitehead, Alfred North, 1, 2, 3–4,
    5, 6, 9, 11, 17, 21, 25, 27–8, 40,
    45–8, 70n, 72n, 73n, 74n, 75n,
    80, 91, 93, 94, 102, 103, 104–6,
    109, 110, 112–13, 119, 123,
    126, 128n, 129n, 130n, 131n,
    133n, 135, 150–4, 155, 156, 157,
    159–60, 161, 165–6, 168, 180n,
    181n, 182n, 183n
Wittgenstein, Ludwig, 45, 46, 49–50,
    55n, 116, 132n, 179n

xenology, 84, 114, 117–18, 119, 121,
    192
xenophilic, 176, 185–6